CONSPIRATORS' HIERARCHY:
THE STORY OF THE COMMITTEE OF 300

Dr. John Coleman

Library of Congress Cataloging-in-Publication Data

Coleman, Dr. John, 1935-
    Conspirators' Hierarchy: The Story of the Committee of 300 by
Dr. John Coleman
    p. cm.
    Includes Index
    ISBN 0-922356-57-2   13 digit: 978-0-922356-57-7
    1. Secret Societies.
    2. Conspiracy.
    I. Title

HS150.C59 1992
366 – dc20
for Library of Congress   92-4441
                                                              CIP

Published By:
Bridger House Publishers, Inc.
PO Box 599, Hayden ID, 83835
1-800-729-4131   www.nohoax.com

Printed in the United States of America
10 9 8

DEDICATION

Dedicated to my wife Lena and our son John who have stood by me throughout years of dangerous and trying times, bearing deprivation and the slings and arrows of outrageous fortune with fortitude and courage.

TABLE OF CONTENTS

FOREWARD

In my career as a professional intelligence officer, I had many occasions to access highly classified documents, but during service as a political science officer in the field in Angola, West Africa, I had the opportunity to view a series of top secret classified documents which were unusually explicit. What I saw filled me with anger and resentment and launched me on a course from which I have not deviated, namely to uncover what power it is that controls and manages the British and United States governments.

I was thoroughly familiar with all of the well known secret societies such as the Royal Institute for International Affairs (RIIA), the Council on Foreign Relations (CFR), the Bilderbergers, Trilaterals, the Zionists, Freemasonry, Bolshevism, Rosicrucianism and all of the spinoffs of these secret societies. As an intelligence officer, and even before that as a young student in the course of my studies at the British Museum in London, I had cut my eye teeth on all of them, plus a good number of others with whom I imagined Americans were familiar.

But when I came to the United States in 1969, I found that names like the Order of St. John of Jerusalem, Club of Rome, the German Marshall Fund, the Cini Foundation, the Round Table, the Fabianists, the Venetian Black Nobility, the Mont Pelerin Society, Hellfire Clubs, and many others were either totally unknown here, or else their true functions were at best but poorly understood, if at all.

i

In 1969-1970 I set about remedying the situation in a series of monographs and cassette tapes. Much to my surprise I soon found plenty of people willing to quote these names as if they had known of them all of their writing careers, but who were not in the least bit knowledgeable about the subjects, yet quite unwilling to state the source of their lately acquired information. I consoled myself with the thought that imitation is the sincerest form of flattery.

I pursued my investigations, pressing on in the face of severe risks, attacks on myself and my wife, financial losses, continual harassment, threats and calumny, all part of a care-fully-crafted and orchestrated program to discredit me, run by government agents and informers, embedded in the so-called Christian rightwing, the "Identity Movement" and rightwing "patriotic" groups. These agents operated, and still operate, under cover of strong and fearless outspoken opposition to Judaism—their main enemy, they would have us believe. These agent-informers are led and controlled by a group of homosexuals who are well-liked and well-respected by political and religious conservatives all across the United States.

Their program of calumny, lies and hatred, disinformation about my work, even lately attributing it to other writers, continues unabated but it has not had the desired effect. I shall carry on with my task until I have finally ripped off the mask of the entire secret upper-level parallel government that runs Britain and the U.S. This book is a part of that ongoing effort.

Dr. John Coleman, November 1991

An Overview and Some Case Histories

Certainly a fair number of us are aware that the people running our government are not the people who are really in control of political and economic matters, domestic and foreign. This has led many to seek the truth in the alternative press, those newsletter writers who, like me, have sought, but not always found what it is that is making the United States terminally ill. "Seek and ye shall find" has not always been the case with this group. What we did find was that the people walk in great darkness, mostly not caring or bothering to find out where their country is headed, firm in the belief that it will always be there for them. This is the way the largest population group has been manipulated to react, and their attitude plays right into the hands of the secret government.

We frequently hear about "they" doing this, that or the other. "They" seem literally to be able to get away with murder. "They" increase taxes, send our sons and daughters to die in wars that do not benefit our country. "They" seem above our reach, out of sight, frustratingly nebulous when it comes to taking action against "them." No one seems able to clearly identify who "they" are. It is a situation that has pertained for decades. During the course of this book, we shall identify the mysterious "they" and then, after that, it is up to the people to remedy their situation.

On 30th April, 1981, I wrote a monograph disclosing the existence of the Club of Rome identifying it as a Committee of

1

300 subversive body. This was the first mention of both of these organizations in the United States. I warned readers not to be fooled by the feeling that the article was far-fetched and I drew a parallel between my article and the warning issued by the Bavarian government when the secret plans of the Illuminati fell into its hands. We shall return to the Club of Rome and the role of the Committee of 300 in U.S. affairs later herein.

Many of the predictions made in that 1981 article have since come to pass, such as the unknown Felipe Gonzalez becoming prime minister of Spain, and Mitterand being returned to power in France; the downfall of Giscard D' Estang and Helmut Schmidt, the return to power of Swedish nobleman and Committee of 300 member Olaf Palme, the nullifying of Reagan's presidency and the destruction of our steel, auto and housing industries in terms of the post-industrial zero-growth orders handed down by the Committee of 300.

The importance of Palme lies in the use made of him by the Club of Rome to deliver technology to the Soviet Union on the forbidden list of the U.S. Customs, and Palme's world-wide communications network employed to train the spotlight on the phony Iran hostage crisis, while he shuttled back and forth between Washington and Teheran in an effort to undermine the sovereign integrity of the U.S. and place the phony crisis in the realm of a Committee of 300 institution, viz, the World Court at The Hague, Holland.

In what is in fact an open conspiracy against God and man, which includes enslaving the majority of humans left on this earth after wars, plagues and mass-murder have done with them is not well hidden. In the intelligence community, it is taught that the best way to hide something is to place it in open view. As an example of the foregoing, when Germany wanted to hide its prize new Messerschmidt fighter plane in 1938, the aircraft was put on display at the Paris Air Show. While secret agents and spies were collecting information from hollow tree trunks and from behind loose bricks in a wall, the information they sought was staring them right in the face.

The upper-level parallel secret government does not operate from dank basements and secret underground chambers. It places itself in full view in the White House, Congress and in Number 10 Downing Street and the Houses of Parliament. It is akin to those weird and supposedly terrifying "monster" films, where the monster appears with distorted features, long hair and even longer teeth, growling and slavering all over the place. This is a distraction, the REAL MONSTERS wear business suits and drive to work on Capitol Hill in limousines.

These men are IN OPEN VIEW. These men are the servants of the One World Government-New World Order. Like the rapist who stops to offer his victim a friendly ride, he does not LOOK like the monster he is. If he did, his intended victim would run off screaming in fright. The same applies to government at all levels. President Bush does not LOOK like a dutiful servant of the upper-level parallel government, but make no mistake about it, he is as much a MONSTER as are those horrors found in horror-movies.

Stop for a moment and consider how President Bush ordered the brutal slaying of 150,000 Iraqi troops, in a convoy of military vehicles carrying white flags, on their way back to Iraq under Geneva Convention rules of agreed disengagement and withdrawal. Imagine the horror of the Iraqi troops when, in spite of waving their white flags, they were mowed down by American aircraft. In another part of the front, 12,000 Iraqi soldiers were buried alive in trenches they occupied. Is that not MONSTROUS in the truest sense of the word? From where did President Bush get his orders to act in this MONSTROUS fashion? He got them from the Royal Institute for International Affairs (RIIA) who received its mandate from the Committee of 300, also known as the "Olympians."

As we shall see, even the "Olympians" do not hide their faces. Often times they put on a show which could be likened to the Paris Air Show, even as conspiracy buffs spend their time in fruitless searching in the wrong places and in the wrong direction. Note how the Queen, Elizabeth II, performs the ceremonial opening of the British Parliament? There, in full view is the head of the Committee of 300. Have you ever witnessed the swearing-in ceremony of a United States President? There in full view is another member of the Committee of 300. The problem is only one of perception.

Who are the conspirators who serve the mighty all-powerful Committee of 300? The better-informed of our citizens are aware that there is a conspiracy and that the conspiracy goes under various names such as the Illuminati, Freemasonry, the Round Table, the Milner Group. To them the CFR and the Trilaterals represent most of what they do not like in regard to domestic and foreign policy. Some even know that the Round Table has a big input into United States affairs through the British ambassador in Washington. The problem is that real hard information on the treasonous activities of members of the invisible government is very hard to come by.

I quote the profound statement made by the prophet Hosea, which is found in the Christian Bible: "My people perish for lack of knowledge." Some may already have heard my expose of the foreign aid scandal, in which work I named several conspiratorial organizations, whose number is legion. Their final objective is the overthrow of the U.S. Constitution and the merging of this country, chosen by God as HIS country, with a godless One World-New World Order Government which will return the world to conditions far worse than existed in the Dark Ages.

Let us talk about actual case histories, the attempt to communize and deindustrialize Italy. The Committee of 300 long ago decreed that there shall be a smaller—much smaller—and better world, that is, their idea of what constitutes a better world. The myriads of useless eaters consuming scarce natural resources were to be culled. Industrial progress supports population growth. Therefore the command to multiply and subdue the earth found in Genesis had to be subverted.

This called for an attack upon Christianity; the slow but sure disintegration of industrial nation states; the destruction of hundreds of millions of people, referred to by the Committee of 300 as "surplus population," and the removal of any leader who dared to stand in the way of the Committee's global planning to reach the foregoing objectives.

Two of the Committee's earliest targets were Italy and Pakistan. The late Aldo Moro, Prime Minister of Italy, was one leader who opposed "zero growth" and population reductions planned for his country, thereby incurring the wrath of the Club of Rome commissioned by the "Olympians" to carry out its policies in this regard. In a Rome courtroom on November 10th, 1982, a close friend of Moro's testified that the former prime minister was threatened by an agent of the Royal Institute for International Affairs (RIIA)—who is also a Committee of 300 member—while he was still the U.S. Secretary of State. The meteoric rise of the man the witness named as Kissinger will be dealt with later.

It will be recalled that Prime Minister Moro was kidnaped by the Red Brigades in 1978 and subsequently brutally shot to death. It was at the trial of members of the Red Brigades that several of them testified to the fact that they knew of high-level U.S. involvement in the plot to kill Moro. When threatening Moro, Kissinger was obviously not carrying out U.S. foreign policy, but rather acting according to instructions received from the Club of Rome, the foreign-policy arm of the Committee of 300.

The witness who delivered the bombshell in open court was a close associate of Moro's, Gorrado Guerzoni. His explosive testimony was broadcast over Italian television and radio on November 10th, 1982, and printed in several Italian newspapers—yet this vital information was suppressed in the U.S. Those famous bastions of freedom with a compelling right to know, the Washington Post and the New York Times, did not think it important to even print a single line of Guerzoni's testimony.

Nor was the news carried by any of the wire services or television stations. The fact that Italy's Aldo Moro had been a leading politician for decades, and who was kidnaped in broad daylight in the spring of 1978, all of his bodyguards butchered in cold blood, was not deemed newsworthy, even though Kissinger stood accused as an accomplice to these crimes? Or was the silence BECAUSE of Kissinger's involvement?

In my 1982 expose of this heinous crime, I demonstrated that Aldo Moro, a loyal member of the Christian Democrat Party, was murdered by assassins controlled by P2 Masonry with the object of bringing Italy into line with Club of Rome orders to deindustrialize the country and considerably reduce its population. Moro's plans to stabilize Italy through full employment and industrial and political peace would have strengthened Catholic opposition to Communism and made the destabilization of the Middle East—a prime goal—that much harder.

From the foregoing it becomes clear just how far ahead the conspirators plan. They do not think in terms of a Five Year Plan. One needs to go back to Weishaupt's statements about the early Catholic Church to understand what was involved in the murder of Aldo Moro. Moro's death removed the roadblocks to the plans to destabilize Italy, and as we now know, enabled conspiracy plans for the Middle East to be carried out in the Gulf War 14 years later.

Italy was chosen as a test-target by the Committee of 300. Italy is important to the conspirators' plans because it is the closest European country to the Middle East linked to Middle East economics and politics. It is also the home of the Catholic Church, which Weishaupt ordered destroyed, and home for some of Europe's most powerful top oligarchical families of the ancient Black Nobility. Should Italy have been weakened by Moro's death, it would have had repercussions in the Middle East which would have weakened U.S. influence in the region. Italy is important for another reason; it is a gateway for drugs entering Europe from Iran and Lebanon, and we shall return to that subject in due course.

Various groups had combined under the name of socialism to bring about the downfall of several Italian governments since the Club of Rome was established in 1968. Among these are the Black Nobility of Venice and Genoa, P2 Masonry and the Red Brigades, all working for the same goals. Police investigators in Rome working on the Red Brigades-Aldo Moro case came across the names of several very prominent Italian families working closely with this terrorist group. The police also discovered evidence that in at least a dozen cases, these powerful and prominent families had allowed their homes and/or property to be used as safe houses for Red Brigades cells.

America's "nobility" were doing their share to destroy the Republic of Italy, a notable contribution having come from Richard Gardner even while in his official capacity as President Carter's ambassador to Rome. At that time Gardner was operating under the direct control of Bettino Craxi, an important member of the Club of Rome and a key man in NATO. Craxi was the leading edge of the conspirators' attempts to destroy the Italian Republic. As we shall see, Craxi was almost successful in ruining Italy, and as the conspirators hierarchy's leading player, was able to get divorce and abortion pushed through the Italian Parliament, resulting in the most far-reaching and destructive religious and social changes ever to strike at the Catholic Church, and consequently, the morals of the Italian nation.

After President Ronald Reagan was elected, an important meeting was held in Washington D.C. in December 1980 under the auspices of the Club of Rome and the Socialist International. Both these organizations are directly responsible to the Committee of 300. The main agenda was to formulate ways and means of how to neutralize the Reagan presidency. A group plan was adopted and, as we look back, it is perfectly clear that the plan the conspirators agreed to follow has been very successful.

In order to get an idea of how vast and how all-pervasive is this conspiracy, it would be appropriate at this point to name the goals set by the Committee of 300 for the pending conquest and control of the world. There are at least 40 known "branch offices" of the Committee of 300, and we shall be listing them all, together with a description of their functions. Once this is studied it becomes easy to understand how one central conspiratorial body is able to operate so successfully and why it is that no power on earth can withstand their onslaught against the very foundations of a civilized, progressive world, based on freedom of the individual, especially as it is declared in the United States Constitution.

Thanks to the sworn testimony of Guerzoni, Italy and Europe—but not the U.S.—learned that Kissinger was behind the death of Aldo Moro. This tragic affair demonstrates the ability of the Committee of 300 to impose its will upon any government without exception. Secure in his position as a member of the most powerful secret society in the world, and I am not talking about Freemasonry, Kissinger not only terrified Moro, but carried through on his threats to "eliminate" Moro if he did not give up his plan to bring economic and industrial progress to Italy.

In June and July of 1982, the wife of Aldo Moro testified in open court that her husband's murder came about as a result of serious threats against his life, made by what she called "a high-ranking United States political figure." Mrs. Eleanora Moro repeated the precise phrase reportedly used by Kissinger in the sworn testimony of Guerzoni: "Either you stop your political line or you will pay dearly for it." Recalled by the judges, Guerzoni was asked if he could identify the person Mrs. Moro was talking about. Guerzoni replied that it was indeed Henry Kissinger as he had previously intimated.

Guerzoni went on to explain to the court that Kissinger had made his threats in Moro's hotel room during the Italian leaders official visit to the U.S. Moro—then Prime Minister and Foreign Minister of Italy, a NATO member-country—was a man of high rank, one who should never have been subjected to Mafia-like pressures and threats. Moro was accompanied on his American visit by the President of Italy in his official capacity. Kissinger was then, and still is, an important agent in the service of the Royal Institute for International Affairs, a member of the Club of Rome and the Council on Foreign Relations.

Kissinger's role in destabilizing the United States by means of three wars, the Middle East, Korea and Vietnam, is well known, as is his role in the Gulf War, in which the U.S. Army acted as mercenaries for the Committee of 300 in bringing Kuwait back under its control and at the same time making an example out of Iraq so that other small nations would not be tempted to work out their own destiny.

Kissinger also threatened the late Ali Bhutto, President of the sovereign nation of Pakistan. Bhutto's "crime" was that he favored nuclear weapons for his country. As a Moslem state, Pakistan felt threatened by continued Israeli aggression in the Middle East. Bhutto was judicially murdered in 1979 by the Council on Foreign Relations representative in the country, General Zia ul Haq.

In his planned ascent to power, ul Haq encouraged a frenzied mob to set fire to the U.S. Embassy in Islamabad in an apparent attempt to show the CFR that he was his own man and to secure more foreign aid and, it was later learned, to murder Richard Helms. Several years later, ul Haq paid with his life for intervening in the war raging in Afghanistan. His C-130 Hercules aircraft was hit by an E.L.F. (electricallow frequency) shot shortly after it took off, causing the aircraft to loop into the ground.

The Club of Rome, acting on Committee of 300 orders to eliminate General ul Haq, had no compunction in sacrificing the lives of a number of U.S. servicemen on board the flight, including a U.S. Army Defense Intelligence Agency group headed by Brigadier General Herber Wassom. General ul Haq had been warned by the Turkish Secret Service not to travel by plane, as he was targeted for a mid-air bombing. With this in mind, ul Haq took the United States team with him as "an insurance policy," as he commented to his inner circle advisors.

In my 1989 work "Terror in the Skies," I gave the following account of what happened: "Shortly before ul Haq's C-130 took off from a Pakistan military base, a suspicious looking truck was seen close to the hangar that had housed the C-130. The control tower warned base security, but by the time action was taken, the C-130 was already airborne and the truck had gone. A few minutes later the plane began looping-the-loop until it hit the ground and exploded in a ball of fire. There is no explanation for such behavior by the C-130, an aircraft with a marvelously reliable record, and a joint Pakistani-United States board of enquiry found no pilot error or mechanical or structural failure. Looping-the-loop is a recognized trade mark of an aircraft hit by E.L.F. fire.

That the Soviet Union has been able to develop high-peak radio frequency devices is known to the West through the work of Soviet scientists who work in the Kurchatov Atomic Energy Institute's Intensive Relatavistic Electron Beam Division. Two of its specialists were Y. A. Vinograov and A. A. Rukhadze. Both scientists worked in the Lededev Physics Institute, which specializes in electronic and X ray lasers.

After receiving this information, I searched for confirmation from other sources and found that in England the International Journal of Electronics had published some material which appeared to confirm the information given to me about the method chosen to shoot down General ul Haq's C-130. In addition, this information was confirmed by two of my intelligence sources. I received some useful information from a Soviet scientific paper on these subjects, published in England under the title "Soviet Radio Electronics and Communications Systems." There was no doubt in my mind that General ul Haq had been murdered. The truck seen near the C-130 hanger undoubtedly carried a mobile E.L.F. device of the type the Soviet Armed Forces are known to possess.

According to written testimony by Bhutto, smuggled out of the country while he was in prison, Kissinger severely threatened him: "I will make a horrible example if you continue with your nation-building policies." Bhutto had fallen afoul of Kissinger and the Club of Rome by calling for a nuclear energy program to bring Pakistan into a modern industrialized state which, in the eyes of the Committee of 300, was a direct contravention of its orders delivered by Kissinger to the Pakistani government. What Kissinger was doing when he threatened Bhutto was not official U.S. policy, but the policy of the modern-day Illuminati.

One needs to have a clear understanding of just why it is that nuclear power is so hated all over the world, and why the fake "environmentalist" movement, established and financially supported by the Club of Rome, was called upon to wage war on nuclear energy. With nuclear energy generating electricity in cheap and abundant supplies, Third World countries would gradually become independent of U.S. foreign aid and begin to assert their sovereignty. Nuclear generated electricity is THE key to bringing Third World countries out of their backward state, a state which the Committee of 300 has ordered to remain in position.

Less foreign aid means less control of a country's natural resources by the I.M.F. It was this idea of developing nations taking charge of their destiny that was an anathema to the Club of Rome and its ruling Committee of 300. We have seen opposition to nuclear power in the United States successfully used to block industrial development in conformity with the Club's "Post-Industrial Zero-Growth" plans.

Dependence upon U.S. foreign aid actually keeps foreign countries in servitude to the Council on Foreign Relations. The people of the recipient countries receive very little of the money as it usually ends up in the pockets of government leaders who allow the natural raw material assets of the country to be savagely stripped by the I.M.F. Mugabe of Zimbabwe, formerly Rhodesia, is a good example of how raw material assets, in this case high grade chrome ore, is controlled through foreign aid. LONRHO, the giant conglomerate run by Angus Ogilvie, an important member of the Committee of 300, on behalf of his cousin, Queen Elizabeth II, now has total control of this valuable resource while the people of the country sink ever deeper into poverty and misery, notwithstanding a hand-out of in excess of $300 million from the United States.

LONRHO now has a monopoly of Rhodesian chrome and charges any price it likes, whereas, under the Smith government, this was not allowed. A reasonable price level was maintained for twenty-five years prior to the Mugabe regime taking power. While there were problems during the 14-year rule of Ian Smith, since his departure unemployment has quadrupled and Zimbabwe is in a state of chaos and de facto bankruptcy. Mugabe received enough foreign aid from the U.S. (in the region of $300 million per annum) to enable him to build three hotels on the French Cote d'Azur, Cap Ferat and Monte Carlo, while his citizens grapple with disease, unemployment and malnutrition, not to mention an iron-fisted dictatorship that allows no complaints. Contrast this with the Smith government which never asked for nor received one red cent in aid from the United States. Thus it is clear that foreign aid is a powerful means of exercising control of countries such as Zimbabwe and indeed all African countries.

It also keeps U.S. citizens in a state of involuntary servitude and therefore less able to mount meaningful opposition to government. David Rockefeller knew what he was doing when his foreign aid bill became law in 1946. It has, since then, become one of the most hated laws on the statute books following public exposure of what it is—a racket run by government and paid for by we, the people.

How can the conspirators maintain their grip upon the world, and more especially, their chokehold over the U.S. and Britain? One of the most asked questions is, "How can any single entity know at all times what is going on and how is control exercised?" This book will attempt to answer these and other questions. The only way we can come to grips with the reality of the conspirator's success is by mentioning and discussing the secret societies, front organizations, government agencies, banks, insurance companies, international businesses, the petroleum industry and the hundreds of thousands of entities and foundations whose leading lights make up the membership of the Committee of 300—the ULTIMATE controlling body that runs the world and has done so for at least a hundred years.

Since there already are scores of books on the Council on Foreign Relations (CFR) and the Trilaterals, we shall go directly to the Club of Rome and the German Marshall Fund. When I introduced these organizations to the United States, few, if any, had heard of them. My first work, "The Club of Rome," published in 1983 attracted almost no attention. Many uninitiated people thought the Club of Rome was something to do with the Catholic Church and that the German Marshall Fund referred to the Marshal Plan.

This is precisely why the Committee chose these names, to confuse and to deflect attention away from what was happening. Not that the U.S. government didn't know, but as it was part of the conspiracy, it helped to keep the lid on information rather than let the truth be known. A few years after I published my work, a few writers saw in it a wealth of hitherto untapped information and began writing and talking about it as though they had always had full knowledge of it.

It came as a revelation to them that the Club of Rome and its financiers under the title of the German Marshall Fund were two highly-organized conspiratorial bodies operating under cover of the North Atlantic Treaty Organization (NATO) and that the majority of Club of Rome executives were drawn from NATO. The Club of Rome formulated all of what NATO claimed as its policies and, through the activities of Committee of 300 member Lord Carrington, was able to split NATO into two factions, a political (left wing) power group and its former military alliance.

The Club of Rome is still one of the most important foreign policy arms of the Committee of 300—the other being the

Bilderbergers. It was put together in 1968 from hard-core members of the original Morgenthau group on the basis of a telephone call made by the late Aurellio Peccei for a new and urgent drive to speed up the plans of the One World Government—now called the New World Order, although I prefer the former name. It is certainly a better job-description than the New World Order, which is somewhat confusing as there have been several "New World Orders" before, but no One World Government.

Peccei's call was answered by the most subversive "future planners" drawn from the United States, France, Sweden, Britain, Switzerland and Japan that could be mustered. During the period 1968-1972, The Club of Rome became a cohesive entity of new-science scientists, globalists, future planners and internationalists of every stripe. As one delegate put it, "We became Joseph's Coat of Many Colors." Peccei's book "Human Quality" formed the basis of the doctrine adopted by NATO's political wing.

The following is extracted from Dr. Peccei's book, "Human Quality":

> "For the first time since the first millennium was approached in Christendom, large masses of people are really in suspense about the impending advent of something unknown which could change their collective fate entirely.... Man does not know how to be a truly modern man.... Man invented the story of the Bad Dragon, but if ever there was a bad dragon, IT IS MAN HIMSELF.... Here we have the human paradox: man trapped by his extraordinary capacity and achievements, as in a quicksand—the more he uses his power the more he needs it.

> "We must never tire of repeating how foolish it is to equate the present profound pathological state and maladjustment of the entire human system to any cyclic crisis or passing circumstances. Since man has opened

Pandora's Box of new technologies, he has suffered uncontrolled human proliferation, the mania for growth, energy crises, actual or potential resource scarcities, degradation of environment, nuclear folly and a host of related afflictions."

This is identical to the program adopted by the much later fake "environmentalist" movement spawned by the same Club of Rome to blunt and turn back industrial development.

Broadly, the anticipated counter-program of the Club of Rome would cover inventing and disseminating "post industrialization" ideas in the United States, coupled with the spread of counterculture movements such as drugs, rock, sex, hedonism, satanism, witchcraft and "environmentalism." Tavistock Institute, Stanford Research Institute and the Institute for Social Relations, in fact the entire wide spectrum of research organizations in applied social psychiatry either had delegates on the board of the Club of Rome, or acted as advisors and played a guiding role in NATO's attempt to adopt the "Aquarian Conspiracy."

The name, New World Order, is seen as something developed as a consequence of the Gulf War in 1991, whereas the One World Government is recognized as being centuries old. The New World Order is not new, it has been around and developing under one or another guise for a very long time but it is perceived as a DEVELOPMENT OF THE FUTURE, which is not the case; the New World Order is PAST AND PRESENT. That is why I said earlier that the term One World Government is, or ought to be, preferred. Aurellio Peccei once confided in his close friend Alexander Haig that he felt like "Adam Weishaupt reincarnated." Peccei had much of Weishaupt's brilliant ability to organize and control the Illuminati of today, and it showed through in Peccei's control of NATO and formulating its policies on a global scale.

Peccei headed the Atlantic Institute's Economic Council for three decades while he was the Chief Executive Officer for

Giovanni Agnelli's Fiat Motor Company. Agnelli, a member of an ancient Italian Black Nobility family of the same name, is one of the most important members of the Committee of 300. He played a leading role in development projects in the Soviet Union. The Club of Rome is a conspiratorial umbrella organization, a marriage between Anglo-American financiers and the old Black Nobility families of Europe, particularly the so-called "nobility" of London, Venice and Genoa. The key to the successful control of the world is their ability to create and manage savage economic recessions and eventual depressions. The Committee of 300 looks to social convulsions on a global scale, followed by depressions, as a softening-up technique for bigger things to come, as its principal method of creating masses of people all over the world who will become its "welfare" recipients of the future.

The committee appears to base much of its important decisions affecting mankind on the philosophy of Polish aristocrat, Felix Dzerzinski, who regarded mankind as being slightly above the level of cattle. As a close friend of British intelligence agent Sydney Reilly (Reilly was actually Dzerzinski's controller during the Bolshevik Revolution's formative years), he often confided in Reilly during his drinking bouts. Dzerzinski was, of course, the beast who ran the Red Terror apparatus. He once told Reilly, while the two were on a drinking binge, that "Man is of no importance. Look at what happens when you starve him. He begins to eat his dead companions to stay alive. Man is only interested in his own survival. That is all that counts. All that Spinoza stuff is a lot of rubbish."

The Club of Rome has its own private intelligence agency and also "borrows" from David Rockefeller's INTERPOL. Every U.S. intelligence agency cooperates very closely with it, as does the KGB and the Mossad. The only agency that remained beyond its reach was the East-German intelligence service, the STASSI. The Club of Rome also has its own highly organized political and economic agencies. It was they who told President Reagan to retain the services of Paul Volcker, yet another important Committee of 300 member. Volcker stayed on as Federal Reserve Board chairman, notwithstanding the faithful promise of candidate Reagan that he would dismiss him as soon as he, Reagan, was elected.

The Club of Rome, after playing a key role in the Cuban Missile Crisis, attempted to sell its "crisis management" (the forerunner of FEMA) program to President Kennedy. Several Tavistock scientists went to see the President to explain what it meant, but the President rejected the advice they gave. The same year that Kennedy was murdered, Tavistock was back in Washington to talk with NASA. This time the talks were successful. Tavistock was given a contract by NASA to evaluate the effect of its coming space program on American public opinion.

The contract was farmed to the Stanford Research Institute and the Rand Corporation. Much of the material produced by Tavistock, Stanford and Rand never saw the light of day and remains sealed until now. Several Senate oversight committees and sub-committees I approached to obtain information told me they had "never heard of it," nor did they have the slightest idea where I might find what I was seeking. Such is the power and prestige of the Committee of 300.

In 1966 I was advised by my intelligence colleagues to approach Dr. Anatol Rappaport who had written a treatise in which the administration was said to be interested. It was a paper intended to bring an end to NASA's space program, which Rapport said had outlived its usefulness. Rappaport was quite happy to give me a copy of his paper which, without going into fine detail, basically claimed that NASA's space program should be scrapped. NASA has too many scientists who were exerting a bad influence on America because they were always eager to lecture schools and university audiences on how rocketry worked, from construction to propulsion. Rappaport claimed that this would produce a generation of adults who would decide to become space scientists, only to find themselves "redundant" as no one would need their services by the year 2000.

No sooner had Rappaport's profiling report on NASA been presented to NATO by the Club of Rome, than the Committee of 300 demanded action. NATO-Club of Rome officials charged with urgent anti-NASA action were Harland Cleveland, Joseph Slater, Claiborne K. Pell, Walter J. Levy, George McGhee, William Watts, Robert Strausz-Hupe (U.S. ambassador to NATO) and Donald Lesh. In May 1967 a meeting was organized by the Scientific and Technological Committee of the North Atlantic Assembly and the Foreign Policy Research Institute. It was called "Conference on Transatlantic Imbalance and Collaboration" and it was held at Queen Elizabeth's palatial property in Deauville, France.

The basic purpose and intent of the conference at Deauville was to end U.S. technological and industrial progress. Out of the conference came two books, one of which is mentioned herein, Brzezinski's "Technotronic Era." The other was written by conference chairman, Aurellio Peccei, entitled "The Chasm Ahead." Peccei largely agreed with Brzezinski, but added that there would be chaos in a future world NOT RULED BY A ONE WORLD GOVERNMENT. In this regard, Peccei insisted that the Soviet Union must be offered "a convergence with NATO," such a convergence ending in an equal partnership in a New World Order with the United States. Both nations would be responsible for future "crisis management and global planning."

The first Club of Rome's "global planning contract" went to the Massachusetts Institute of Technology (MIT), one of the premiere Committee of 300's research institutes. Jay Forrestor and Dennis Meadows were placed in charge of the project.

What was their report all about? It did not differ fundamentally from what Malthus and Von Hayek preached, namely the old question of not enough natural resources to go around. The Forrestor-Meadows Report was a complete fraud. What it did not say was that man's proven inventive genius would in all likelihood work its way around "shortages." Fusion energy, the DEADLY enemy of the Committee of 300, could be applied to CREATING natural resources. A fusion torch could produce from one square mile of ordinary rock enough aluminum, for example, to fill our needs for 4 years.

Peccei never tired of preaching against the nation-state and how destructive they are for the progress of mankind. He called for "collective responsibility." Nationalism was a cancer on man was the theme of several important speeches delivered by Peccei. His close friend Ervin Lazlo produced a work in 1977 in a similar vein which was called "Goals of Mankind," a landmark study for the Club of Rome. The entire position paper was a vitriolic attack on industrial expansion and urban growth. Throughout these years, Kissinger, as the designated contact man, kept in close touch with Moscow on behalf of the RIIA. "Global modeling" papers were regularly shared with Kissinger's friends in the Kremlin.

With regard to the Third World, the Club of Rome's Harland Cleveland prepared a report which was the height of cynicism. At the time, Cleveland was United States Ambassador to NATO. Essentially, the paper said it would be up to Third World nations to decide among themselves which populations should be eliminated. As Peccei later wrote (based on the Cleveland Report): "Damaged by conflicting policies of three major countries and blocs, roughly patched up here and there, the existing international economic order is visibly coming apart at the seams.... The prospect of the necessity of the recourse to triage—deciding who must be saved—is a very grim one indeed. But, if lamentably, events should come to such a pass, the right to make such decisions cannot be left to just a few nations because it would lend themselves to ominous power over life of the world's hungry."

In this is found the committee policy of deliberately starving African nations to death, as evidenced in the sub-Sahara nations. This was cynicism at its worst, because the Committee of

300 had already abrogated the decisions of life and death unto itself, and Peccei knew it. He had previously so indicated in his book "Limits of Growth." Peccei completely dismissed industrial and agricultural progress and in its place demanded that the world come under one coordinating council, to whit, the Club of Rome and its NATO institutions, in a One World Government. Natural resources would have to be allocated under the auspices of global planning. Nation states could either accept Club of Rome domination or else survive by the law of the jungle and fight to survive. In its first "test case," Meadows and Forrestor planned the 1973 Arab-Israeli War on behalf of the RIIA to sharply bring home to the world that natural resources like petroleum would in the future come under global planners' control, meaning of course, under the control of the Committee of 300.

Tavistock Institute called for a consultation with Peccei to which McGeorge Bundy, Homer Perlmutter and Dr. Alexander King were invited. From London Peccei traveled to the White House where he met with the President and his cabinet, followed by a visit to the State Department where he conferred with the Secretary of State, the State Department's intelligence service and State's Policy Planning Council. Thus, from the very beginning, the United States government was fully aware of the Committee of 300's plans for this country. That should answer the often asked question, "Why would our government allow the Club of Rome to operate in a subversive manner in the United States?"

Volcker's economic and monetary policies were a reflection of those of Sir Geoffrey Howe, Chancellor of the exchequer and member of the Committee of 300. This serves to illustrate how Britain has controlled the United States, beginning from soon after the War of 1812, and continues to exercise control over this country through the policies of the Committee of 300.

What are the goals of the secret elite group, the inheritors of Illuminism (Moriah Conquering Wind), the Cult of Dionysius, the Cult of Isis, Catharism, Bogomilism? This elite group that also calls itself the OLYMPIANS (they truly believe they are equal in power and stature to the legendary gods of Olympus, who have, like Lucifer their god, set themselves above our true God) absolutely believe they have been charged with implementing the following by divine right:

(1) A One World Government-New World Order with a unified church and monetary system under their direction. Not many people are aware that the One World Government began setting up its "church" in the 1920's/ 1930's, for they realized the need for a religious belief inherent in mankind to have an outlet and, therefore, set up a "church" body to channel that belief in the direction they desired.

(2) The utter destruction of all national identity and national pride.

(3) The destruction of religion and more especially the Christian religion, with the one exception, their own creation mentioned above.

(4) Control of each and every person through means of mind control and what Brzezinski call "technotronics" which would create human-like robots and a system of terror beside which Felix Dzerzinski's Red Terror will look like children at play.

(5) An end to all industrialization and the production of nuclear generated electric power in what they call "the post-industrial zero-growth society." Exempted are the computer and service industries. United States industries that remain will be exported to countries such as Mexico where abundant slave labor is available. Unemployables in the wake of industrial destruction will either become opium-heroin and or cocaine addicts, or become statistics in the elimination process we know today as Global 2000.

(6) Legalization of drugs and pornography.

(7) Depopulation of large cities according to the trial run carried out by the Pol Pot regime in Cambodia. It is interesting to note that Pol Pot's genocidal plans were drawn up here in the United States by one of the Club of Rome's research foundations. It is also interesting that the Committee is presently seeking to reinstate the Pol Pot butchers in Cambodia.

(8) Suppression of all scientific development except for those deemed beneficial by the Committee. Especially targeted is nuclear energy for peaceful purposes. Particularly hated are the fusion experiments presently being scorned and ridiculed by the Committee and its jackals of the press. Development of the fusion torch would blow the Committee's conception of "limited natural resources" right out of the window. A fusion torch properly used could create unlimited untapped natural resources from the most ordinary substances. Fusion torch uses are legion and would benefit mankind in a manner which is as yet not even remotely comprehended by the public.

(9) Cause by means of limited wars in the advanced countries, and by means of starvation and diseases in Third World countries, the death of 3 billion people by the year 2000, people they call "useless eaters." The Committee of 300 commissioned Cyrus Vance to write a paper on this subject of how best to bring about such genocide. The paper was produced under the title the "Global 2000 Report" and was accepted and approved for action by President Carter, for and on behalf of the U.S. Government, and accepted by Edwin Muskie, then Secretary of State. Under the terms of the Global 2000 Report, the population of the United States is to be reduced by 100 million by the year 2050.

(10) To weaken the moral fiber of the nation and to demoralize workers in the labor class by creating mass unem-

ployment. As jobs dwindle due to the post industrial zero growth policies introduced by the Club of Rome, demoralized and discouraged workers will resort to alcohol and drugs. The youth of the land will be encouraged by means of rock music and drugs to rebel against the status quo, thus undermining and eventually destroying the family unit. In this regard The Committee of 300 commissioned Tavistock Institute to prepare a blueprint as to how this could be achieved. Tavistock directed Stanford Research to undertake the work under the direction of Professor Willis Harmon. This work later became known as "The Aquarian Conspiracy."

(11) To keep people everywhere from deciding their own destinies by means of one created crisis after another and then "managing" such crises. This will confuse and demoralize the population to the extent where faced with too many choices, apathy on a massive scale will result. In the case of the United States, an agency for crisis management is already in place. It is called the Federal Emergency Management Agency (FEMA), whose existence I first disclosed in 1980. There will be more on FEMA as we proceed.

(12) To introduce new cults and continue to boost those already functioning which includes rock "music" gangsters such as the filthy, degenerate Mick Jagger's "Rolling Stones" (a gangster group much favored by European Black Nobility) and all of the Tavistock-created "rock" groups which began with "The Beatles."

(13) To continue to build up the cult of Christian fundamentalism begun by the British East India Company's servant, Darby, which will be misused to strengthen the Zionist state of Israel through identifying with the Jews through the myth of "God's Chosen People" and by donating very substantial amounts of money to what they mistakenly believe is a religious cause in the

furtherance of Christianity.

(14) To press for the spread of religious cults such as the Moslem Brotherhood, Moslem fundamentalism, the Sikhs, and to carry out experiments of the Jim Jones and "Son of Sam" type of murders. It is worth noting that the late Ayatollah Khomeini was a creation of British Intelligence Military Intelligence Division 6, commonly known as MI6, as I reported in my 1985 work, "What Really Happened In Iran."

(15) To export "religious liberation" ideas around the world so as to undermine all existing religions but more especially the Christian religion. This began with "Jesuit Liberation Theology" which brought about the downfall of the Somoza family rule in Nicaragua and which is today destroying El Salvador, now 25 years into a "civil war," Costa Rica and Honduras. One very active entity engaged in so-called liberation theology is the Communist oriented Mary Knoll Mission. This accounts for the extensive media attention to the murder of four of Mary Knoll's so-called nuns in El Salvador a few years ago.

The four nuns were Communist subversive agents and their activities were widely documented by the government of El Salvador. The United States press and news media refused to give any space or coverage to the mass of documentation in possession of the Salvadorian government, documentation which proved what the Mary Knoll Mission nuns were doing in the country. Mary Knoll is in service in many countries, and played a leading role in bringing Communism to Rhodesia, Mozambique, Angola and South Africa.

(16) To cause a total collapse of the world's economies and engender total political chaos.

(17) To take control of all foreign and domestic policies of the United States.

(18) To give the fullest support to supranational institutions such as the United Nations (UN), the International Monetary Fund (IMF), the Bank of International Settlements (BIS), the World Court and, as far as possible, make local institutions of lesser effect by gradually phasing them out or bringing them under the mantle of the United Nations.

(19) Penetrate and subvert all governments, and work from within them to destroy the sovereign integrity of nations represented by them.

(20) Organize a world-wide terrorist apparatus and negotiate with terrorists whenever terrorist activities take place. It will be recalled that it was Bettino Craxi who persuaded the Italian and U.S. governments to negotiate with the Red Brigades kidnapers of Prime Minister Moro and General Dozier. As an aside, General Dozier is under orders not to talk about what happened to him. Should he break that silence, he will no doubt be made "a horrible example of" in the manner in which Kissinger dealt with Aldo Moro, Ali Bhutto and General Zia ul Haq.

(21) Take control of education in America with the intent and purpose of utterly and completely destroying it.

Much of these goals, which I first enumerated in 1969, have since been achieved or are well on their way to being achieved. Of special interest in the Committee of 300 program is the core of their economic policy, which is largely based on the teachings of Malthus, the son of an English country parson who was pushed to prominence by the British East India Company upon which the Committee of 300 is modeled.

Malthus maintained that man's progress is tied to the earth's natural ability to support a given number of people, beyond which point earth's limited resources would rapidly be depleted. Once these natural resources have been consumed, it will be impossible to replace them. Hence, Malthus observed, it is necessary to limit populations within the boundaries of decreasing natural resources. It goes without saying that the elite will not allow themselves to be threatened by a burgeoning population of "useless eaters," hence culling must be practiced. As I have previously stated, "culling" is going on today, using the methods mandated in the "Global 2000 Report."

All economic plans of the Committee meet at the crossroads of Malthus and Frederick Von Hayek, another doom and gloom economist who is sponsored by the Club of Rome. The Austrian born Von Hayek has long been under the control of David Rockefeller, and Von Hayek theories are fairly widely accepted in the United States. According to Von Hayek, the United States economic platform must be based on (a) Urban Black Markets, (b) Small Hong Kong-type industries utilizing sweat-shop labor, (c) The Tourist Trade, (d) Free Enterprise Zones where speculators can operate unhindered and where the drug trade can flourish, (e) End of all industrial activity and (f) Close down all nuclear energy plants.

Von Hayek's ideas dove-tail perfectly with those of the Club of Rome, which is perhaps why he is so well promoted in rightwing circles in this country. The mantle of Von Hayek is being passed to a new, younger economist, Jeoffrey Sachs, who was sent to Poland to take up where Von Hayek left off. It will be recalled that the Club of Rome organized the Polish economic crisis which led to political destabilization of the country. The exact same economic planning, if one dare call it that, will be forced upon Russia, but if widespread opposition is encountered, the old price-support system will quickly be restored.

The Committee of 300 ordered the Club of Rome to use Polish nationalism as a tool to destroy the Catholic Church and pave the way for Russian troops to reoccupy the country. The "Solidarity" movement was a creation of the Committee of 300's Zbigniew Brzezinski, who chose the name for the "trade union" and selected its office holders and organizers. Solidarity is no "labor" movement, although Gdansk shipyard workers were used to launch it, but rather, it was a high-profile POLITI-CAL organization, created to bring forced changes in preparation for the advent of the One World Government.

Most of Solidarity's leaders were descendants of Bolshevik Jews from Odessa and were not noted for hating Communism. This helps to understand the saturation coverage provided by the American news media. Professor Sachs has taken the process a step further, ensuring economic slavery for a Poland recently freed from the domination of the USSR. Poland will now become the economic slave of the United States. All that has happened is that the master has changed.

Brzezinski is the author of a book that should have been read by every American interested in the future of this country. Entitled "The Technotronic Era," it was commissioned by the Club of Rome. The book is an open announcement of the manner and methods to be used to control the United States in the future. It also gave notice of cloning and "robotoids," i.e., people who acted like people and who seemed to be people, but who were not. Brzezinski, speaking for the Committee of 300 said the United States was moving "into an era unlike any of its predecessors; we were moving toward a technotronic era that could easily become a dictatorship." I reported fully on "the Technotronic Era" in 1981 and mentioned it in my newsletters a number of times.

Brzezinski went on to say that our society "is now in an information revolution based on amusement focus, spectator spectacles (saturation coverage by television of sporting events) which provide an opiate for an increasingly purposeless mass." Was Brzezinski another seer and a prophet? Could he see into the future? The answer is NO; what he wrote in his book was simply copied from the Committee of 300's blueprint given to the Club of Rome for execution. Isn't it true that by 1991 we already have a purposeless mass of citizens? We could say that 30 million unemployed and 4 million homeless people are a "purposeless mass," or at least the nucleus of one.

In addition to religion, "the opiate of the masses" which Lenin and Marx acknowledged was needed, we now have the opiates of mass spectator sport, unbridled sexual lusts, rock music and a whole new generation of drug addicts. Mindless sex and an epidemic of drug usage was created to distract people from what is happening all around them. In "The Technotronic Era" Brzezinski talks about "the masses" as if people are some inanimate object—which is possibly how we are viewed by the Committee of 300. He continually refers to the necessity of controlling us "masses."

At one point, he lets the cat out of the bag:

"At the same time the capacity to assert social and political control over the individual will vastly increase. It will soon be possible to assert almost continuous control over every citizen and to maintain up-to-date files, containing even the most personal details about health and personal behavior of every citizen in addition to the more customary data.

"These files will be subject to instantaneous retrieval by the authorities. Power will gravitate into the hands of those who control information. Our existing institutions will be supplanted by pre-crisis management institutions, the task of which will be to identify in advance likely social crises and to develop programs to cope with them. (This describes the structure of FEMA which came much later.)

"This will encourage tendencies through the next several decades toward a TECHNOTRONIC ERA, A DICTATORSHIP, leaving even less room for political procedures as we know them. Finally, looking ahead to the end of the century, the possibility of BIOCHEMICAL MIND CONTROL AND GENETIC TINKERING WITH MAN, INCLUDING BEINGS WHICH WILL FUNCTION LIKE MEN AND REASON LIKE THEM AS WELL, COULD GIVE RISE TO SOME DIFFICULT QUESTIONS."

Brzezinski was not writing as a private citizen but as Carter's National Security Advisor and a leading member of the Club of

Rome and a member of the Committee of 300, a member of the CFR and as a member of the old Polish Black Nobility. His book explains how America must leave its industrial base behind and enter into what he called "a distinct new historical era."

"What makes America unique is its willingness to experience the future, be it pop-art or LSD. Today, America is the creative society, the others, consciously or unconsciously, are emulative." What he should have said was that America is the proving ground for Committee of 300 policies which lead directly to a dissolution of the old order and an entry into the One World Government-New World Order.

One of the chapters in "The Technotronic Era" explains how new technology will bring in its wake intense confrontation that will strain social and international peace. Oddly enough we are already under intense strains through surveillance. Lourdes in Cuba is one place where this is happening. The other is NATO headquarters in Brussels, Belgium, where a giant computer designated "666" can store data of every type mentioned by Brzezinski, plus possessing an expanded capacity to take in data for several billions more people than presently exist, if it ever comes to that, but which, in the light of the Global 2000 genocidal report, will probably never need to be utilized.

Retrieval of data will be simple in the United States where social security and or driver licence numbers could simply be added to 666 to provide the surveillance recording announced by Brzezinski and his Committee of 300 colleagues. The Committee already in 1981 warned governments, including the government of the USSR, that there "will be chaos unless the Committee of 300 takes complete control of preparations for the New World Order. CONTROL WILL BE EXERCISED THROUGH OUR COMMITTEE AND THROUGH GLOBAL PLANNING AND CRISIS MANAGEMENT." I reported this factual information a few months after I received it in 1981. Another item I reported back then was that RUSSIA HAD BEEN INVITED TO JOIN THE PREPARATIONS FOR THE

COMING ONE WORLD GOVERNMENT.

When I wrote these things in 1981, the conspirators' global plans were already in an advanced state of preparedness. Looking back over the past 10 years, it can be seen just how rapidly the Committee's plans have advanced. If the information provided in 1981 was alarming, then it should be even more alarming today as we near the final stages of the demise of the United States as we know it. With unlimited funding, with several hundred think tanks and 5000 social engineers, the media, banking and control of most governments a reality, we can see that we are facing a problem of immense proportions, one that cannot be opposed by any nation at this time.

As I have so often stated, we have been misled into believing that the problem I am talking about has its origin in Moscow. We have been brainwashed into believing that Communism is the greatest danger we Americans are facing. This is simply not so. The greatest danger arises from the mass of traitors in our midst. Our Constitution warns us to be watchful of the enemy within our gates. These enemies are the servants of the Committee of 300 who occupy high positions within our governmental structure. The UNITED STATES is where we MUST begin our fight to turn back the tide threatening to engulf us, and where we must meet, and defeat these internal conspirators.

The Club of Rome also had a direct hand in creating the 25-year old war in El Salvador, as an integral part of the wider plan drawn up by Elliot Abrams of the U.S. State Department. It was Committee of 300 member Willy Brandt, leader of the Socialist International and a former chancellor of West Germany, who paid for the "final offensive" by the Salvadorian guerrillas which, fortunately, was not successful. El Salvador was chosen by the committee to turn Central America into a zone for a new Thirty-Year War, which task was allocated to Kissinger to carry out under the innocuous title of "The Andes Plan."

Just to demonstrate how the conspirators operate across all national boundaries, the "final offensive" action planned by

Willy Brandt came about as a result of a visit to Cuba by Felipe Gonzalez, who at the time was preparing himself for his Club of Rome-ordained role as Spain's future prime minister. Apart from myself and one or two of my intelligence colleagues and former colleagues, no one appeared to have heard of Gonzalez before he surfaced in Cuba. Gonzalez was the Club of Rome's case officer for El Salvador, and the first Socialist to be elevated to political power in Spain since the death of General Franco.

Gonzalez was on his way to Washington to attend the Club of Rome Socialist "get Reagan" meeting which took place in December 1980. Present at the Gonzalez-Castro meeting was the left-wing guerrilla, Guillermo Ungo, run by the Institute for Policy Studies (IPS), the Committee of 300's most notorious Washington-based leftwing think tank. Ungo was run by an IPS fellow who died in a mysterious plane crash while enroute from Washington to Havana to visit Castro.

As most of us know, both the left and the right of the political spectrum is controlled by the same people, which will help to explain the fact that Ungo was a life-long friend of the late Napoleon Duarte, leader of the rightwing in El Salvador. It was after the Cuban meeting that the "final offensive" by the Salvadorian guerrillas was carried out.

The polarizing of South America and the U.S was a special assignment given to Kissinger by the Committee of 300. The Malvinas War (also known as the Falklands War) and the subsequent overthrow of the Argentine government, followed by economic chaos and political upheavals, were planned by Kissinger Associates acting in concert with Lord Carrington, a top-ranking member of the Committee of 300.

One of the principal Committee of 300 assets in the U.S., the Aspen Institute of Colorado, also helped plan events in Argentina, even as it did in the case of the fall of the Shah of Iran. Latin America is important to the United States, not only because we have so many mutual defense treaties with countries there, but also because it has the potential of providing a huge market for

American exports of technology, heavy industrial equipment, which would have galvanized many of our faltering companies and provided thousands of new jobs. This was to be prevented at all costs, even if it meant 30 years of war.

Instead of seeing this huge potential in a positive light, the Committee of 300 saw it as a dangerous threat to its post-industrial zero-growth U.S. plans and immediately acted to make an example of Argentina as a warning to other Latin American nations to forget any ideas they may have had to promote nationalism, independence and sovereign integrity. This is the reason why so many Latin American countries turned to drugs as their sole means of support, which may very well have been the intention of the conspirators in the first place.

Americans in general look down on Mexico, which is precisely the attitude with which the Committee wants the people of the United States to regard Mexico. What we need to do is change our thinking about Mexico and South America in general. Mexico represents a potentially huge market for all types of U.S. goods which could mean thousands of jobs for Americans and Mexicans alike. Transferring our industries "south of the border" and paying the maquiladores slave wages is not in the interests of either country. It benefits nobody but the "Olympians."

Mexico received most of its nuclear power technology from Argentina, but the Malvinas War put an end to that. The Club of Rome decreed back in 1986 that it would stop exports of nuclear technology to developing countries. With nuclear power stations generating abundant cheap electricity, Mexico would have become the "Germany of Latin America." Such a state of affairs would have been a disaster for the conspirators who have, by 1991, stopped all exports of nuclear technology except that destined for Israel.

What the Committee of 300 has in mind for Mexico is a feudal peasantry, a condition that allows for easy management and looting of Mexican oil. A stable and prosperous Mexico can only be a plus for the United States. This is what the conspirators wish to prevent, so they have engaged in decades of innuendo, slander and direct economic war on Mexico. Before former President Lopes Portillo took office and nationalized the banks, Mexico was losing $200 million a day to capital flight, organized and orchestrated by the Committee of 300's representatives in banks and brokerage houses on Wall Street.

If only we in the United States had statesmen and not politicians running the country, we could act together and set back the One World Government-New World Order plans to return Mexico to a state of helplessness. If we were able to defeat the Club of Rome's plans for Mexico, it would come as a shock to the Committee of 300, a shock from which they would take a long time to recover. The inheritors of the Illuminati pose as great a threat to the United States as they do to Mexico. By seeking common ground with Mexican patriotic movements, we in the United States could forge a formidable force to be reckoned with. But such action requires leadership, and we are more lacking in leadership than in any other area of endeavor.

The Committee of 300 through its many affiliated organizations was able to nullify the Reagan presidency. Here is what Stuart Butler of the Heritage Foundation had to say on the subject: "The right thought it had won in 1980 but in fact it had lost." What Butler was referring to was the situation in which the Right found itself when it realized that every single position of importance in the Reagan administration was filled by Fabianist appointees recommended by the Heritage Foundation. Butler went on to say that Heritage would use rightwing ideas to impose leftwing radical principles upon the United States, the same radical ideas which Sir Peter Vickers Hall, top Fabianist in the U.S. and the number one man at Heritage, had been openly discussing during the election year.

Sir Peter Vickers Hall remained an active Fabianist even though he was running a conservative "think tank." As a member of the British oligarchical Vickers armament manufacturing family, he had position and power. The Vickers family supplied both sides in the First World War and again during Hitler's rise to power. Vickers' official cover was the University of California's Urban and Regional Development Institute. He was a longtime confidant of British Labour leader and Committee of 300 member Anthony Wedgewood Benn.

Both Vickers and Benn are integrated with the Tavistock Institute for Human Relations, the premiere brainwashing institution in the world. Vickers uses his Tavistock training to very good effect when speech-making. Consider the following example:

"There are two Americas. One is the nineteenth century heavy-industry based society. The other is the growing post industrial society, in some cases built on the shards of the old America. It is the crisis between these two worlds which will produce the economic and social catastrophe of the next decade. The two worlds are in fundamental opposition, they cannot co-exist. In the end the post industrial world must crush and obliterate the other one." Remember, this speech was made in 1981 and we can see from the state of our economy and our industries just how accurate was Sir Peter's prediction. When concerned people ask me how long the 1991 recession will last, I refer them to Sir Peter's statements and add my own opinion that it will not end until 1995/1996, and even then what emerges will not be the America we knew in the 1960's and 1970's. That America has already been destroyed.

I reported Sir Peter's speech in my newsletter soon after it was delivered. How prophetic it was, but then it was easy to predict a future already written for America by the Committee of 300 and its executive Club of Rome. What was Sir Peter saying in a euphemistic manner? Translated into ordinary everyday English, he was saying that the old American way of life, our true and trusted republican form of government based upon our Constitution, was going to be crushed by the New World Order. America as we knew it was going to have to go, or be crushed to pieces.

As I said, Committee of 300 members often make themselves highly visible. Sir Peter was no exception. To make it clearly understood where he was coming from, Sir Peter rounded off his speech by declaring:

"I am perfectly happy working with the Heritage Foundation and groups like that. True Fabians look to the New Right to push through some of their more radical ideas. For more than a decade the British population has been subject to a constant propaganda barrage of how it was on the industrial skids. All of this is true, but the net effect of the propaganda was to demoralize the population. (Exactly as intended by the new-science scientists at Tavistock.)

"This will happen in the United States as the economy worsens. This (demoralizing process) is necessary to make people accept difficult choices. If there is no planning for the future or if constituencies block progress there will be social chaos on a scale which is currently hard to imagine. The outlook for urban America is bleak. There is a possibility of doing something with the inner cities, but basically the cities will shrink and the manufacturing base will decline. This will produce social convulsions."

Was Sir Peter a psychic, a magician of great report or merely a charlatan fortune teller with a great deal of luck? The answer is "none of these." All Sir Peter was doing was reading off the blueprint of the Committee of 300-Club of Rome for slow death of the United States as a former industrial giant. Looking back over the ten years of Sir Peter's predictions, can anybody doubt that the Committee of 300's plans for the demise of an industrialized United States has become a fait accompli?

Haven't Sir Peter's predictions proved to be remarkably accurate? Indeed they have, almost down to the last word. It is worth noting that Sir Peter Vickers (Sir Peter Vickers-Hall's father-in-law) worked on the Stanford Research paper, "Changing Images of Man," from which much of the 3000 pages of material advice sent to the Reagan Administration was taken. Moreover, as a senior MI6 British intelligence officer, Sir Peter Vickers was in a position to give Heritage a great deal of advance information.

As a member of the Committee of 300 and NATO, Sir Peter Vickers was around when NATO directed the Club of Rome to develop a social program which would utterly change the direction in which America wanted to go. The Club of Rome, under Tavistock direction, ordered Stanford Research Institute (SRI) to develop such a program, not only for America, but for every nation in the Atlantic Alliance and the OECD nations.

It was Sir Peter's protege, Stuart Butler, who gave President Reagan 3000 pages of "recommendations," which no doubt contained some opinions expressed by Anthony Wedgewood Benn, a member of parliament and a ranking member of the Committee of 300. Benn told members of the Socialist International who met in Washington on December 8, 1980: "You can thrive under Volcker's credit collapse if you profile Reagan to intensify the credit collapse."

That Butler's advice was taken and applied to the Reagan administration can be seen in the collapse of the Savings and Loan and banking industries which accelerated under Reagan economic policies. While Benn called it "profiling," he really meant that Reagan should be brainwashed. It is worth noting that Von Hayek—who is a founder member of Heritage—used his student, Milton Friedman, to preside over the Club of Rome's plans to deindustrialize America using the Reagan presidency to accelerate the collapse of first the steel industry, and then the auto and housing industries, for example.

In this regard a French Black Nobility member, Etienne D'Avignon, as a member of the Committee of 300, was assigned the task of collapsing the steel industry in this country. It is doubtful that any of the hundreds of thousands of steel workers and shipyard workers who have been without jobs for the past decade have ever heard of D'Avignon. I fully reported the

D'Avignon Plan in April 1981 World Economic Review. Attending that fateful December 10th Club of Rome meeting in Washington D.C. was a mystery man from Iran who turned out to be Bani Sadr, the Ayatollah Khomeini's special envoy.

One speech in particular at the December 10th, 1980 conclave caught my attention, mainly because it came from Francois Mitterand, a man the French establishment had discarded and thought to be washed up. But my intelligence source had previously told me that Mitterand was in the process of being picked up, dusted off and returned to power, so what he said carried a good deal of weight for me:

"Industrial capitalist development is the opposite of freedom. We must put an end to it. The economic systems of the 20th and 21st century will use machines to crush man, first in the domain of nuclear energy which is already producing formidable results." Mitterand's return to the Elysee Palace was a great triumph for socialism. It proved that the Committee of 300 was powerful enough to predict happenings and then make them happen, by force, or by whatever means it took to make its point that it could crush any and all opposition even if, as in the case of Mitterand, he had been totally rejected a few short days before by a discerning political power group in Paris.

Another group representative at the December 1980 Washington meetings with "observer status" was John Graham, also known as "Irwin Suall," head of the fact-finding committee of the Anti-Defamation League (ADL). The ADL is an outright British intelligence operation run by all three branches of British intelligence, that is, MI6 and the JIO. Suall's extensive bag of dirty tricks was garnered from the sewers of the East End of London. Suall is still a member of the super-secret SIS, an elite James Bond type of operation. Let nobody underestimate the power of the ADL, nor its long reach.

Suall works closely with Hall and other Fabianists. He was singled out as useful to British intelligence while at Ruskin Labour College at Oxford University in England, the same communist education center that gave us Milner, Rhodes, Burgess, McLean and Kim Philby. Oxford and Cambridge Universities have long been the province of the sons and daughters of the elite, those whose parents belong to the "upper crust" of British high society. While at Oxford, Suall joined the Young People's Socialist League, and was recruited by British intelligence shortly thereafter.

Suall was posted to the United States where he came under the protection and sponsorship of one of the most insidious leftists in the country, Walter Lippmann. Lippmann founded and ran the League for Industrial Democracy, and Students for a Democratic Society, both leftist spoiler operations to set industrial workers at variance with what it called "the Capitalist class" and management. Both of Lippmann's projects were an integral part of the Committee of 300 apparat that stretched right across America, of which Lippmann was a most important member.

Suall has strong connections with the Justice Department and can secure FBI profiles of any person he targets. The Justice Department has orders to give Suall everything he wants when he wants it. Most of Suall's activities centre around "keeping an eye on rightwing groups and individuals." The ADL has an open door to the State Department and makes good use of State's impressive intelligence agency.

The State Department has a layer of agents in the right wing, posing as "fearless anti-Semitic fighters." There are four leaders in this group of informers, three of whom are discreet Jewish homosexuals. This spy group has been in operation for the past two decades. They publish virulently anti-Jewish "newspapers" and sell a wide variety of anti-Semitic books. One of the principal operators works out of Louisiana. A member of this group is a writer who is dearly beloved in Christian rightwing circles. The group and the individuals who go to make it up are under the protection of the ADL. Suall was deeply involved in ABSCAM and is often called upon by law enforcement agencies to assist them in investigations and sting operations.

Suall was assigned to "dog Reagan," in terms of the course laid out for the newly-elected President by the Heritage Foundation, and to figuratively fire a few warning shots if Reagan looked like deviating or taking off his blinders at any time. Suall helped to get rid of any troublesome rightwing advisor not beholden to Heritage for his or her job with the Reagan administration. Such a person was Ray Donovan, Reagan's Secretary of Labor, who was eventually removed from his post thanks to the Dirty Tricks department of the ADL. James Baker III, one of those on the list of 3000 recommendations made by the Heritage Foundation, was the go-between who carried Suall's messages of hate about Donovan to the President.

Another important conspirator was Philip Agee, the so-called CIA "defector." Although not a member of the Committee, he was nevertheless its case officer for Mexico, and run by the Royal Institute for International Affairs (RIIA) and the Council on Foreign Relations. For the record, nothing that happens in the U.S. happens without the sanction of the RIIA. It is a continuing and ongoing agreement first OPENLY entered into (there were many such secret agreements before that) by Churchill and Roosevelt in 1938, under the terms of which U.S. intelligence services are obliged to share intelligence secrets with British intelligence.

This is the basis of the so-called "special relationship" between the two countries about which Churchill and Lord Halifax boasted and which "special relationship" was responsible for the U.S. fighting the Gulf War against Iraq for and on behalf of British interests, more especially British Petroleum, one of the most important companies in the Committee of 300 in which Queen Elizabeth's immediate family has a big stake.

No intelligence activity has taken place since 1938 except through this special joint command structure. Philip Agee joined the CIA after graduating from Notre Dame where he was inducted into its Jesuit Freemason ring. Agee first came to my attention in 1968 as the intelligence officer behind the riots at the University of Mexico. One of the most important things about the Mexican student riots was that they occurred at the same time as student rioting in New York, Bonn, Prague and West Berlin.

With the coordination expertise and its special intelligence network of which INTERPOL is an integral part, it is not as difficult as it might seem at first sight for the Committee to set in motion carefully timed global actions, whether they be student rioting or deposing leaders of supposedly sovereign nations. It is all in a day's work for the "Olympians." From Mexico, Agee moved on to align himself with Puerto Rican terrorist groups. During this time he became a trusted confidant of the Cuban dictator, Fidel Castro.

It should not be imagined that while Agee was carrying out these operations, he was doing so as a "rogue" agent. On the contrary, he was working for the CIA all during these assignments. Trouble came when Castro's DGI (Cuban intelligence service) was able to "turn" him. Agee continued to work in his capacity as a member of the CIA until his double role was uncovered. This involved the biggest Soviet listening post in the West located at Lourdes, Cuba. Staffed by 3000 Soviet specialists in signals monitoring and deciphering, Lourdes has the capability of monitoring thousands of electronic signals simultaneously. Many a private phone conversation between a member of Congress and his mistress was picked up at Lourdes and used to telling effect.

Although we are told today in 1991 that "Communism is dead," the United States has done nothing to close down this vast spy operation which sits on our doorstep. Incidentally, Lourdes has the capability of picking up even the weakest "tempest" signal, which is the type given off by a fax machine or an electric typewriter which, when deciphered, will give the contents of whatever is being typed or faxed. Lourdes remains a dagger in the heart of the United States. There is absolutely no reason for its continued existence. If the U.S. and the USSR are truly at peace with each other, why the continued need for so massive a spy operation? The simple truth is that, rather than retrenching personnel as we are led to believe, the KGB has taken on additional recruits during 1990 and 1991.

Bernard Levin is probably not a name that is well-known in the United States. Unlike decadent "pop stars" or Hollywood's latest miserable "discovery," academics seldom if ever come before the public eye. Of the hundreds of academics in the United States working under the Control of the Club of Rome, Levin is worthy of special mention, if for no reason other than his role in undermining Iran, the Philippines, South Africa, Nicaragua and South Korea. The demise of the Shah of Iran was run to a plan devised by Bernard Levin and Richard Falk, and supervised by Robert Anderson's Aspen Institute.

Levin was the author of a work entitled "Time Perspective and Morale" which is a Club of Rome publication concerning how to break down the morale of nations and individual leaders. Here is an extract of the document:

"One of the main techniques for breaking morale through a strategy of terror consists in exactly this tactic: keep the person hazy as to where he stands and just what he may expect. In addition, if frequent vacillations between severe disciplinary measures and promise of good treatment together with the spreading of contradictory news make the structure of the situation unclear, then the individual may cease to know whether a particular plan would lead toward or away from his goal. Under these conditions, even those individuals who have definite goals and are ready to take risks are paralyzed by the severe inner conflict in regard to what to do."

This Club of Rome blueprint applies to COUNTRIES as well as to individuals, particular the government leaders of those countries. We in the U.S. need not think that "Oh well, this is America, and those kinds of things just do not happen here." Let me assure you that they ARE happening in the U.S., and perhaps more so than in any other country.

The Levin-Club of Rome plan is designed to demoralize us all so that in the end we feel we should follow whatever it is that is planned for us. We WILL follow Club of Rome orders like sheep. Any seemingly strong leader who SUDDENLY APPEARS to "rescue" the nation must be regarded with the utmost suspicion. Remember that Khomeini was groomed for years by British intelligence, especially during his time in Paris, before he suddenly appeared as the savior of Iran. Boris Yeltsin is from the same MI6-SIS stable.

The Club of Rome feels confident that it has carried out its Committee of 300 mandate to "soften up" the United States. After 45 years of waging war on the people of this nation, who will doubt that it has indeed accomplished its task? Look around and see how we have been demoralized. Drugs, pornography, rock and roll "music," free sex, the family unit all but totally undermined, lesbianism, homosexuality and finally the ghastly murder of millions of innocent babies by their own mothers. Has there ever been a crime so vile as mass abortion?

With the U.S. spiritually, morally bankrupted, with our industrial base destroyed throwing 30 million people out of work, with our big cities ghastly cesspools of every imaginable crime, with a murder rate almost three times higher than any other country, with 4 million homeless, with corruption in government reaching endemic proportions, who will gainsay that the United States is ready to collapse from within, into the waiting arms of the New Dark Age One World Government?

The Club of Rome has succeeded in splitting the Christian churches; it has succeeded in building up an army of charismatics, fundamentalists and evangelicals who will fight for the Zionist State of Israel. During the Gulf War of genocide I received scores of letters asking me how I could oppose "a just Christian war against Iraq." How could I doubt that Christian fundamentalist support for the (Committee of 300's) war against Iraq was not Biblical—after all didn't Billy Graham pray with President

Bush just before the shooting started? Doesn't the Bible speak of "wars and rumors of wars"? These letters give an insight into just how well the Tavistock Institute has done its work. The Christian fundamentalists will be a formidable force behind the state of Israel, exactly as planned. How sad that these fine people do not realize that they have been GROSSLY MISUSED by the Club of Rome and that their opinions and beliefs are NOT THEIR OWN, but those created for them by the hundreds of Committee of 300 "think tanks" that dot the American landscape. In other words, like any other segment of the United States population, the Christian fundamentalists and evangelicals have been thoroughly brainwashed.

We as a nation are ready to accept the demise of the United States of America and the American way of life, once the envy of the entire world. Do not think this has happened on its own—the old "times are changing" syndrome. Time does not change anything, PEOPLE do. It is a mistake to think of the Committee of 300 and the Club of Rome as European institutions. The Club of Rome exercises great influence and power in the United States, and has its own chapter based in Washington D.C.

Senator Claiborne Pell is its leader, and one of its members is Frank M. Potter, a one-time staff director of the House Sub-committee on Energy. It is not difficult to see how the Club of Rome has maintained its grip on U.S. energy policies and where "environmentalist" opposition to nuclear energy is coming from. Perhaps the Club's greatest success story is its hold over Congress in regard to nuclear energy which has had the effect of preventing the U.S. from entering the 21st century as a strong industrial nation. The effect of the anti-nuclear policy of the Club of Rome can be measured in terms of silent blast furnaces, derelict railroad yards, rusting steel mills, shipyards long since closed down and a valuable trained work force scattered across the United States, which may never again be assembled.

Other Club of Rome members in the U.S. are Walter A.

Hahn of the Congressional Research Service, Ann Cheatham and Douglas Ross, both senior economists. Ross's task, in his own words, was to "translate Club of Rome perspectives into legislation to help the country get away from the illusion of plenty." Ann Cheatham was the director of an organization called "Congressional Clearing House For The Future."

Her task was to profile members of Congress who would be susceptible to astrology and New Age mumbo-jumbo. At one stage she had in excess of 100 Congressmen in her classes. Daily sessions were held in which a variety of astrological "forecasts" were made based on her "occult perceptions." Besides Congressmen, other prominent people who attended her sessions were Michael Walsh, Thornton Bradshaw—A LEADING MEMBER OF THE COMMITTEE OF 300—and David Sternlight, a senior vice-president of Allstate Insurance Company.

Some of the more important members of the Committee of 300 are also members of NATO, a fact which we ought to remember. These Committee of 300 members often hold several offices. Among the NATO-Club of Rome membership are found Harland Cleveland, a former U.S. ambassador to NATO, Joseph Slater, a director of the Aspen Institute, Donald Lesh, a former staffer in the U.S. National Security Agency, George McGhee and Claiborne Pell, to name a few examples.

It is important that we remember these names, make a list of them if you wish, so as to recall who they are and what they stand for when their names come up in television programs and news services. Following intelligence modus vivendi, leaders of the Committee often appear on television, usually in the most innocent of guises. We ought to be aware that nothing they do is innocent.

The Committee of 300 has planted its agents in the muscle and sinew of the United States, in its government, in Congress, in advisory posts around the President, as ambassadors and as Secretaries of State. From time to time the Club of Rome holds gatherings and conferences which, although they appear under innocuous titles, break up into action committees, each of which is assigned a specific task and a specific target date by which time their assignments must be completed. If it does nothing else, the Committee of 300 is working to a very specific time-table.

The first Club of Rome conference in the United States was called by the Committee of 300 in 1969 under the title: "The Association of the Club of Rome." The next meeting was held in 1970 under the title "Riverdale Center of Religious Research" and was directed by Thomas Burney. Then followed the Woodlands Conference held in Houston, Texas, starting in 1971. Thereafter, regular conferences have been held at Woodlands every year.

Also in 1971, at a later date, the Mitchell Energy and Development Corporation held its energy strategy meeting for the Club of Rome: The recurring theme: LIMIT THE GROWTH OF THE U.S.A. Then to crown it all, the First Global Conference on the Future was held in July of 1980, attended by 4000 social engineers and members of think tanks, all of whom were members of or affiliated with various institutions operating under Club of Rome umbrella organizations.

The First Global Conference on the Future had the blessing of the White House which held its own conference based on the transcripts of the First Global Conference forum. It was called the "White House Commission on the 1980's" and OFFICIALLY recommended the policies of the Club of Rome "as a guide to future U.S. policies" and even went so far as to say that the United States economy is moving out of the industrial phase. This echoed the theme of Sir Peter Vickers Hall and Zbigniew Brzezinsky and provides further proof of the control exercised by the Committee of 300 over U.S. affairs, both domestic and foreign.

As I said in 1981, we are set up, politically, socially and economically so that we remain locked into the Club of Rome's plans. Everything is RIGGED against us. If we are to survive, then we must break the stranglehold the Committee of 300 has on our government. In every election since Calvin Coolidge ran for the White House, the Committee of 300 has been able to plant its agents in key positions in government so that it matters not who gets the White House post. For example, every one of the candidates who ran for the Presidency, from the time of Franklin D. Roosevelt, were selected, some like to call it "hand-picked," by the Council on Foreign Relations acting on the instructions of the RIIA.

Especially in the 1980 election, every candidate for the highest office in the United States was run by the CFR. Therefore, it was of no consequence to the conspirators who won the presidential race. Through such Trojan Horses as the Heritage Foundation and the CFR, ALL key policy making positions in the new administrations were filled by the Council on Foreign Relations nominees, and before that, since the 1960's, by NATO-Club of Rome yes-men, thereby ensuring that key policy decisions bore the indelible stamp of the Club of Rome and the CFR, acting as the executive arms of the Committee of 300.

Both the 1984 and 1988 elections followed this long-established pattern. Secretary of State George Schultz was the perfect choice of the Committee of 300 for the office of Secretary of State. Schultz was always a creature of Henry Kissinger, the ruling order-giver for the CFR. Moreover, his position with Bechtel, a key Committee of 300 company of global dimensions, gave him access to countries that might otherwise have been suspicious of his Kissinger connection. The Carter Administration accelerated the process of key pro-conspiracy personnel in key positions. Before Carter was elected, his key campaign strategist, Hamilton Jordan, said that if Cyrus Vance or Brzezinski received appointments in the Carter cabinet, he, Jordan, would resign. They did. Jordan did not resign.

Carter's choice of Paul Volcker (in fact he was told to appoint Volcker by David Rockefeller) started the collapse of the U.S. economy according to the plan laid down by the Club of Rome. We are up against powerful forces who are dedicated to the goal of a One World Government. We have been engaged in a devastatingly crippling war for the past 45 years, only it is not perceived as such. We are brainwashed, methodically and systematically, without ever being aware of it. The Tavistock Institute provided the system for this to take place, and then set its operations in motion.

The only way we can fight back is by exposing the conspirators and their multiplicity of front organizations. We need men with experience who can formulate strategy to defend our priceless heritage which, once lost, will never again reappear. We need to learn the methods the conspirators use; learn them and adopt counter-measures. Only a crash program will stop the rot which is consuming our nation.

Some may have difficulty in accepting the idea of a global conspiracy because so many writers have made financial gain from it. Others doubt that activity on a global scale can be successfully advanced. They see the huge bureaucracy of our government and then say, "Well, how are we supposed to believe that private people can do more than the government does?" This overlooks the fact that government is part of the conspiracy. Hard evidence is what they want and hard evidence is difficult to come by.

Others say, "So what. What do I care about a conspiracy, I don't even bother to vote." That is exactly the way the general population of America was profiled to react. Our people have become discouraged and confused, the results of 45 years of warfare conducted against us. How this is done is explained in Bernard Lewin's book, but how many people would bother to read an academic's non-fiction book? We are reacting exactly as we were profiled to act. Demoralized and confused people will be far more ready to welcome the sudden appearance of a great man who promises to solve every problem and guarantee a well-ordered society in which people are fully employed and domestic strife is minimal. Their dictator, for that is who it will be, will be welcomed with open arms.

Knowing WHO the enemy is is a vital necessity. No one can

fight and win against an unidentified enemy. This book could be used as a military field manual. Study its content and memorize all names. I have mentioned profiling techniques quite frequently in this chapter. A full explanation of "profiling" is contained in the next chapter. One of the most profound pieces of information to come out of the science of profiling is the relative ease in which this can be accomplished in individuals, party groups, political entities and so on right on down the line. Once we wake up as to how easy this is to do, the conspiracy will no longer be more than we can comprehend. The assassination of President Kennedy and the attempt on the life of President Reagan become easy to understand.

INSTITUTIONS THROUGH WHICH CONTROL IS EXERCISED

Profiling is a technique developed in 1922 on command of the Royal Institute for International Affairs (RIIA). Major John Rawlings Reese, a British Army technician, was instructed to set up the largest brainwashing facility in the world at the Tavistock Institute for Human Relations as a part of Sussex University. This became the core of Britain's Psychological Warfare Bureau. When I first introduced the names of Reese and Tavistock into the United States in 1970, very little interest was shown. But over the years, as I revealed more and more about Tavistock and its vital role in the conspiracy, it has become popular to imitate my earlier research.

Britain's Psychological Warfare Bureau made extensive use of the work done by Reese on his 80,000 British Army guinea pigs, captive soldiers who underwent many forms of testing. It was Tavistock-designed methods that got the United States into the Second World War and which, under the guidance of Dr. Kurt Lewin, established the OSS, the forerunner of the CIA. Lewin became the director of the Strategic Bombing Survey, which was a plan for the Royal Air Force to concentrate on bombing German worker housing while leaving military targets, such as munition plants, alone. The munition plants on both sides belonged to the international bankers who had no wish to see their assets destroyed.

Later, after the war was over, NATO ordered Sussex University to establish a very special brainwashing center which became part of Britain's Psychological Warfare Bureau, only now, its research was directed toward civilian rather than military applications. We shall return to that super secret unit which was called Science Policy Research Institute (SPRI) under our chapters on drugs.

The idea behind saturation bombing of civilian worker housing was to break the morale of the German worker. It was not designed to affect the war effort against the German military machine. Lewin and his team of actuaries reached a target figure, that if 65% of German worker housing was destroyed by nightly RAF bombing, the morale of the civilian population would collapse. The actual document was prepared by the Prudential Assurance Company.

The RAF, under the command of "Bomber" Harris, carried out Lewin's plans, culminating in the terror firestorm bombing of Dresden, in which over 125,000, mainly old men, women and children, were killed. The truth of "Bomber" Harris's horror raids on German civilians was a well kept secret until long after the end of WW II.

Tavistock provided most of the detailed programs that led to the establishing of the Office of Naval Intelligence, (ONI) the number one intelligence service in the United States, one which dwarfs the CIA in size and scope. Contracts worth *billions* of dollars were given to Tavistock by the United States Government and Tavistock's strategic planners provide most of what the Pentagon uses for our defense establishment, even today. Here again is illustrated the grip the Committee of 300 has on the United States, and the majority of our institutions. Tavistock runs over 30 research institutions in the United States, all of which we will name in our charts at the end of the book.

These Tavistock-U.S. institutions have in many cases grown into gargantuan monsters, penetrating every aspect of our government agencies and taking command of all policy making. One of Tavistock's chief wreckers of our way of life was Dr. Alexander King, a founder member of NATO and a favorite with the Committee of 300, as well as an outstanding member of the Club of Rome. Dr. King was assigned by the Club of Rome to destroy America's education by taking control of the National Teachers Association and working in close conjunction with certain law makers and judges. If it was not generally known how all-pervading is the influence of the Committee of 300, this book should dispel every vestige of that doubt.

The trial run for the Federal Emergency Management Agency (FEMA)—a Club of Rome creation—came in a test run against the nuclear power station at Three Mile Island, Harrisburg, Pennsylvania. Termed "an accident" by the hysterical media, this was not an accident but a deliberately designed crisis test for FEMA. An additional benefit was the fear and hysteria created by the news media which had people fleeing the area when in fact they were never in any danger.

It was considered a success by FEMA and it scored a lot of points for the anti-nuclear forces. TMI became the rallying point for the so-called "environmentalists," a highly financed and controlled group run out of Aspen Institute on behalf of the Club of Rome. Coverage was provided free of charge by William Paley of CBS television, a former British intelligence agent.

FEMA is a natural successor to the Strategic Bombing Survey of WW II. Dr. Kurt Lewin, theoretician for what the Tavistock conspirators called crisis management, was deeply involved in the study. There is an unbroken chain between Lewin and Tavistock that stretches back for thirty-seven years. Lewin incorporated the Strategic Bombing Survey into FEMA, with only a few small adjustments proving necessary, one of the changes being the target, WHICH WAS NO LONGER GERMANY BUT THE UNITED STATES OF AMERICA. Forty-five years after the end of WW II it is still Tavistock that has its hands on the trigger, and the weapon is pointed at the United States. The late Margaret Mead conducted an intensive study of the German and Japanese population, under the aegis of Tavistock, on how they reacted to stress caused by aerial bombardment. Irving Janus was an associate professor on the project which was supervised by Dr. John Rawlings Reese, promoted to Brigadier-General in the British Army. The test results were given to FEMA. The Irving Janus report was of great value in formulating FEMA policies. Janus used it in a book which he later wrote entitled *AIR WAR AND STRESS*. The ideas in his book were followed TO THE LETTER BY FEMA DURING THE THREE MILE ISLAND "CRISIS." Janus had a really simple idea: Simulate a succession of crises and manipulate the population following the Lewin terror tactics and they will do exactly as required.

In carrying out this exercise, Lewin discovered something new, that social control on a wide scale can be achieved by using the news media to bring home the horrors of a nuclear war via the television media. It was discovered that women's magazines were very effective in dramatizing the terrors of a nuclear war. A trial run conducted by Janus had Betty Bumpers, wife of Senator Dale Bumpers of Arkansas, "writing" for *McCalls* magazine on that subject.

The article appeared in *McCalls* January 1983 issue. Actually, Mrs. Bumpers did not write the article, it was created for her by a group of writers at Tavistock whose speciality such subject matters are. It was a collection of untruths, non-facts, innuendoes and conjectures based entirely upon false premises. The Bumpers article was typical of the kind of psychological manipulation at which Tavistock is so very good. Not one of the ladies who read *McCalls* could have failed to be impressed by the terror-horror story of what a nuclear war looks like.

The Committee of 300 has a major bureaucracy at its disposal made up of hundreds of think tanks and front organizations that run the whole gamut of private business and government leaders. I will mention as many as I can fit in, starting with the German Marshall Fund. Its members, and remember they are also members of NATO and the Club of Rome, consist of David Rockefeller of Chase Manhattan Bank, Gabriel Hague of the prestigious Manufactures Hanover Trust and Finance Corporation, Milton Katz of the Ford Foundation, Willy Brandt, leader of Socialist International, KGB agent and member of the Committee of 300, Irving Bluestone, chairman of the United Auto Workers Executive Board, Russell Train, U.S. president of the Club of Rome and Prince Philip's World Wildlife Fund, Elizabeth Midgely, CBS programs producer, B. R. Gifford, director of the Russell Sage Foundation, Guido Goldman of the Aspen Institute, the late Averill Harriman, Committee of 300 extraordinary member, Thomas L. Hughes of the Carnegie Endowment Fund, Dennis Meadows and Jay Forrestor of MIT "world dynamics."

The Committee of 300, although in existence for over 150 years, did not take on its present form until around 1897. It was always given to issuing orders through other fronts, such as the Royal Institute for International Affairs. When it was decided that a super-body would control European affairs, the RIIA founded the Tavistock Institute, which in turn created NATO. For five years NATO was financed by the German Marshall Fund. Perhaps the most important member of the Bilderbergers, a foreign policy body of the Committee, was Joseph Rettinger, said to have been its founder and organizer, whose annual meetings have delighted conspiracy hunters for several decades.

Rettinger was a well-trained Jesuit priest and a 33rd Degree Freemason. Mrs. Katherine Meyer Graham who is suspected of having murdered her husband in order to get control of the *Washington Post*, was another ranking member of the Club of Rome, as was Paul G. Hoffman of the New York Life Insurance Company, one of the largest insurance companies in the United

States and a leading Rank company, with ties directly to Queen Elizabeth of England's immediate family. John J. McCloy, the man who attempted to wipe post-World War II Germany off the map and last but not least, James A. Perkins of the Carnegie Corporation, were also founding members of the Bilderbergers and the Club of Rome.

What a star-studded cast! Yet strangely enough, few if any outside of genuine intelligence agencies had ever heard of this organization until recent times. The power exercised by these important personages and the corporations, television stations, newspapers, insurance companies and banks they represent matches the power and prestige of at least two European countries, and still this is only the tip of The Committee of 300's enormous cross-gridding and interfaced interests.

Not mentioned in the foregoing line-up is Richard Gardner who, although an early member of the Committee of 300, was sent to Rome on a special assignment. Gardner married into one of the oldest Black Nobility families of Venice, thus providing the Venetian aristocracy a direct line to the White House. The late Averill Harriman was another of the committee's direct links with the Kremlin and the White House, a position which Kissinger inherited after the death of Harriman.

The Club of Rome is indeed a formidable agency of the Committee of 300. Although ostensibly working on American affairs, the group overlaps other Committee of 300 agencies and its United States members are often found working with "problems" in Japan and Germany. Some of the front organizations operated by the above committee include the following, although not limited to them:

LEAGUE OF INDUSTRIAL DEMOCRACY

Officials: Michael Novak, Jeane Kirkpatrick, Eugene Rostow, IRWIN SUALL, Lane Kirkland, Albert Schenker.

Purpose: To disrupt and disturb normal labor relations between workers and employees by brainwashing labor unions to make impossible demands with special attention to steel, automobile and housing industries.

FREEDOM HOUSE
Officials: Leo Churn and Carl Gershman.

Purpose: To spread socialist disinformation among American blue collar workers, spread dissension and dissatisfaction. Now that these objectives have been largely realized, Gershman has been drafted by Lawrence Eagleburger to CEDC, a newly created body to stop a united Germany from expanding its trade into the Danube Basin.

COMMITTEE FOR A DEMOCRATIC MAJORITY
Officials: Ben Wattenburg, Jean Kirkpatrick, Elmo Zumwalt and Midge Dector.

Purpose: To provide a connecting link between the educated socialist class and minority groups with the intent of setting up a solid block of voters who can be counted on to vote for leftwing candidates at election time. It was really a Fabianist operation from start to finish.

FOREIGN POLICY RESEARCH INSTITUTE
Officials: Robert Strausz Hupe.

Purpose: To undermine and eventually end NASA space program.

SOCIAL DEMOCRATS U.S.A.
Officials: Bayard Rustin, Lane Kirkland, Jay Lovestone, Carl Gershman, Howard Samuel, Sidney Hook.

Purpose: To spread radical socialism, especially among minority groups, and forge links between similar organizations in socialist countries. Lovestone was for decades the leading advisor to U.S. presidents on Soviet affairs and a strong direct link with Moscow.

INSTITUTE FOR SOCIAL RELATIONS
Officials: Harland Cleveland, Willis Harmon.
Purpose: Change the way America thinks.

THE CITIZENS LEAGUE
Officials: Barry Commoner.
Purpose: To bring "common cause" legal suits against various government agencies, especially in the defense industries.

WAR RESISTERS LEAGUE
Officials: Noam Chomsky and David McReynolds.
Purpose: To organize resistance to the Vietnam War among leftwing groups, students and the Hollywood "in crowd."

THE DEMOCRATIC SOCIALIST ORGANIZING COMMITTEE OF THE INSTITUTE FOR DEMOCRATIC SOCIALISM
Officials: Frank Zeider, Arthur Redier and David McReynolds.
Purpose: A clearing house for leftwing socialist ideas and activities in the U.S and Europe.

ANTI-DEFAMATION LEAGUE—FACT FINDING DIVISION
Officials: IRWIN SUALL, also known as John Graham.
Purpose: A joint FBI-British intelligence operation designed to single out rightwing groups and their leaders and put them out of business before they grow too large and too influential.

INTERNATIONAL ASSOCIATION OF MACHINISTS
Purpose: A labor oriented front for the Socialist International and a hot-bed of organized labor unrest polarizing workers and management.

AMALGAMATED CLOTHING WORKERS
Officials: Murray Findley, IRWIN SUALL and Jacob Scheinkman.
Purpose: Much the same as the Machinists Union, to socialize and polarize workers in the garment trade.

A. PHILIP RANDOLPH INSTITUTE
Officials: Bayard Rustin.
Purpose: To provide a means of coordinating organizations with a common purpose, an example of which would be the spread of socialist ideas among college students and workers.

CAMBRIDGE POLICY STUDIES INSTITUTE
Officials: Gar Apelrovitz.
Purpose: To expand on the work being done at the Institute for Policy Studies. Founded in February 1969 by international socialist, Gar Apelrovitz, former assistant to Senator Gaylord Nelson. Apelrovitz wrote the controversial book *ATOMIC DI-PLOMACY* for the Club of Rome which work was financed by the German Marshall Fund. It concentrates on research and action projects, with a stated goal of fundamentally changing American society, i.e., to create a Fabianist United States in preparation of the coming One World Government.

ECONOMIC COMMITTEE OF THE NORTH ATLANTIC INSTITUTE
Officials: Dr. Aurellio Peccei.
Purpose: NATO think-tank on global economic issues.

CENTER FOR THE STUDY OF DEMOCRATIC INSTITUTIONS
Officials: Founder Robert Hutchins of the Committee of 300, Harry Ashmore, Frank Kelly and a large group of "Fellows."
Purpose: To spread ideas that will bring on social reforms

of the liberal kind with democracy as an ideology. One of its activities is to draft a new constitution for the U.S. which will be strongly monarchical and socialistic as found in Denmark. The Center is an "Olympian" stronghold. Located in Santa Barbara, it is housed in what is affectionately called "the Parthenon." Former Representative John Rarick called it "an outfit loaded with Communists." By 1973 work on a new United States Constitution was in its thirty-fifth draft which proposes an amendment guaranteeing "environmental right," the thrust of which is to reduce the industrial base of the U.S. to a mere whisper of what it was in 1969. In other words, this institution is carrying out Club of Rome zero-growth post-industrial policies laid down by the Committee of 300.

Some of its other aims are control of economic cycles, welfare, regulation of business and national public works, control of pollution. Speaking on behalf of the Committee of 300, Ashmore says the function of the CSDI is to find ways and means of making our political system work more effectively. " We must change education and we must consider a new U.S. Constitution and a Constitution for the world," Ashmore says.

Further goals enunciated by Ashmore are as follows:

(1) Membership of the U.N. must be made universal.

(2) The U.N. must be strengthened.

(3) South East Asia must be neutralized. (For neutralized, read "Communized.")

(4) Cold War must be ended.

(5) Racial discrimination must be abolished.

(6) Developing nations must be assisted. (Meaning assisted to destruct.)

(7) No military solutions to problems. (Pity they didn't tell George Bush that before the Gulf War.)

(8) National solutions are not adequate.

(9) Coexistence is necessary.

HARVARD PSYCHOLOGICAL CLINIC

Officials: Dr. Kurt Lewin and staff of 15 new-science scientists.

Purpose: To create a climate where the Committee of 300 can take unlimited power over the U.S.

INSTITUTE FOR SOCIAL RESEARCH

Officials: Dr. Kurt Lewin and staff of 20 new-science scientists.

Purpose: To devise a whole new set of social programs to steer America away from industry.

SCIENCE POLICY RESEARCH UNIT

Officials: Leland Bradford, Kenneth Dam, Ronald Lippert.

Purpose: A "Future Shocks" research institution at Sussex University in England and part of the Tavistock network.

SYSTEMS DEVELOPMENT CORPORATION

Officials: Sheldon Arenberg and a staff of hundreds, too numerous to mention here.

Purpose: To coordinate all elements of the intelligence communities of the U.S.A. and Britain. It analyzess what "players" have to be assigned the role of a national entity; for example, Spain would come under a supine watered-down Catholic Church, the U.N. under the Secretary General and so forth. It developed the system of "X RAY 2" where think tank personnel, military installations and law enforcement centers are all linked to the Pentagon through a nation-wide network of teletypes and computers: To apply surveillance techniques on a nation-wide scale. Arenberg says his ideas are non-military, but his techniques are mainly those he learned from the military. He was responsible for the New York State Identification and Intelligence System, a typical George Orwell "1984" project, which is completely illegal under our Constitution. The NYSIIS system is in the process of being adopted nationwide. It is what Brzezinski referred to as the ability to almost instantaneously retrieve data about any person. NYSIIS shares data with all law enforcement and government agencies in the state. It provides storage and rapid retrieval of individual records, criminal and social. It is a TYPICAL Committee of 300 project. There is a crying need for a full investigation to be conducted into just what it is that Systems Development Corporation is doing, but that is beyond the scope of this book. One thing is sure, SDC is not there to preserve freedom and liberty guaranteed by the U.S. Constitution. How convenient that it should be located in Santa Barbara in easy reach of Robert Hutchins' "Parthenon." Some publications put out by these Club of Rome institutions are as follows:

"Center Magazine"
"Counterspy"
"Coventry"
"Covert Action Information Bulletin"
"Dissent"
"Human Relations"
"Industrial Research"
"Inquiry"
"Mother Jones"
"One"
"Progressive"
"Raconteur"
"The New Republic"
"Working Papers for a New Society"

These are by no means all of the publications issued under the auspices of the Club of Rome. There are many hundreds more, in fact each of the foundations puts out its own publication. Given the number of foundations run by the Tavistock Institute and the Club of Rome, a partial listing is all we can include here. Some of the more important foundations and think tanks are in the following list, which includes Army think tanks.

The American public would be astounded if it only knew

how deeply the Army is involved in "new war tactics" research with Committee of 300 "think tanks." Americans are not aware that in 1946 the Club of Rome was ordered by the Committee of 300 to further the progress of think tanks which it said offered a new means of spreading the Committee's philosophy. The impact of these think tanks upon our military, just since 1959 when they suddenly proliferated, is truly astounding. There is no doubt that they will play an even greater role in the daily affairs of this nation as we come to the close of the 20th century

THE MONT PELERIN SOCIETY

Mont Pelerin is an economic foundation devoted to issuing misleading economic theories and influencing economists in the Western world to follow models it lays out from time to time. Its leading practitioners are Von Hayek and Milton Friedman.

THE HOOVER INSTITUTION

Founded originally to fight Communism, the institution has slowly but surely turned toward Socialism. It has an annual budget of $2 million, funded by companies under the umbrella of the Committee of 300. It now concentrates on "peaceful changes" with emphasis on arms control and domestic U.S. problems. It is frequently used by the news media as a "conservative" organization whose views they seek when a conservative viewpoint is needed. The Hoover Institution is far from that, and following the 1953 take-over of the Institution by a group allied to the Club of Rome, it has become a One World-New World Order outlet for "desirable" policies.

HERITAGE FOUNDATION

Founded by brewery magnate Joseph Coors to act as a conservative think tank, Heritage was soon taken over by Fabianists Sir Peter Vickers Hall, Stuart Butler, Steven Ayzler, Robert Moss and Frederich Von Hayek under the direction of the Club of Rome. This institute played a major role in carrying out British Labour leader Anthony Wedgewood Benn's order to "Thatcherize Reagan." Heritage is certainly not a conservative operation although at times it may look and sound like one.

HUMAN RESOURCES RESEARCH OFFICE. This is an Army research establishment dealing in "psychotechnology." Most of its personnel are Tavistock-trained. "Psychotechnology" covers GI motivation, morale and music used by the enemy. In fact a lot of what George Orwell wrote about in his book "1984" appears to be remarkably similar to what is taught at HUMRRO. In 1969, the Committee of 300 took over this important institution and turned it into a private non-profit organization run under the auspices of the Club of Rome. It is the largest behavioral research group in the U.S.

One of its specialities is the study of small groups under stress and HUMRRO teaches the Army that a soldier is merely an extension of his equipment and has brought great influence to bear on the "man/weapon" system and its "human quality control," so widely accepted by the United States Army. HUMRRO has had a very pronounced effect on how the Army conducts itself. Its mind-bending techniques are straight out of Tavistock. HUMRRO'S applied psychology courses are supposed to teach Army brass how to make the human weapon work. A good example of this is the manner in which soldiers in the war against Iraq were willing to disobey their field manual standing orders and bury 12,000 Iraqi soldiers alive.

This type of brainwashing is terribly dangerous because, today, it is applied to the Army, the Army applies it to brutally destroy thousands of "enemy" soldiers, and tomorrow the Army could be told that civilian population groups opposed to government policies are "the enemy." We are already a mindless brainwashed flock of sheep, yet it seems that HUMRRO can take mind bending and mind control a step further. HUMRRO is a valuable adjunct to Tavistock and many of the lessons taught at HUMRRO were applied in the Gulf War, which makes it a little easier to understand how it came to be that American soldiers behaved as ruthless and heartless killers, a far cry from the concept of the traditional American fighting man.

RESEARCH ANALYSIS CORPORATION.

This is HUMRRO'S sister "1984" organization situated in McLean, Virginia. Established in 1948, it was taken over by the Committee of 300 in 1961 when it became part of the Johns Hopkins bloc. It has worked on over 600 projects, including integrating Negroes into the Army, the tactical use of nuclear weapons, psychological warfare programs and mass population control.

Obviously there are many more major think tanks, and we shall come to most of them in this book. One of the most important areas of cooperation between what think tanks turn out and what becomes government and public policy are the "pollsters." It is the job of the polling companies to mold and shape public opinion in the way that suits the conspirators. Polls are constantly being taken by CBS-NBC-ABC, the *New York Times*, the *Washington Post*. Most of these efforts are coordinated at the National Opinion Research Center where, as much as it will amaze most of us, a psychological profile was developed for the entire nation.

Findings are fed into the computers of Gallup Poll and Yankelovich, Skelley and White for comparative evaluation. Much of what we read in our newspapers or see on television has first been cleared by the polling companies. WHAT WE SEE IS WHAT THE POLLSTERS THINK WE SHOULD SEE. This is called "public opinion making." The whole idea behind this bit of social conditioning is to find out how responsive the public is to POLICY DIRECTIVES handed down by the Committee of 300. We are called "targeted population groups" and what is measured by the pollsters is how much resistance is generated to what appears in the "Nightly News." Later, we shall learn exactly how this deceptive practice got started and who is responsible for it.

It is all part of the elaborate opinion-making process created at Tavistock. Today our people believe they are well-informed but what they do not realize is that the opinions they believe are their own were in fact created in the research institutions and think tanks of America and that none of us are free to form our own opinions because of the information we are provided with by the media and the pollsters.

Polling was brought to a fine art just before the United States entered the Second World War. Americans, unbeknown to themselves, were conditioned to look upon Germany and Japan as dangerous enemies who had to be stopped. In a sense, this was true, and that makes conditioned thinking all the more dangerous, because based on the INFORMATION fed to them, the enemy did indeed appear to be Germany and Japan. Just recently we saw how well Tavistock's conditioning process works when Americans were conditioned to perceive Iraq as a threat and Saddam Hussein as a personal enemy of the United States.

Such a conditioning process is technically described as "the message reaching the sense organs of persons to be influenced." One of the most respected of all pollsters is Committee of 300 member Daniel Yankelovich, of the company, Yankelovich, Skelley and White. Yankelovich is proud to tell his students that polling is a tool to change public opinion, although this is not original, Yankelovich having drawn his inspiration from David Naisbett's book "TREND REPORT" which was commissioned by the Club of Rome.

In his book Naisbett describes all of the techniques used by public opinion makers to bring about the public opinion desired by the Committee of 300. Public opinion making is the jewel in the crown of the OLYMPIANS, for with their thousands of new-science social scientists at their beck and call, and with the news media firmly in their hands, NEW public opinions on almost any subject can be created and disseminated around the world in a matter of two weeks.

This is precisely what happened when their servant George Bush was ordered to make war on Iraq. Within two weeks, not only the U.S. but almost the entire world public opinion was turned against Iraq and its President Saddam Hussein. These media change artists and news manipulators report directly to the Club of Rome which in turn reports to the Committee of 300 at whose head sits the Queen of England ruling over a vast network of closely-linked corporations who never pay taxes and are answerable to no one, who fund their research institutions through foundations whose joint activities have almost total control over our daily lives.

Together with their interlocking companies, insurance business, banks, finance corporations, oil companies, newspapers, magazines, radio and television, this vast apparatus sits astride the United States and the world. There is not a politician in Washington D.C. who is not, somehow, beholden to it. The Left rails against it, calling it "imperialism" which indeed it is, but the left is run by the same people, the very same ones who control the right, so that the left is no more free than we are!

Scientists engaged in the process of conditioning are called "social engineers" or "new-science social scientists" and they play an integral part in what we see, hear and read. The "old school" social engineers were Kurt K. Lewin, Professor Hadley Cantril, Margaret Meade, Professor Derwin Cartwright and Professor Lipssitt who, together with John Rawlings Reese, made up the backbone of new-science scientists at Tavistock Institute.

During the Second World War, there were over 100 researchers at work under the direction of Kurt Lewin, copying slavishly the methods adopted by Reinhard Heydrich of the S.S. The OSS was based on Heydrich's methodology and, as we know, the OSS was the forerunner of the Central Intelligence Agency. The point of all this is that the governments of Britain and the United States already have the machinery in place to bring us into line in a New World Order with only a slight modicum of resistance materializing, and this machinery has been in place since 1946. Each passing year has added new refinements.

It is this Committee of 300 which has established control networks and mechanisms far more binding than anything ever seen in this world. Chains and ropes are not needed to restrain us. Our fear of what is to come does that job far more efficiently than any physical means of restraint. We have been brainwashed to give up our Constitutional right to bear arms; to give up our Constitution itself; to allow the United Nations to exercise control over our foreign policies and the IMF to take control of our fiscal and monetary policies; to permit the President to break United States law with impunity and to invade a foreign country and kidnap its head-of-state. In short we have been brainwashed to the extent where we, as a nation, will accept each and every lawless act carried out by our government almost without question.

I for one know that **we will soon have to fight to reclaim our country from the Committee, or lose it forever.** BUT when it comes right down to it, how many will actually take up arms? In 1776 only 3% of the populace took up arms against King George III. This time around, 3% will be woefully inadequate. We should not allow ourselves to be led down dead-end roads, for that is what our mind controllers have planned for us by confronting us with such a complexity of issues that we simply succumb to long range penetration and make no decisions at all on many vital issues.

We shall be looking at the names of those who make up the Committee of 300 but, before we do that, we should examine the massive interfacing of all important institutions, companies and banks under the Committee's control. We must mark them well because these are the people who are deciding who shall live and who shall be eliminated as "useless eaters"; where we will worship God, what we must wear and even what we shall eat. According to Brzezinski, we shall be under endless surveillance around the clock for 365 days a year ad infinitum.

That we have been betrayed from within is being accepted by more and more people each year, and that is good, because it is through knowledge, a word translated from the word BELIEF, that we shall be able to defeat the enemies of all mankind. While we were being distracted by the bogeymen in the Kremlin, the Trojan Horse was moved into position in Washington D.C. The greatest danger free people face today is not from Moscow but from Washington D.C. We need first to conquer the DOMESTIC ENEMY, and after that we will be strong enough to mount an offensive to remove Communism from the earth, together with all of its attendant "isms."

The Carter Administration accelerated the collapse of our economy and our military strength, the latter begun by Club of Rome and Lucis Trust member Robert Strange McNamara. In spite of his promises, Reagan continued to undermine our industrial base, starting where Carter left off. While we need to keep our defenses strong, we cannot do that from a weak industrial base for, without a well-run military-industrial complex, we cannot have a viable defense system. The Committee of 300 recognizes this and planned from 1953 its zero-growth post-industrial policies now in full flower.

Thanks to the Club of Rome our technology potential has dropped below that of Japan and Germany, nations we are supposed to have defeated in the Second World War. How has this come about? Because of men like Dr. Alexander King and our blindfolded state of mind, we have failed to recognize the destruction of our educational institutions and systems of teaching. As a result of our blindness, we are no longer training engineers and scientist in sufficient numbers to keep us among the industrialized nations of the world. Thanks to Dr. King, a man very few people in America know about, education in the U.S. is at its lowest level since 1786. Statistics produced by the Institute for Higher Learning show that the reading and writing capabilities of high school children in the United States are LOWER than they were among high school children in 1786.

What we face today is not only the loss of our freedom and the very fabric of our nation, but far worse, the possibility of the loss of our souls. The steady chipping away at the foundation upon which this republic rests has left an empty void, which satanists and cultists are rushing to fill with their synthetic soul material. This truth is difficult to accept and appreciate because there was nothing SUDDEN about these events. If a sudden shock were to hit us, a cultural and religious shock, we would be shaken out of our apathy.

But gradualism—which is what Fabianism is, does nothing to raise the alarm. Because the vast majority of Americans can see no MOTIVATION for the things I have described, they cannot accept it, and so the conspiracy is scorned and often mocked. By creating chaos through presenting hundreds of daily choices our people have to make, we have come down to a position where, unless motivation can be clearly shown, all information is rejected.

This is both the weak and the strong link in the conspiratorial chain. Most thrust aside anything that has no motive, so the conspirators feel safe behind the ridicule poured upon those who point to the coming crisis in our nation and our individual lives. However, if we can get enough people to see the truth, the motivation block gets weaker until it will eventually be forced aside as more and more people become enlightened and the notion that "this cannot happen in America" is dispensed with.

The Committee of 300 is counting on our maladaptive responses to govern our reaction to created events, and it will not be disappointed as long as we as a nation continue in the present way we respond. We must turn responses to created crises into ADAPTIVE responses by identifying the conspirators and exposing their plans for us, so that these things become public knowledge. The Club of Rome has already made THE TRANSITION TO BARBARISM. Instead of waiting to be "raptured," we must stop the Committee of 300 before it can accomplish its goal of making us prisoners of the" New Dark Age" planned for us. It is not up to God, IT IS UP TO US. We have to take the necessary action.

All information that I provide in this book comes from years of research backed up by impeccable intelligence sources. Nothing is exaggerated. It is factual and precise so do not fall into the trap set by the enemy that this material is "disinformation." For the past two decades I have provided information which has proved to be highly accurate and which has explained a lot of puzzling events. My hope is that through this book, a better, clearer and wider understanding of the conspiratorial forces ranged against this nation will come about. That hope is being realized as more and more young people are beginning to ask questions and seek information about what is REALLY going on.

It is difficult for people to comprehend that these conspirators are real and that they have the power I and many others have attributed to them. Many have written to ask how it is that our government does nothing about the terrible threat to civilization? The problem is that our government is PART of the problem, part of the conspiracy, and nowhere and at no time has this become more clearly evident than during the Bush Presidency. Of course President Bush knows precisely what the Committee of 300 is doing to us. HE WORKS FOR THEM. Others have written to say, "We thought we were fighting the government." Of course we are, but behind government stands a force so powerful and all-encompassing that intelligence agencies are even afraid to mention the name "Olympians."

Proof of the Committee of 300 is found in the vast number of powerful institutions owned and controlled by it. Listed here are some of the more important ones, all of which come under the MOTHER OF ALL THINK TANKS AND RESEARCH INSTITUTIONS, THE TAVISTOCK INSTITUTE OF HUMAN RELATIONS with its far-flung network of hundreds of "branches."

STANFORD RESEARCH CENTER

Stanford Research Center (SRC) was founded in 1946 by the Tavistock Institute For Human Relations. Stanford was created to help Robert O. Anderson and his ARCO oil company, who had secured for the Committee of 300 the oil rights on the North Slope of Alaska. Basically, the job was too large for Anderson's Aspen Institute to handle, so a new center had to be founded and funded. That new center was Stanford Research Center. Alaska sold its rights on a downpayment of $900 million, a relatively small amount for the Committee of 300. The governor of Alaska was steered to SRI for help and advice. This was no accident but the result of judicious planning and a process of long-range conditioning.

Following the governor's call for help, three SRI scientists set up shop in Alaska where they met with the Alaskan Secretary of State and the State Planning Office. Francis Greehan, who headed the SRI team, assured the Governor that his problem of how to handle the rich oil find would be safe in the hands of SRI. Naturally Greehan did not mention the Committee of 300 or the Club of Rome. In less than a month Greehan assembled a team of economists, petroleum scientists and new-science scientists numbering in the hundreds. The report SRI gave to the Governor ran to eighty-eight pages.

The proposal was adopted virtually without change by the Alaska legislature in 1970. Greehan had indeed done a remarkable job for the Committee of 300. From this beginning SRI developed into an institution employing 4000 people with an annual budget of $160 million plus. Its President, Charles A. Anderson, has seen much of this growth during his tenure, as has Professor Willis Harmon, director of the SRI Center for the Study of Social Policies, employing hundreds of new-science scientists, many of the top staffers having been transferred from Tavistock's London base. One of those was RCA board chairman and former British intelligence agent, David Sarnoff, who was closely involved with Harmon and his team for twenty-five years. Sarnoff was something of a "watchdog" for the mother institute in Sussex.

Stanford claims to make no moral judgments on projects it accepts, working for Israel and the Arabs, South Africa and Libya but, as one would imagine, by adopting this attitude it ensures an "inside edge" with foreign governments that the CIA has found most useful. In Jim Ridgeway's book, "THE CLOSED CORPORATION," SRI spokesman Gibson brags about SRI's non-discriminatory stance. Although not on the Federal Contract Research Center lists, SRI is today the largest military think tank, dwarfing Hudson and Rand. Among SRI's speciality departments are chemical and biological warfare experimental centers.

One of Stanford's more dangerous activities is counter-insurgency operations aimed at civilian populations—just the sort of "1984" things government is already using against its own people. The U.S. government pays SRI millions of dollars each year for this kind of highly controversial "research." Following student protests against chemical warfare experiments conducted at Stanford, SRI "sold" itself to a private group for just $25 million. Of course nothing really changed, SRI was still a Tavistock project and the Committee of 300 still owned it, but the gullible appeared to be satisfied by this meaningless cosmetic change.

In 1958 a startling new development arose. Advanced Research Products Agency (ARPA), a contracting agency for the Defense Department, approached SRI with a top secret proposal. John Foster at the Pentagon told SRI that what was needed was a program to insure the United States against "technological surprise." Foster wanted to perfect a condition where the environment became a weapon; special bombs to trigger volcanoes and/or earthquakes, behavioral research on potential enemies and minerals and metals with potential for new weapons. The project was accepted by SRI and code-named "SHAKY."

The massive electronic brain in SHAKY was capable of

carrying out many commands, its computers having been constructed by IBM for SRI. Twenty-eight scientists worked on what is called "Human Augmentation." The IBM computer even has the capability to solve problems by analogy and recognizes and identifies scientists who work with it. The "special applications" of this tool can be better imagined than described. Brzezinski knew what he was talking about when he wrote "THE TECHNOTRONIC ERA."

Stanford Research Institute works closely with scores of civilian consulting firms, trying to apply military technology to domestic situations. This has not always been a success, but as techniques improve, the prospects for massive all-pervading surveillance, as described by Brzezinski, daily becomes more real. IT ALREADY EXISTS AND IS IN USE, EVEN THOUGH SLIGHT MALFUNCTIONS FROM TIME TO TIME HAVE TO BE IRONED OUT. One such civilian consulting firm was Schriever McKee Associates of McLean, Virginia, run by retired General Bernard A. Schriever, a former chief of the Air Force Systems Command, who developed the Titan, Thor, Atlas and Minuteman rockets.

Schriever put together a consortium of Lockheed, Emmerson Electric, Northrop, Control Data, Raytheon and TRW under the name of URBAN SYSTEMS ASSOCIATES, INC. The purpose of the consortium? To solve social and psychological "urban problems" by means of military techniques using advanced electronic systems. It is interesting to note that TRW became the largest credit information collecting company in the credit-reporting business as a result and an outcome of its work with Urban Systems Associates, Inc.

This should tell us a great deal about just how far this nation is already under TOTAL SURVEILLANCE, which is the first requirement of the Committee of 300. No dictatorship, especially not one on a global scale, can function without total control over each and every individual. SRI was well on its way to becoming a key Committee of 300 research organization.

By the 1980's, 60% of SRI's contracts were devoted to "futurism" with both military and civilian applications. Its major clients were the U.S. Department of Defense-Directorate of Defense Research and Engineering, Office of Aerospace Research which dealt with "Applications of the Behavioral Sciences to Research Management," Executive Office of the President, Office of Science and Technology, U.S. Department of Health. On behalf of the Department of Health, SRI ran a program called "Patterns in ESDEA Title I Reading Achievement Tests." Other clients were the U.S. Department of Energy, the U.S. Department of Labor, U.S. Department of Transportation and the National Science Foundation (NSF). Of significance was the paper developed for NSF, entitled "Assessment of Future and International Problems."

Stanford Research, under the tutelage of Tavistock Institute in London, put together a far reaching and chilling system it called "Business Intelligence Program." In excess of 600 companies in the U.S. and abroad became subscribers. The program covered research in Japanese Foreign Business Relations, Consumer Marketing in a Period of Change, The Mounting Challenge of International Terrorism, Sensory Evaluation in Consumer Products, Electronic Funds Transfer System, Opto-Electric Sensing, Exploratory Planning Methods, the U.S. Defense Industry and Capital Availability. Among the TOP Committee of 300 companies who became clients of this program were Bechtel Corporation (George Schultz was on its board), Hewlett Packard, TRW, Bank of America, Shell Company, RCA, Blyth, Eastman Dillon, Saga Foods Corporation, McDonnell Douglas, Crown Zellerbach, Wells Fargo Bank and Kaiser Industries.

But one of the most sinister of all SRI programs with the possibilities of doing tremendous damage in altering the direction in which the United States will go, socially, morally and religiously, was Stanford's Charles F. Kettering Foundation's "CHANGING IMAGES OF MAN" under Stanford official reference "Contract Number URH (489)-2150 Policy Research

Report Number 4/4/74, Prepared by SRI Center for the Study of Social Policy, Director Willis Harmon." This is probably one of the most far-reaching investigations into how man might be changed that has ever been conducted. The report, covering 319 pages, was written by 14 new-science scientists under the supervision of Tavistock and 23 top controllers including B. F. Skinner, Margaret Meade, Ervin Lazlo and Sir Geoffrey Vickers, a high-level British intelligence officer in MI6. It will be recalled that his son-in-law, Sir Peter Vickers Hall, was a founding member of the so-called conservative "Heritage Foundation." Much of the 3000 pages of "recommendations" given to the Reagan administration in January 1981 were based upon material taken from Willis Harmon's "CHANGING IMAGES OF MAN."

I was privileged to receive a copy of "THE CHANGING IMAGES OF MAN" from my intelligence colleagues five days after it was accepted by the United States government. What I read shocked me, as I realized I was looking at a blueprint for a future America, unlike anything I had ever seen before. The nation was to be programmed to change and become so accustomed to such planned changes that it would hardly be noticeable when profound changes did occur. We have gone downhill so fast since "THE AQUARIAN CONSPIRACY" (the book title of Willis Harmon's technical paper) was written, that today, divorce draws no stigma, suicide is at an all time high and raises few eyebrows, social deviations from the norm and sexual aberrations, once unmentionable in decent circles, are now commonplace and excite no special protest.

As a nation we have not noticed how "CHANGING IMAGES OF MANKIND" has radically altered our American way of life forever. Somehow we were overcome by the "Watergate Syndrome." For a while we were shocked and dismayed to learn that Nixon was nothing but a cheap crook who hobnobbed with Earl Warren's Mafia friends at the beautiful home they built for him adjoining the Nixon estate. When too many "future shocks" and news headlines demanded our attention, we lost our way, or rather, the huge number of choices with which we were and still are daily confronted, confused us to such a degree that we were no longer able to make the necessary choices.

Worse yet, having been subjected to a barrage of crimes in high places, plus the trauma of the Vietnam War, our nation seemed no longer to want truths. Such reaction is carefully explained in Willis Harmon's technical paper, in short, the American nation was reacting exactly as profiled. Worse yet, in not wishing to accept truth, we took matters a step further: We looked to government to shield us from the truth.

The corrupt stench of the Reagan-Bush Administrations we wanted covered with six feet of earth. The crimes committed under the title of Iran/Contra affair (or scandals), we didn't want uncovered. We let our President lie to us regarding his whereabouts in the period October 20-23rd, 1980. Yet these crimes far exceed in quantity and scope anything Nixon did while he was in office. Do we as a nation recognize it as going downhill with our brakes off?

No, we do not. When those whose business it is to bring the truth to the American people that a private, well-organized little government inside the White House was busy committing one crime after another, crimes which attacked the very soul of this nation and the republican institutions upon which it rested, we were told not to bother the public with such things. "We really don't want to know about all this *speculation*," became a standard response.

When the highest elected official of the land blatantly put U.N. law above the Constitution of the United States—an impeachable offense, the majority accepted it as "normal." When the highest elected official of the land went to war without a Congressional declaration of war, the fact was censored out by the news media and, again, we accepted it rather than face the truth.

When the Gulf War, which our President plotted and planned, began, not only were we happy with censorship of the most blatant kind, we even took it to our hearts, believing that it was "good for the war effort." Our President lied, April Glaspie lied, the State Department lied. They said the war was justified because President Hussein had been warned to leave Kuwait alone. When Glaspie's cables to the State Department were finally made public, one United States Senator after another went charging to defend Glaspie, the harlot. It mattered not that they came from both the Democrats and the Republicans. We, the people, let them get away with their vile lies.

In this public attitude of the American people, the wildest dreams of Willis Harmon and his teams of scientists became a reality. The Tavistock Institute was elated at its success in destroying the self respect and self esteem of this once great nation. We are told that we won the Gulf War. What is not yet perceived by the vast majority of Americans is that, in winning the war, it cost the self respect and honor of our nation. That lies rotting in the desert sands of Kuwait and Iraq, alongside the corpses of the Iraqi soldiers we butchered in the agreed retreat from Kuwait and Basra—we could not keep our word that we would abide by the Geneva Conventions and not attack them. "What do you want," our controllers asked us, "victory or self respect? You can't have both."

One hundred years ago, this could not have happened, but now it has happened and excites no comment. We have succumbed to the long range penetration warfare waged against this nation by Tavistock. Like the German nation, defeated by the Prudential Bombing Survey, enough of us have succumbed to make this nation the kind that totalitarian regimes of the past would have only envisaged in their dreams. "Here," they would say, "is a nation, one of the largest in the world, that doesn't want the truth. All of our propaganda agencies can be dispensed with. We don't have to struggle to keep the truth from this nation, they have willingly rejected it of their own volition. This nation is a pushover."

Our once proud Republic of the United States of America

became no more than a series of criminal front organizations, which history shows is always the start of totalitarianism. This is the stage of permanent alteration we are at in America as 1991 drew to a close. We live in a throw-away society, programmed not to last. We do not even flinch at the 4 million homeless nor the 30 million jobless, nor the 15 million babies murdered thus far. They are "throw-aways" of the Age of Aquarius, a conspiracy so damnable that, when first confronted with it, the majority will disavow its existence, rationalizing these events as "times have changed."

This is how the Tavistock Institute and Willis Harmon programmed us to react. Dismantling of our ideals goes on without protest. The spiritual and intellectual drive of our people has been destroyed! On May 27th, 1991, President Bush made a very profound statement, the thrust of which appears to have been totally misused by most political commentators:

"The moral dimension of American policy requires us to chart a moral course through a world of lesser evils. That is the real world, not black and white. Very few moral absolutes."

What else could we expect from a President who is most probably the most evil man ever to occupy the White House?

Consider this in the light of his order to the military to bury alive 12,000 Iraqi soldiers. Consider this in the light of his ongoing war of genocide against the Iraqi people. President Bush was delighted to characterize President Saddam Hussein as the "Hitler of our times." He never bothered to offer a single scrap of proof. It was not needed. Because President Bush made the statement, we accepted it without question. Consider this in the bright light of truth, that he did all of these things in the name of the American people while secretly taking his orders from the Committee of 300.

But, more than anything else, consider this: President Bush

and his controllers feel so secure that they no longer deem it necessary to hide their evil control of the American people, or to lie about it. This is self-evident in the statement that he, as our leader, will make all manner of compromises with truth, honesty and decency if his controllers (and ours) deem it necessary. On May 27th, 1991, the President of the United States abandoned each and every principle embodied in our Constitution and boldly proclaimed that he was no longer bound by it. This is a great victory for the Tavistock Institute and the Prudential Bombing Survey, whose target changed from German worker housing in 1945 to the soul of the American people in a war that began in 1946 and runs through to 1992.

Increased pressure on this nation for change was applied by Stanford Research Institute in the early 1960's. SRI's offensive gathered power and momentum. Switch on your television set and you will see Stanford's victory in front of your very eyes: Talk shows featuring heavy sexual details, special video channels where perversion, rock and roll and drugs reign supreme. Where once John Wayne ruled, we now have a made-over apology for a man (or is he?) called Michael Jackson, a parody of a human being who is held up as a hero, as he gyrates, shuffles, mumbles and screams his way across television screens in millions of American homes.

A woman who has been through a series of marriages gets national coverage. One filthy, half-washed drug-ridden decadent rock band after another has hours of air time devoted to its inane sounds and mad gyrations, clothes fashions and language aberrations. Soap operas showing as near as "dammit" is to swearing pornographic scenes, draw no comment. Whereas in early 1960 this would never have been tolerated, today it is accepted as normal. We have been subjected and we have succumbed to what Tavistock Institute calls "future shocks" whose future is NOW and we are so numbed by one cultural shock after another that to protest seems like a futile gesture and, therefore, logically we think, it does no good to protest.

In 1986 the Committee of 300 ordered the pressure turned up. The U.S. was not going down fast enough. The United States began the process of "recognizing" the butchers of Cambodia, the criminal Pol Pot regime, self confessors to the murder of 2 million Cambodian citizens. In 1991, the wheel turned the full circle. The United States went to war against a friendly nation that had been programmed to trust the Washington traitors. We accused President Hussein of the small nation of Iraq of all manner of evil, NONE OF WHICH WAS EVEN REMOTELY TRUE. We killed and maimed its children, we left them to starve and to die of all manner of diseases.

In the same breath we sent the Bush emissaries of the Committee of 300 to Cambodia to RECOGNIZE THE EVIL MASS MURDERERS OF 2 MILLION CAMBODIANS, who were sacrificed by the Committee of 300's depopulation of cities experiment, which the big cities of the United States will experience in the not too distant future. Now, President Bush and his Committee of 300-ridden administration say, in effect, "Look people, what do you want from me? I told you that I will compromise where I see fit, even when that means sleeping with the Pol Pot murderers. SO WHAT—KISS MY HIPS."

The level of pressure for change will reach its peak in 1993 and we shall witness scenes such as we would never have thought possible. Punch drunk America will react, but ever so slightly. Not even the latest threat to our freedom, the personal computer card disturbs us. Willis Harman's "CHANGING IM-AGES OF MAN" would have been too technical for most so the service of Marilyn Ferguson was obtained to make it more easily understood. "THE AGE OF AQUARIUS" heralded nude stage shows and a song which made the top of the charts: "The Dawning of the Age of the Aquarius" swept the globe.

The personal computer card which, when fully distributed, will deprive us of our familiar environment and, as we shall see, environment means a lot more than the usually accepted meaning of the word. The United States has gone through a period of intense trauma such as has never been visited upon any other nation in the history of the world, and the worst is yet to come. Everything is going according to what Tavistock ordered and what the social scientists at Stanford mapped out. Times do not change; they are made to change. All changes are preplanned and come as the result of careful action. We have been changed, gradually at first, but now the pace of change is picking up. The United States is being transformed from One Nation Under God to a polyglot of nations under several gods. The U.S. is no longer One nation under God. The framers of the Constitution have lost the battle.

Our forebears spoke a common language and believed in a common religion—Christianity, and held common ideals. There were no aliens in our midst; that came later in a deliberately planned attempt to break up the United States into a series of fragmented nationalities, cultures and beliefs. If you doubt this, go down to the East Side of New York, or the West Side of Los Angeles, on any given Saturday and look around you. The United States has become several nations struggling to coexist under a common system of government. When the floodgates of immigration were opened wide by Franklin D. Roosevelt, a cousin of the head of the Committee of 300, the cultural shock caused great confusion and dislocation and made "One Nation" an unworkable concept. The Club of Rome and NATO have exacerbated the situation. "Love thy neighbor" is an ideal that will not work unless your neighbor "is as yourself."

To the framers of our Constitution, the truths they laid out for future generations were "self evident"—to themselves. Being unsure that future generations would also find the truths to which they bound this nation self evident, THEY SET ABOUT SPELLING THEM OUT. IT SEEMS THAT THEY WERE AFRAID OF A TIME THAT MIGHT COME WHEN THE TRUTHS THEY ESPOUSED WOULD NO LONGER BE SELF-EVIDENT. The Tavistock Institute for Human Relations has made sure that what the framers feared might come to pass has indeed come to pass. That time has arrived with Bush and his "no absolutes" and his New World Order under the Committee of 300.

This is part of the concept of social changes forced upon Americans which Harmon and the Club of Rome said would make for severe trauma and a great building up of pressure. The social upheavals that have taken place since the advent of Tavistock, the Club of Rome and NATO will continue in the U.S. for as long as the limit of absorption is ignored. Nations are made up of individuals and, like individuals, there is a limit to their ability to absorb changes, no matter how robust they may be.

This psychological truth was well proven by the Strategic Bombing Survey which called for saturation bombing of German worker housing. As mentioned earlier, the project was the work of the Prudential Insurance Company and no one doubts today that Germany suffered its defeat because of this operation. Many of the scientists who worked on that project are working on saturation bombing of America, or else they have passed on, leaving their skilled techniques in the hands of others who followed behind them.

The legacy they left behind them can be found in the fact that we have not so much lost our way as a nation, but that we have been steered in a direction opposite to that which the framers of the Declaration guided us for over 200 years. We have, in short, lost contact with our historical genes, our faith, which inspired countless generations of Americans to move forward as a nation, benefiting from the patrimony left to us by the framers of the Declaration of Independence and the United States Constitution. That we are lost is clear to all who seek the truth, as unpleasant as it may be.

With President Bush and his "no absolute morals" guiding us, we blunder ahead as lost nations and individuals tend to do. We are collaborating with the Committee of 300 for our own downfall and our own enslavement. Some sense it—and feel a strong sense of unease. The various conspiracy theories they are familiar with do not seem to cover it all. This is because they know nothing of the Conspirators' Hierarchy, The Committee of 300.

These souls who feel a deep sense of unease and that something is radically wrong, yet cannot put their collective fingers on the problem, walk in darkness. They look to a future they see slipping away from them. The American dream has become a mirage. They place their faith in religion but take no steps to help that faith along by ACTION. Americans will never experience a retracing of steps such as the Europeans experienced when at the height of the Dark Ages. By determined ACTION, they awoke in themselves a spirit of renewal which resulted in the glorious Renaissance.

The enemy that has directed them to this point decided to make a strong move against the United States in 1980, so that a Renaissance of America would be impossible. Who is the enemy? The enemy is no faceless "they." The enemy is clearly identifiable as the Committee of 300, the Club of Rome, NATO and all of its affiliated organizations, the think tanks and research institutions controlled by Tavistock. There is no need to use "they" or "the enemy" except as shorthand. WE KNOW WHO "THEY," THE ENEMY, IS. The Committee of 300 with its Eastern Liberal Establishment "aristocracy," its banks, insurance companies, giant corporations, foundations, communications networks, presided over by a HIERARCHY OF CONSPIRATORS—THIS IS THE ENEMY.

This is the power that brought to life the reign of terror in Russia, the Bolshevik Revolution, World Wars I and II, Korea, Vietnam, the fall of Rhodesia, South Africa, Nicaragua, and the Philippines. This is the secret upper-level government that brought into existence the controlled disintegration of the U.S. economy and deindustrialized what was once the greatest industrial power, for good, that the world had ever known.

America today can be compared with a soldier who falls asleep in the thick of battle. We Americans have fallen asleep, given way to apathy caused by being confronted with a multiplicity of choices which has confused us. These are the changes that alter our environment, break down our resistance to change, so that we become dazed, apathetic and eventually fall asleep in the thick of battle.

There is a technical term for this condition. It is called "long range penetration strain." The art of subjecting a very large group of people to continued long range penetration strain was developed by scientists working out of the Tavistock Institute of Human Relations and their U.S. subsidiaries, Stanford Research and Rand Corporation, and at least another 150 research institutions here in the U.S.

Dr. Kurt Lewin, the scientist who developed this fiendish warfare, has caused the average American patriot to fret over various conspiracy theories, leaving him or her with a feeling of uncertainty and insecurity, isolated and perhaps even afraid, as he searches, but fails to understand the decay and rot caused by "THE CHANGING IMAGES OF MANKIND," unable to identify or combat the social, moral, economic and political changes he deems undesirable and does not want, yet which increase in intensity on every hand.

Dr. Lewin's name will not be found in any of our establishment history books which, in any event, are a record of events mostly from the side of the ruling class or the victors of wars. Therefore, it is with pride that I introduce his name to you. As mentioned before, Dr. Lewin organized the Harvard Psychological Clinic and the Institute for Social Research under the auspices of the Tavistock Institute. The names do not give much indication of the purpose of the two organizations.

This reminds me of the infamous bill to reform coinage and mint laws passed in 1827. The title of the bill was harmless enough, or sounded harmless, which was the intention of its backers. Through this Act, Senator John Sherman betrayed the nation into the hands of the international bankers. Sherman allegedly sponsored the bill "without reading it." As we know, the bill's true purpose was to demonetize silver and give the thieving bankers unlimited power over the credit of our nation; powers to which the bankers were clearly not entitled under the clear and unmistakable terms of the U.S. Constitution.

Kurt Lewin gave the Tavistock Institute, the Club of Rome and NATO unlimited power over America, to which no organization, entity or society is entitled. These institutions have used the usurped powers to destroy the will of the nation to resist the plans and intentions of the conspirators to rob us of the fruits of the American Revolution and steer us on a course leading directly to a New Dark Ages under a One World Government.

Lewin's colleagues in this long range penetration objective were Richard Crossman, Eric Trist, H. V. Dicks, Willis Harmon, Charles Anderson, Garner Lindsay, Richard Price and W. R. Bion. Again, these names never appear in the evening news; in fact, they only appear in scientific journals—so very few Americans are aware of them and not at all aware of what the men behind the names have done and are doing to the United States.

President Jefferson once said he pitied those who thought they knew what was taking place through reading the newspaper. Disraeli, the British prime minister, said much the same thing. Indeed, down through the ages, rulers have delighted in running things from behind the scenes. Man has always felt the need to dominate and nowhere and at no time is the desire more prevalent than in this modern era.

If it were not so, why all the need for secret societies? If we are ruled by an open system run by democratically elected officials, why the need for a secret Masonic order in every village, town and city across the United States? How is it that Freemasonry can operate so openly and yet keep its secrets so well hidden? We can't ask the Nine Unknown Men of the Nine Sisters Lodge in Paris that question, nor can we ask it of their nine fellows in the Quatuar Coronati Lodge in London. Yet these eighteen men form part of an even more secret government, the RIIA, and beyond that, the Committee of 300.

How is it that the Scottish Rite of Freemasonry could brainwash John Hinckley to shoot President Reagan? Why do we have such secret orders as the Knights of St. John of Jerusalem, the Round Table, the Milner Group and so on down line upon line of secret societies? They form part of a world-wide chain of command and control running through the Club of Rome, NATO, the RIIA and finally right up to the Conspirators' Hierarchy, The Committee of 300. Men need these secret societies because their deeds are evil and must be hidden. Evil cannot stand in the light of truth.

In this book we shall find an almost complete list of the conspirators, their institutions, fronts and publications. In 1980 the Aquarian Conspiracy was in full swing and its success can be seen in every facet of our private and national life. The overwhelming rise in mindless violence, serial killers, teenage suicides, the unmistakable signs of lethargy—"long range penetration" is a part of our new environment, as dangerous, if not more so, than the polluted air that we breathe.

The coming of the Age of Aquarius caught America totally unprepared. We as a nation were not prepared for the changes about to be forced upon us. Who ever had heard of Tavistock, Kurt Lewin, Willis Harmon and John Rawlings Reese? They were not even on the American political scene. What we would have noticed, if we bothered to look at all, was a falling off of our ability to withstand futuristic shock as we became more fatigued, distressed and eventually entered a period of psychological shock followed by widespread apathy as an outward manifestation of long range penetration warfare.

The Age of Aquarius was best described by Tavistock Institute as the vehicle for delivering turbulence: "There are three distinct phases in the response and reaction to stress displayed by large social groups. First, there is superficiality; the population under attack will defend itself with slogans; this does not identify the source of the crisis and therefore does nothing to address it, hence the crisis will persist. The second is fragmentation. This occurs as the crisis continues and social order breaks down. Then, there is the third phase where the population group goes into 'self realization' and turns away from the induced crisis and there follows a maladaptive response, accompanied with active synoptic idealism and disassociation."

Who can deny that with the huge increase in drug usage— "crack" making thousands of instant new addicts each day—the shocking rise in the murder of infants each day (aborticide), which by now far exceeds casualties suffered by our armed forces in both World Wars, Korea and Vietnam, the open acceptance of homosexuality and lesbianism whose "rights" are protected by more and more laws each year, the terrible plague we call "AIDS" washing over our towns and cities, total failure of our education system, the stunning increase in the divorce rate, a murder rate that shocks the rest of the world into disbelief, satanic serial killings, the disappearance of thousands of young children, snatched off our streets by perverts, a virtual tidal wave of pornography accompanied by "permissiveness" on our television screens—who can deny that this nation is in crisis, which we are not addressing and from which we are turning away.

Well-meaning people who specialize in these things blame a lot of the problem on education, or what passes for it in the United States. Criminals now abound in the age groups 9-15. Rapists are quite commonly as young as 10. Our social specialists, our teacher's unions, our churches say it is all due to a faulty education system. Witness how test scores keep dropping. The specialists bewail the fact that the United States now ranks around 39th in the level of education in the world.

Why do we bemoan what is so obvious? OUR EDUCATION SYSTEM WAS PROGRAMMED TO SELF-DESTRUCT. THAT WAS WHAT DR. ALEXANDER KING WAS SENT HERE BY NATO TO ARRANGE. THAT IS WHAT JUSTICE HUGO BLACK WAS ORDERED TO ARRANGE. THE FACT IS, THE COMMITTEE OF 300, WITH THE APPROVAL OF OUR GOVERNMENT, DOES NOT WANT OUR YOUTH TO

BE PROPERLY EDUCATED. The education that Freemason Justice Hugo Black, Alexander King, Gunnar Myrdal and his wife came to give the children of the United States is that CRIME PAYS, EXPEDIENCY IS WHAT COUNTS.

They taught our children that United States law is unequally applied, and that is perfectly in order. Our children were properly educated by a decade of corrupt examples; Ronald Reagan and George Bush were ruled by greed and became totally corrupted by it. Our education system hasn't failed. Under the guidance of King, Black and the Myrdals it is actually a great success, but it all depends from whose point of view we look at it. The Committee of 300 is DELIGHTED with our education system, and will not allow one comma of it to be changed.

According to Stanford and Willis Harmon, the induced trauma of long range penetration—of which our education is a part, has been going on for 45 years, yet how many are aware of the insidious pressures being applied to our society and the constant exposure to brainwashing that goes on every day? The mysterious gang wars that broke out in New York in the 1950's is an example of how the conspirators can create and stage-manage any type of disruptive elements they like. Where those gang wars came from nobody knew until the 1980's when researchers uncovered the hidden controllers who directed the so-called "social phenomena."

Gang wars were carefully planned at Stanford, deliberately designed to shock society and cause ripples of disturbances. By 1958 there were in excess of 200 of these gangs. They were made popular by a musical and a Hollywood movie, "West Side Story." After making the news for a decade, suddenly, in 1966, they disappeared off the streets of New York, Los Angeles, Newark, New Jersey, Philadelphia and Chicago.

Throughout the near decade of gang violence, the public reacted according to the profiled response Stanford expected; society as a whole could not comprehend gang warfare and the public responded in a maladaptive manner. Had there been those wise enough to recognize in gang wars a Stanford experiment in social engineering and brainwashing, the conspirator's plot would have been exposed. Either we did not have trained specialists who could see what was going on—which is highly unlikely—or else they were threatened and remained silent. The cooperation with Stanford by the news media brought to light a "new age" attack on our environment just as predicted by the social engineers and new-science scientists at Tavistock.

In 1989 gang warfare, as a social conditioning to change, was reintroduced to the streets of Los Angeles. Within a few short months of the first incidents, gangs began to proliferate—first in the scores, then in the hundreds on the streets of the East Side of Los Angeles. Crack houses and rampant prostitution proliferated; drug dealers dominated the streets. Anybody who got in their way was gunned down. The outcry in the press was loud and long. Stanford's targeted large population group began defending itself with slogans. This is what Tavistock called the first phase, with the targeted group failing to identify the source of the crisis.

The second phase of the gang war crisis was "fragmentation." People not living in the areas frequented by gangs said, "Thank God they are not in our neighborhood." This ignored the fact that the crisis continued with or without recognition and that social order in Los Angeles had begun to break down. As profiled by Tavistock, those groups not affected by gang war "broke away to defend themselves" because the source of the crisis was not identified, the so called "maladaptation" process, the period of disassociation.

Apart from the proliferation of drug sales, what is the purpose of gang wars? First, it is to show the targeted group that they are not safe, i.e., insecurity is generated. Secondly, it is to show that organized society is helpless in the face of such violence and thirdly, to bring about a recognition of the fact that our social order is collapsing. The present wave of gang violence will go away just as quickly as it started, once the three phases of the

Stanford program are completed.

An outstanding example of social conditioning to accept change, even when it is recognized as unwelcome change by the large population group in the sights of Stanford Research Institute, was the "advent" of the BEATLES. The Beatles were brought to the United States as part of a social experiment which would subject large population groups to brainwashing of which they were not even aware.

When Tavistock brought the Beatles to the United States nobody could have imagined the cultural disaster that was to follow in their wake. The Beatles were an integral part of "THE AQUARIAN CONSPIRACY," a living organism which sprang from "THE CHANGING IMAGES OF MAN," URH (489)-2150-Policy Research Report No. 4/4/74. Policy Report prepared by SRI Center for the study of Social Policy, Director, Professor Willis Harmon.

The phenomenon of the Beatles was not a spontaneous rebellion by youth against the old social system. Instead it was a carefully crafted plot to introduce by a conspiratorial body which could not be identified, a highly destructive and divisive element into a large population group targeted for change against its will. New words and new phrases—prepared by Tavistock—were introduced to America along with the Beatles. Words such as "rock" in relation to music sounds, "teenager," "cool," "discovered" and "pop music" were a lexicon of disguised code words signifying the acceptance of drugs and arrived with and accompanied the Beatles wherever they went, to be "discovered" by "teenagers." Incidentally, the word "teenagers" was never used until just before the Beatles arrived on the scene, courtesy of the Tavistock Institute for Human Relations.

As in the case of gang wars, nothing could or would have been accomplished without the cooperation of the media, especially the electronic media and, in particular, the scurrilous Ed Sullivan who had been coached by the conspirators as to the role he was to play. Nobody would have paid much attention to the motley crew from Liverpool and the 12-atonal system of "music" that was to follow had it not been for an overabundance of press exposure. The 12-atonal system consisted of heavy, repetitive sounds, taken from the music of the cult of Dionysus and the Baal priesthood by Adorno and given a "modern" flavor by this special friend of the Queen of England and hence the Committee of 300.

Tavistock and its Stanford Research Center created trigger words which then came into general usage around "rock music" and its fans. Trigger words created a distinct new break-away largely young population group which was persuaded by social engineering and conditioning to believe that the Beatles really were their favorite group. All trigger words devised in the context of "rock music" were designed for mass control of the new targeted group, the youth of America.

The Beatles did a perfect job, or perhaps it would be more correct to say that Tavistock and Stanford did a perfect job, the Beatles merely reacting like trained robots "with a little help from their friends"—code words for using drugs and making it "cool." The Beatles became a highly visible "new type"—more Tavistock jargon—and as such it was not long before the group made new styles (fads in clothing, hairstyles and language usage) which upset the older generation, as was intended. This was part of the "fragmentation-maladaptation" process worked out by Willis Harmon and his team of social scientists and genetic engineering tinkerers and put into action.

The role of the print and electronic media in our society is crucial to the success of brainwashing large population groups. Gang wars ended in Los Angeles in 1966 as the media withdrew its coverage. The same thing will happen with the current wave of gang wars in Los Angeles. Street gangs will wither on the vine once media saturation coverage is toned down and then completely withdrawn. As in 1966, the issue would become "burned out." Street gangs will have served their purpose of creating turbulence and insecurity. Exactly the same pattern will be followed in the case of "rock" music. Deprived of media attention, it will eventually take its place in history.

Following the Beatles, who incidentally were put together by the Tavistock Institute, came other "Made in England" rock groups, who, like the Beatles, had Theo Adorno write their cult lyrics and compose all the "music." I hate to use these beautiful words in the context of "Beatlemania"; it reminds me of how wrongly the word "lover" is used when referring to the filthy interaction between two homosexuals writhing in pigswill. To call "rock" music, is an insult, likewise the language used in "rock lyrics."

Tavistock and Stanford Research then embarked on the second phase of the work commissioned by the Committee of 300. This new phase turned up the heat for social change in America. As quickly as the Beatles had appeared on the American scene, so too did the "beat generation," trigger words designed to separate and fragment society. The media now focused its attention on the "beat generation." Other Tavistock-coined words came seemingly out of nowhere: "beatniks," "hippies," "flower children" became part of the vocabulary of America. It became popular to "drop out" and wear dirty jeans, go about with long unwashed hair. The "beat generation" cut itself off from mainstream America. They became just as infamous as the cleaner Beatles before them.

The newly-created group and its "lifestyle" swept millions of young Americans into the cult. American youth underwent a radical revolution without ever being aware of it, while the older generation stood by helplessly, unable to identify the source of the crisis, and thus reacting in a maladaptive manner against its manifestation, which were drugs of all types, marijuana, and later Lysergic acid, "LSD," so conveniently provided for them by the Swiss pharmaceutical company, SANDOZ, following the discovery by one of its chemists, Albert Hoffman, how to make synthetic ergotamine, a powerful mind-altering drug. The Committee of 300 financed the project through one of their banks, S. C. Warburg, and the drug was carried to America by the philosopher, Aldous Huxley.

The new "wonder drug" was promptly distributed in "sample" size packages, handed out free of charge on college campuses across the United States and at "rock" concerts, which became the leading vehicle for proliferating the use of drugs. The question that cries out for an answer is, what was the Drug Enforcement Agency (DEA) doing at the time? There is compelling circumstantial evidence that would appear to indicate that the DEA knew what was going on but was ordered not to take any action. With very substantial numbers of new British "rock" bands arriving in the U.S., rock concerts began to become a fixture on the social calender of American youth. In tandem with these "concerts," the use of drugs among the youth rose in proportion. The devilish bedlam of discordant heavy beat sounds numbed the minds of listeners so that they were easily persuaded to try the new drug on the basis that "everybody is doing it." Peer pressure is a very strong weapon. The "new culture" received maximum coverage from the jackal media, which cost the conspirators not one single thin dime.

Great anger was felt by a number of civic leaders and churchmen over the new cult but their energies were misdirected against the RESULT of what was going on and not against the CAUSE. Critics of the rock cult made the same mistakes that had been made in the prohibition era, they criticized law enforcement agencies, teachers, parents—anybody but the conspirators.

Because of the anger and resentment I feel toward the great drug plague, I make no apology for using language which is not customary for me to use. One of the worst drug slobs ever to walk the streets of America was Alan Ginsberg. This Ginsberg pushed the use of LSD through advertising which cost him nothing, although under normal circumstances it would have cost millions of dollars in TV advertising revenues. This free advertising for drugs, and LSD in particular, reached a new high in the late 1960's, thanks to the ever-willing cooperation of the media. The effect of Ginsberg's mass advertising campaign was devastating; the American public was subjected to one cultural future shock after another in rapid succession.

We became over-exposed and over stimulated and, again, may I remind you that this is Tavistock jargon, lifted from the Tavistock training manual, overwhelmed by its new development and, when we reached that point, our minds began to lapse into apathy; it was just too much to cope with, that is to say, "long range penetration had taken hold of us." Ginsberg claimed to be a poet but no greater rubbish was ever written by anyone who ever aspired to becoming a poet. Ginsberg's designated task had little to do with poetry; his main function was to push the new subculture and force acceptance of it upon the large targeted population group.

To assist him in his task, Ginsberg coopted the services of Norman Mailer, a writer of sorts who had spent some time in a mental institution. Mailer was a favorite of the leftwing Hollywood crowd and so had no problem with getting maximum television time for Ginsberg. Naturally Mailer had to have a pretext—not even he could blatantly come out with the true nature of Ginsberg's television appearances. So a charade was adopted: Mailer would talk "seriously" on camera with Ginsberg about poetry and literature.

This method of getting wide television coverage at no cost to themselves was followed by every rock group and concert promoter who followed the example set by Ginsberg. The electronic media moguls had big hearts when it came to giving free time to these dirty verminous creatures and their even dirtier products and filthy ideas. Their promotion of horrible garbage spoke volumes and, without abundant help from the print and electronic media, the drug trade could not have spread as rapidly as it did in the late 1960's-early 1970's, and probably would have been confined to a few small local areas.

Ginsberg was able to give several nationally televised performances extolling the virtues of LSD and marijuana, under the guise of "new ideas" and "new cultures" developing in the art and music world. Not to be outdone by the electronic media, Ginsberg's admirers wrote glowing articles about "this colorful man" in the art and social columns of all of America's largest newspapers and magazines. There had never been such an across-the-media-board free advertising campaign in the history of newspaper, radio and television and it cost the promoters of the Aquarian conspiracy, NATO and the Club of Rome not one red cent. It was all absolutely free advertising for LSD, only thinly disguised as "art" and "culture."

One of Ginsberg's closest friends, Kenny Love, published a five-page report in the *New York Times*. This is in accordance with the methodology used by Tavistock and Stanford Research: If something is to be promoted which the public has not yet been fully brainwashed to accept, then have someone write an article, covering all sides of the subject matter. The other method is to have live television talk shows in which a panel of experts promotes the product and or idea under the pretext of "discussing" it. There are point and counter-point, both pro and con participants airing their support or opposition. When it is all over, the subject to be promoted has been dinned into the public mind. While this was new in the early 1970's, today it is standard practice on which talk shows thrive.

Love's five-page pro LSD pro Ginsberg article was duly printed by the *New York Times*. Had Ginsberg tried to buy the same amount of space in an advertisement, it would have cost him at least $50,000. But Ginsberg didn't have to worry; thanks to his friend Kenny Love, Ginsberg got the massive advertising all for free. With newspapers like the *New York Times* and the *Washington Post* under the control of the Committee of 300, this kind of free advertising is given to any subject matter, and more especially to those promoting decadent life styles—drugs-hedonism—anything that will confuse the American people. After the trial run with Ginsberg and LSD, it became standard Club of Rome practice to call upon major newspapers in America to give free advertising on demand to people and ideas they were promoting.

Worse yet—or better yet, depending upon the viewpoint— United Press (UP) picked up Kenny Love's free advertising for Ginsberg and LSD and telexed it to HUNDREDS of newspapers and magazines around the country under the guise of a "news" story. Even such highly respectable establishment magazines as "Harpers Bazaar" and "TIME" made Mr. Ginsberg respectable. If a nation-wide campaign of this magnitude were presented to Ginsberg and the promoters of LSD by an advertising agency, the price tag would have run into at least $1 million in terms of 1970 dollars. Today the price tag would be nothing less than $15-$16 million dollars. It is no wonder that I refer to the news media as "jackals."

I suggest that we try to find any media outlet to do an expose on the Federal Reserve Board, which is what I did. I took my article, which was a good expose of the greatest swindle on earth, to every major newspaper, radio and television station, magazine house and several talk-show hosts. A few made promises that sounded good—they would definitely air the article and have me discuss it—give them about a week and they would get back to me. Not one of them ever did, nor did my article ever appear in the pages of their newspapers and journals. It was as if a blanket of silence had been thrown over me and the subject I was endeavoring to promote, and indeed that was precisely what had happened.

Without massive media hype, and without almost around the clock coverage, the hippy-beatnik rock, drug cult would never have gotten off the ground; it would have remained a localized oddity. The Beatles, with their twanging guitars, silly expressions, drug language and weird clothes, would not have amounted to a hill of beans. Instead, because the Beatles were given saturation coverage by the media, the United States has suffered one cultural shock after another.

The men buried in the think tanks and research institutions, whose names and faces are still not known to but a few people, made sure that the press played its part. Conversely, the media's important role in not exposing the power behind the future cultural shocks made certain that the source of the crisis was never identified. Thus was our society driven mad through psychological shocks and stress. "Driven mad" is taken from Tavistock's training manual. From its modest beginnings in 1921, Tavistock was ready in 1966 to launch a major irreversible cultural revolution in America, which has not yet ended. The Aquarian Conspiracy is part of it.

Thus softened up, our nation was now deemed ripe for the introduction of drugs which was to rival the prohibition era in scope and the huge amounts of money to be made. This too was an integral part of the Aquarian Conspiracy. The proliferation of drug usage was one of the subjects under study at the Science Policy Research Unit (SPRU) at Tavistock's Sussex University facility. It was known as the "future shocks" center, a title given to so-called future oriented psychology designed to manipulate whole population groups to induce "future shocks." It was the first of several such institutions set up by Tavistock.

"Future shocks" is described as a series of events which come so fast that the human brain cannot absorb the information. As I said earlier, science has shown that there are clearly marked limits to the amount of changes and the nature of them that the mind can deal with. After continuous shocks, the large targeted population group discovers that it does not want to make choices any more. Apathy takes over, often preceded by mindless violence such as is characteristic of the Los Angeles street gangs, serial killers, rapists and child kidnapers.

Such a group becomes easy to control and will docilely follow orders without rebelling, which is the object of the exercise. "Future shocks," says SPRU, "is defined as physical and psychological distress arising from the excess load on the decision-making mechanism of the human mind." That is Tavistock jargon lifted straight from Tavistock manuals—which they don't know I have.

Just as an overloaded electrical circuit will activate a trip switch, so do humans "trip out," which is a syndrome that medical science is only now beginning to understand, although John Rawlings Reese conducted experiments in this field as far back as the 1920's. As can be appreciated, such a targeted group is ready to "trip out" and take to drugs as a means of escape from the pressures of so many choices having to be made. This is how drug usage was spread so rapidly through America's "beat generation." What started with the Beatles and sample packages of LSD has grown into a flood-tide of drug usage which is swamping America.

The drug trade is controlled by the Committee of 300 from the top down. The drug trade started with the British East India Company and was closely followed by the Dutch East India Company. Both were controlled by a "Council of 300." The list of names of members and stockholders of the BEIC read like something out of Debretts Peerage. BEIC established the "China Inland Mission," whose job it was to get the Chinese peasants, or coolies, as they were called, addicted to opium. This created the market for opium which the BEIC then filled.

In much the same way the Committee of 300 used "The Beatles" to popularize "social drugs" with the youth of America and the Hollywood "in-crowd." Ed Sullivan was sent to England to become acquainted with the first Tavistock Institute "rock group" to hit the shores of the United States. Sullivan then returned to the United States to draft the strategy for the electronic media on how to package and sell the group. Without the full cooperation of the electronic media and Ed Sullivan, in particular, "The Beatles" and their "music" would have died on the vine. Instead, our national life and the character of the United States was forever changed.

Now that we know, it is all too clear how successful the "Beatles" campaign to proliferate the use of drugs became. The fact that "The Beatles" had their music and lyrics written for them by Theo Adorno was concealed from public view. The prime function of "The Beatles" was to be discovered by teenagers, who where then subjected to a non-stop barrage of "Beatlemusic," until they became convinced that they liked the sound and adopted it, along with all that accompanied it. The Liverpool group performed up to expectations, and with "a little help from their friends," i.e., illegal substances we call drugs, created a whole new class of young Americans in the precise mold ordained by the Tavistock Institute.

Tavistock had created a highly visible "new type" to act as their drug-runners. The China Inland Mission "Christian missionaries" would not have fitted in with the 1960's. "New type" is social-science scientist jargon; what it meant was that the Beatles created new social patterns, first and foremost being to normalize and popularize the use of drugs, new tastes in clothes and hair styles which really distinguished them from the older generation as was intended by Tavistock.

It is important to note the deliberate fragmentation-inducing language used by Tavistock. The "teenagers" never once dreamed that all the "different" things they aspired to were the products of older scientists working in think tanks in England and Stanford Research. How mortified they would have been if they had discovered that most of their "cool" habits and expressions were deliberately created for their use by a group of older social science scientists!

The role of the media was, and remains, very important in promoting the use of drugs on a nation-wide scale. When coverage of the street warfare gangs was abruptly terminated by the media, they became "burned out" as a social phenomena; the "new age" of drugs followed. The media has always served as a catalyst and has always pushed "new causes" and now media attention was focused on drug usage and its supporters, the "beat generation," yet another phrase fashioned at Tavistock, in its determined efforts to bring about social changes in The United States.

Drug usage now became an accepted part of everyday life in America. This Tavistock-designed program took in millions of American youth, and the older generation began to believe that America was undergoing a natural social revolution, failing all the while to realize that what was happening to their children was not a spontaneous movement, but a highly artificial creation designed to force changes in America's social and political life.

The descendants of the British East India Company were delighted with the success of their drug pushing program. Their disciples became adept in the use of lysergic acid (LSD) so conveniently made available by patrons of the drug trade like Aldous Huxley, courtesy of the highly respected Sandoz company of Switzerland and financed by the great Warburg banking dynasty. The new "wonder drug" was promptly distributed at all rock concerts and on college campuses in free sample packages. The question that begs to be asked is, "What was the FBI doing while all this was going on?"

The purpose of the Beatles had become abundantly clear. The British East India Company's descendants in the upper-class society in London must have felt very good about the billions of dollars that began rolling in. With the coming of "rock" which shall henceforth be used as shorthand to describe Adorno's fiendish satanic music, a tremendous increase in the use of social drugs, especially marijuana, was observed. The entire dope business was expanded under the control and direction of the Science Policy Research Unit (SPRU).

SPRU was run by Leland Bradford, Kenneth Damm and Ronald Lippert, under whose expert guidance a large number of new-science scientists were trained to promote "future shocks," one of the chief being the dramatic increase in the use of drugs by America's teenagers. SPRU's policy papers, planted in various government agencies, including the Drug Enforcement Agency (DEA), dictated the course of the disastrous "drug war" allegedly waged by the Reagan and Bush Administrations.

This was the forerunner of how the United States is run

today, by one committee and/or council after another, by an inner-government fed on Tavistock papers which they firmly believe are their own opinions. These virtual unknowns are making decisions that will forever change our form of government and the quality of life here in the United States. Through "crisis adaptation" we have already been changed so much as to barely compare with what we were in the 1950's. Also, our environment has been changed.

There is much talk about environment these days and, while it mostly refers to green surroundings, pure rivers and fresh air, there is another, equally important environment, namely, the drug environment. The environment of our life style has become polluted; our thinking has become polluted. Our ability to control our destiny has become polluted. We are confronted by changes that pollute our thinking to the extent that we do not know what to make of it all. The "Environment of Change" is crippling the nation; we appear to have so little control that it has produced anxiety and confusion.

We now look to group solutions instead of individual solutions to our problems. We do not make use of our own resources to solve problems. In this the prolific rise in drug usage is playing a leading role. The strategy is a deliberate one, devised by the new-science scientists, the social engineers and tinkerers, aimed at the most vulnerable of all areas, our self-image, or how we perceive ourselves, which leads us eventually to become like sheep being led to the slaughter. We have become confused by the many choices we have to make, and we have become apathetic.

We are manipulated by unscrupulous men without ever being aware of it. This is particularly true of the drug trade and we are now in the transition stage where we can be set up for a change from the present constitutional form of government, which has taken a giant step forward under the Bush administration. While there are those who still persist, in the face of all of the evidence to the contrary in saying, "It can't happen in America," the fact is: IT HAS ALREADY HAPPENED. Our will to resist events not to our liking has been steadily eroded and undermined. We will resist, some of us say, but not so many of us will do that, and we will be in the minority.

The drug trade has insidiously changed our environment. The alleged "war on drugs" is a farce; it does not exist in qualitative measure to make the slightest difference to the descendants of the British East India Company. Combined with computerization, we are almost fully brainwashed, robbed of our ability to resist forced changes. Which brings us to another environment, PEOPLE CONTROL, also known as personal information control, without which governments cannot play their numbers game.

As matters stand, we the people have absolutely no way of knowing just what government does or does not know about us. Government computer files are not subject to scrutiny by the public at large. Do we foolishly believe that personal information is sacrosanct? Remember, in every society there are rich and powerful families who control law enforcement agencies. I have proved the existence of such families. Do not think that if these families wanted to find out about us, they could not do so. These are the families who often have a member in the Committee of 300.

Take Kissinger, for instance, who has his own private dossiers on hundreds of thousands of people, not only in the U.S. but all over the world. Are we on Kissinger's enemy list? Is this far fetched? Not at all. Take P2 Masonic and Committee Monte Carlo who have such lists which run into tens of thousands of names. Incidentally, Kissinger is one of them. There are other "private" intelligence agencies, such as INTEL, whom we shall meet later.

One of the ways heroin is moved into Europe is through the Principality of Monaco. The heroin comes from Corsica carried in ferries that ply a busy trade between Corsica and Monte Carlo during the summer. There is no check of what goes on or comes off these ferries. As there is no border between France and Monaco, drugs, and more especially heroin (partly processed opium), flows through the open border of Monaco into laboratories in France, or else if it has already been processed into heroin, it goes directly to the distributors.

The Grimaldi family has been in the drug smuggling business for centuries. Because Prince Ranier got greedy and began skimming heavily and would not desist after three warnings, his wife, Princess Grace, was murdered in a car "accident." Ranier underestimated the power of the Committee of which he is a member. The Rover car in which she was traveling had the brake fluid chambers tampered with in such a way that each time the brakes were depressed, fluid was released in measured amount, until by the time the car reached the most dangerous of several hairpin bends, there was no stopping power, and it sailed over a stone wall, hitting the ground fifty feet below in a sickening smash.

Everything possible was done by the Committee of 300 operatives to conceal the truth about the murder of Princess Grace. To this day the Rover car remains in the custody of French police, shrouded under a cover on a trailer which no one is allowed to approach, let alone examine. The signal for the execution of Princess Grace was picked up by the British Army listening post in Cyprus and it is believed by well placed sources that the Committee Monte Carlo and P2 gave the order.

The drug trade, controlled by the Committee of 300, is a crime against humanity, but having been conditioned and softened up by years of incessant bombardment by Tavistock Institute, we have more or less accepted our changed environment, regarding the drug trade as a problem that is "too big" to handle. This is not the case. If we could marshal an entire nation, equip and send millions of American soldiers to fight in a war in Europe in which he had no business intervening, if we could defeat a major power, then we can smash the drug trade, using the same WW II tactics.

The logistical problems that had to be solved when we entered the Second World War are even today still mind-boggling.

Yet we successfully overcame all problems. Why then is it impossible to defeat a well-defined enemy, far smaller and weaker than Germany, given the immensely improved weapons and surveillance equipment we have today? The real reason that the drug problem is not eradicated is because it is being run by the highest families in the entire world as part of a coordinated gigantic money-making machine.

In 1930, British capital invested in South America greatly exceeded capital investment in British "dominions." Graham, an authority on British investments abroad, stated that British investment in South America "exceeded one trillion pounds." Remember, this was 1930, and one trillion pounds was a staggering sum of money in those days. What was the reason for such heavy investment in South America? In a word it was drugs.

The plutocracy controlling British banks held the purse strings and then, as now, put up a most respectable facade to cover their true business. No one ever caught them with dirtied hands. They always had front men, even as they do today, willing to take the blame if things went awry. Then as now the connections with the drug trade were tenuous at best. No one was ever able to lay a finger on the respectable and "noble" banking families of Britain, whose members are on the Committee of 300.

There is great significance in that only 15 members of Parliament were the controllers of that vast empire, of which the most prominent were Sir Charles Barry and the Chamberlain family. These overlords of finance were busy in places like Argentina, Jamaica and Trinidad, which became big money-spinners for them through the drug trade. In these countries, British plutocrats kept "the locals" as they were contemptuously called, at bare subsistence levels, hardly above slavery. The fortunes extracted from the drug trade in the Caribbean were vast.

The plutocrats hid behind faces like Trinidad Leaseholds Limited, but the REAL MEAT, then as now, was drugs. This is true of today where we find that Jamaica's Gross National

Product (GNP) is made up almost entirely of sales of ganja, a very potent form of marijuana. The mechanism for handling the ganja trade was set up by David Rockefeller and Henry Kissinger under the title "Caribbean Basin Initiative."

Up until a relatively short time ago, the true history of the China opium trade was quite unknown, having been as well covered up as it is possible to do. Many of my former students, in the days when I was lecturing, would come and ask me why the Chinese were so fond of smoking opium? They were puzzled, as are many still today, over contradictory accounts of what had actually taken place in China. Most thought it was merely a case of the Chinese workers buying opium on an open market and smoking it, or going to some of the thousands of opium dens and forgetting their terrible existence for a while.

The truth is that the supply of opium to China was a British monopoly, an OFFICIAL monopoly of the British government and official British policy. The Indo-British opium trade in China was one of the best kept secrets, around which many misleading legends grew up, such as "Clive of India" and the tales of derring-do by the British Army in India for the glory of "the Empire," so well written by Rudyard Kipling, and tales of "Tea Clippers" racing across the oceans with their cargoes of China tea for the high society drawing rooms of Victorian England. In reality, the history of British occupation of India and Britain's Opium Wars are some of the most dastardly blots on Western civilization.

Almost 13% of the income of India under British rule was derived from the sale of good quality Bengal opium to the British-run opium distributors in China. "The Beatles" of the day, the China Inland Mission, had done a great job in proliferating the use of opium among the poor Chinese laborers (coolies, as they were called). These addicts did not suddenly materialize out of thin air, any more than did teenager addicts in the U.S. THE POINT TO REMEMBER IS THAT BOTH WERE CREATED. In China a market for opium was first created and then filled by opium from Bengal. In the same way, a market for marijuana and LSD was first created in the United States by methods already described, and then filled by British plutocrats and their American cousins with the help of the overlords of the British banking establishment.

The lucrative drug trade is one of the worst examples of making money out of human misery; the other being the legal drug trade run by the pharmaceutical drug houses under Rockefeller ownership, in the U.S. for the most part, but with substantial companies operating in Switzerland, France and Britain and fully backed by the American Medical Association (AMA). The dirty dope transactions and the money it generates flows through the City of London, together with Hong Kong, Dubai and latterly, Lebanon, thanks to the invasion of that country by Israel.

There will be those who doubt this statement. "Look at the business columns of tae *Financial Times,*" they will tell us. "Don't tell me that this is all related to drug money"? OF COURSE IT IS, but don't imagine for one minute that the noble lords and ladies of England are going to advertise the fact. Remember the British East India Company? Officially, its business was trading in tea!

The London "Times" never dared tell the British public that it was impossible to make VAST PROFITS from tea, nor did that illustrious paper even hint at a trade in opium being plied by those who spent their time in London's fashionable clubs or playing a chukka of polo at the Royal Windsor Club, or that the gentlemen officers who went out to India in the service of the Empire were financed SOLELY by the enormous income derived from the misery of the millions of Chinese coolies addicted to opium.

The trade was conducted by the illustrious British East India Company, whose meddling in political, religious and economic affairs of the United States has cost us very dearly for over 200 years. The 300 members of the British East India Company's board were a cut above the common herd. They were so mighty, as Lord Bertrand Russell once observed, "They could even give God advice when he had trouble in Heaven." Nor should we imagine that anything has changed in the intervening years. EXACTLY the same attitude prevails today among members of the Committee of 300, which is why they often refer to themselves as the "Olympians."

Later the British Crown, i.e., the Royal Family, joined the British East India Company's trade, and used it as a vehicle to produce opium in Bengal, and elsewhere in India, controlling exports through what was called "transit duties," that is, the Crown levied a tax on all producers of opium duly registered with the state authority, who were sending their opium to China.

Prior to 1896, when the trade was still "illegal"—a word used to extract greater tribute from the producers of opium—there never having been the slightest attempt to stop the trade, colossal amounts of opium were shipped out of India on board "China Tea Clippers," those sailing ships around which legend and lore were built, which supposedly carried chests of tea from India and China to the London exchanges.

So audacious did the British East India Company lords and ladies become that they tried to sell this lethal substance to the Union and Confederate Armies in pill form as a pain killer. Is it difficult to imagine just what would have happened had their plan succeeded? All those hundreds of thousands of soldiers would have left the battlefields totally hooked on opium. "The Beatles" were much more successful in turning out millions of teenage addicts in later years.

The Bengal merchants and their British controllers and bankers grew fat and intolerant on the enormous amounts of money that poured into the coffers of the British East India Company from the wretched Chinese coolies opium trade. BEIC profits, even in those years, far exceeded the combined profits made in a single year by General Motors, Ford and Chrysler in their heydays. The trend in making huge profits out of drugs was carried over into the 1960's by such "legal" drug death merchants as Sandoz, the makers of LSD and Hoffman la Roche, manufacturers of Valium. The cost of the raw material and manufacturing of Valium to Hoffman la Roche is $3 per kilo (2.2 pounds). It is sold to their distributors for $20,000 per kilo. By the time it reaches the consumer, the price of Valium has risen to $50,000 per kilo. Valium is used in huge quantities in Europe and the United States. It is possibly the most used drug of its kind in the world.

Hoffman la Roche does the same thing with Vitamin C, which costs them less than 1 cent a kilo to produce. It is sold for a profit of 10,000 percent. When a friend of mine blew the whistle on this criminal company, which had entered into a monopoly agreement with other producers, in contravention of European Economic Community laws, he was arrested on the Swiss-Italian border and hustled into prison; his wife was threatened by the Swiss police until she committed suicide. As a British national he was rescued by the British consul in Berne as soon as word of his plight was received, removed from prison and flown out of the country. He lost his wife, his job and his pension because he dared to disclose Hoffman La Roche secrets. The Swiss take their Industrial Espionage law very seriously.

Remember this the next time you see those lovely advertisements of Swiss ski slopes, beautiful watches, pristine mountains and cuckoo clocks. That is not what Switzerland is about. It is about dirty multi-billion dollar money laundering which is carried out by major Swiss banking houses. It is about the Committee of 300—"legal" drug manufacturers. Switzerland is the Committee's ultimate "safe haven" for money and protection of their bodies in time of global calamity.

Now mind you, one could get into serious trouble with the Swiss authorities for giving out any information on these nefarious activities. The Swiss regard it as "industrial espionage" which usually carries a 5-year term in prison. It is safer to pretend that Switzerland is a nice clean country rather than look under the covers or inside its garbage can banks.

In 1931 the managing directors of the so-called "big Five" British companies were rewarded by being made Peers of the Realm for their activities in drug money laundering. Who decides such matters and bestows such honors? It is the Queen of England who bestows honors upon the men in the top positions in the drug trade. British banks engaged in this terrible trade are too numerous to mention, but a few of the top ones are:

The British Bank of the Middle East.

Midland Bank.

National and Westminster Bank.

Barclays Bank.

Royal Bank of Canada.

Hong Kong and Shanghai Bank.

Baring Brothers Bank.

Many of the merchant banks are up to their hocks in pigswill drug trade profits, banks such as Hambros for example, run by Sir Jocelyn Hambro. For a really interesting major study of the Chinese opium trade, one would need access to India Office in London. I was able to get in there because of my intelligence service and received great assistance from the trustee of the papers of the late Professor Frederick Wells Williamson, which provided much information on the opium trade carried on by the British East India Company in India and China in the 18th and 19th centuries. If only those papers could be made public, what a storm would burst over the heads of the crowned vipers of Europe.

Today the trade has shifted somewhat in that less expensive cocaine has taken over a good part of the North American market. In the 1960's the flood of heroin coming from Hong Kong, Lebanon and Dubai threatened to engulf the United States and Western Europe. When demand outpaced supply, there was a switch to cocaine. But now, at the end of 1991, that trend has been reversed; today it is heroin that is back in favor, although it is true that cocaine still enjoys great favor among the poorer classes.

Heroin, we are told, is more satisfying to addicts; the effects are far more intense and last longer than the effects of cocaine and there is less international attention on heroin producers than there is on Colombian cocaine shippers. Besides which, it is hardly likely that the U.S. would make any real effort to stop the production of opium in the Golden Triangle which is under the control of the Chinese military, a serious war would erupt if any country tried to interdict the trade. A serious attack on the opium trade would bring Chinese military intervention.

The British know this; they have no quarrel with China, except for an occasional squabble over who gets the larger share of the pie. Britain has been involved in the China opium trade for over two centuries. No one is going to be so foolish as to rock the boat when millions upon millions of dollars flow into the bank accounts of the British oligarchists and more gold is traded on the Hong Kong gold market than the combined total traded in London and New York.

Those individuals who fondly imagine they can do some kind of a deal with a minor Chinese or Burmese overlord in the hills of the Golden Triangle apparently have no idea of what is involved. If they had known, they would never have talked about stopping the opium trade. Such talk reveals little knowledge of the immensity and complexity of China's opium trade.

British plutocrats, the Russian KGB, the CIA, and U.S. bankers are all in league with China. Could one man stop or even make a small dent in the trade? It would be absurd to imagine it. What is heroin and why is it favored over cocaine these days? According to the noted authority on the subject, Professor Galen, heroin is a derivative of opium, a drug that stupefies the senses and induces long periods of sleep. This is what most addicts like, it is called "being in the arms of Morpheus." Opium is the most habit-forming drug known to man. Many pharmaceutical drugs contain opium in various degrees, and it is believed that paper used in the manufacture of cigarettes is first impregnated with opium, which is why smokers become so addicted to their habit.

The poppy seed from which it is derived was long known to the Moguls of India, who used the seeds mixed in tea offered to a difficult opponent. It is also used as a pain-killing drug which largely replaced chloroform and other older anesthetics of a bygone era. Opium was popular in all of the fashionable clubs of Victorian London and it was no secret that men like the Huxley brothers used it extensively. Members of the Orphic-Dionysus cults of Hellenic Greece and the Osiris-Horus cults of Ptolemaic Egypt which Victorian society embraced, all smoked opium; it was the "in" thing to do.

So did some of those who met at St. Ermins Hotel in 1903 to decide what sort of a world we would have. The descendants of the St. Ermins crowd are found today in the Committee of 300. It is these so-called world leaders who brought about such a change in our environment that enabled drug usage to proliferate to the point where it can no longer be stopped by regular law enforcement tactics and policies. This is especially true in big cities where big populations can conceal a great deal of what transpires.

Many in the circles of royalty were regular opium users. One of their favorites was the writer Coudenhove-Kalergi who wrote a book in 1932 entitled "REVOLUTION THROUGH TECHNOLOGY" which was a blueprint for the return of the world to a medieval society. The book, in fact, became a working paper for the Committee of 300's plan to deindustrialize the world, starting with the United States. Claiming that pressures of over-population are a serious problem, Kalergi advised a return to what he called "open spaces." Does this sound like the Khmer Rouge and Pol Pot? Here are some extracts from the book:

> "In its facilities, the city of the future will resemble the city of the Middle Ages...and he who is not condemned to live in a city because of his occupation, will go to the countryside. Our civilization is a culture of the major cities; therefore it is a marsh plant, born by degenerated, sickly and decadent people, who have vol-

untarily, or involuntarily, ended up in this dead-end street of life." Isn't that very close to what "AnkarWat" gave as "his" reasons for depopulating Phnom Penh?

The first opium shipments reached England from Bengal in 1683, carried in British East India Company "Tea Clippers." Opium was brought to England as a test, an experiment, to see whether the common folk of England, the yeomen and the lower classes, could be induced into taking the drug. It was what we could call today "test marketing" of a new product. But the sturdy yeomen and the much derided "lower classes" were made of stern stuff, and the test marketing experiment was a total flop. The "lower classes" of British society firmly rejected opium smoking.

The plutocrats and oligarchists in high society in London began casting about for a market that would not be so resistant, so unbending. They found such a market in China. In the papers I studied at the India Office under the heading "Miscellaneous Old Records," I found all the confirmation I could have wished for in proving that the opium trade in China really took off following the founding of the British East India Company-funded "China Inland Mission," ostensibly a Christian missionary society but in reality the "promotion" men and women for the new product being introduced into the market, that new product being OPIUM.

This was later confirmed when I was given access to the papers of Sir George Birdwood in India Office records. Soon after the China Inland Mission missionaries set out to give away their sample packages and show the coolies how to smoke opium, vast quantities of opium began to arrive in China. "The Beatles" could not have done a better job. (In both cases the trade was sanctioned by the British royal family, who openly supported the Beatles.) Where the British East India Company had failed in England, it now succeeded beyond its wildest expectations in China, whose teeming millions of poor looked upon smoking opium as an escape from their life of misery. Opium dens began proliferating all across China, and in the big cities like Shanghai and Canton, hundreds of thousands of miserable Chinese found that a pipe of opium seemingly made life bearable. The British East India Company had a clear run for over a 100 years before the Chinese government woke up to what was happening. It was only in 1729 that the first laws against opium smoking were passed. The 300 board members of BEIC did not like it one bit and, never one to back down, the Company was soon engaged in a running battle with the Chinese government.

The BEIC had developed poppy seeds that brought the finest quality opium from the poppy fields of Benares and Bihar in the Ganges Basin in India, a country they fully controlled. This fetched top price, while the lower grades of opium from other areas of India were sold for less. Not about to lose their lucrative market, the British Crown engaged in running battles with Chinese forces, and defeated them. In the same manner, the U.S. government is supposedly fighting a running battle against today's drug barons and, like the Chinese, are losing heavily. There is however one big difference: The Chinese government fought to win whereas the United States government is under no compunction to win the battle which explains why staff turnover in the Drug Enforcement Agency (DEA) is so high.

Latterly, high grade quality opium has come out of Pakistan via Makra on the desolate coastline of the country from whence ships take the cargo to Dubai where it is exchanged for gold. This is said to account in part for heroin being favored over cocaine today. The heroin trade is more discreet, there is no murder of prominent officials such as became an almost daily occurrence in Colombia. Pakistani opium does not sell for as much as Golden Triangle or Golden Crescent (Iranian) opium. This has greatly spurred heroin production and sales which threaten to overtake cocaine as the number one seller.

The vile opium trade was talked about in the upper-crust

circles of English society for many years as "the spoils of the Empire." The tall tales of valor in the Khyber Pass covered a vast trade in opium. The British Army was stationed in the Khyber Pass to protect caravans carrying raw opium from being pillaged by hill tribesmen. Did the British royal family know this? They must have, what else would induce the Crown to keep an army in this region where there was nothing of much worth other than the lucrative opium trade? It was very expensive to keep men under arms in a far away country. Her Majesty must have asked why these military units were there? Certainly not to play polo or billiards in the officers' mess.

The BEIC was jealous of its monopoly in opium. Would-be competitors received short shrift. In a noted trial in 1791, a certain Warren Hastings was put on charges that he helped a friend to get into the opium trade at the expense of the BEIC. The actual wording which I found in the records of the case housed in India Office gives some insight into the vast opium trade: "The charge is that Hastings has granted a contract for the Provision of Opium for four years to Stephen Sullivan, without advertising for the same, on terms glaringly obvious and wantonly profuse, for the purpose of creating an INSTANT FORTUNE for the said William Sullivan Esq." (Emphasis added.)

As the BEIC-British government held the monopoly in opium trading, the only people allowed to make instant fortunes were the "nobility," the "aristocracy," the plutocrats and oligarchical families of England, many of whose descendants sit on the Committee of 300 just as their forbears sat on the Council of 300 who ran the BEIC. Outsiders like Mr. Sullivan soon found themselves in trouble with the Crown if they were so bold as to try and help themselves get into the multi-billion pound Sterling opium business.

The honorable men of the BEIC with its list of 300 counselors were members of all the famous gentlemen's clubs in London and they were for the most part members of parliament, while others, both in India and at home, were magistrates. Company passports were required to land in China. When a few busybodies arrived in China to investigate the British Crown's involvement in the lucrative trade, BEIC magistrates promptly revoked their passports, thus effectively denying them entry into China. Friction with the Chinese government was common. The Chinese had passed a law, the Yung Cheng Edict of 1729, forbidding the importation of opium, yet the BEIC managed to keep opium as an entry in the Chinese Customs Tariff books until 1753, the duty being three taels per chest of opium. Even then British special secret service (the 007 of the day) saw to it that troublesome Chinese officials were bought off, and in cases where that was not possible, they were simply murdered.

Every British monarch since 1729 has benefited immensely from the drug trade and this holds good for the present occupant of the throne. Their ministers saw to it that wealth flowed into their family coffers. One such minister of Victoria's was Lord Palmerston. He clung obstinately to the belief that nothing should be allowed to stop Britain's opium trade with China. Palmerston's plan was to supply the Chinese government with enough opium to make individual members become greedy. Then the British would withhold supplies and when the Chinese government was on its knees, supplies would be resumed—but at a much higher price, thus retaining a monopoly through the Chinese government itself, but the plan failed.

The Chinese government responded by destroying large cargoes of opium stored in warehouses, and British merchants were required to sign INDIVIDUAL agreements not to import any more opium into Canton. BEIC responded by sending scores of fully-loaded opium carrying ships to lie in the roads of Macao. Companies beholden to BEIC, rather than individuals, then sold these cargoes. Chinese Commissioner Lin said, "There is so much opium on board English vessels now lying in the roads of this place (Macao) which will never be returned to the country from which it came, and I shall not be surprised to hear of its being smuggled in under American colors." Lin's prophecy proved to be remarkably accurate.

The Opium Wars against China were designed to "put the Chinese in their place" as Lord Palmerston once said, and the British Army did that. There was simply no stopping the vast, lucrative trade which provided the British oligarchical feudal lords with untold billions, while leaving China with millions of opium addicts. In later years the Chinese appealed to Britain for help with their immense problem and received it. Thereafter, respective Chinese governments realized the value in cooperating instead of fighting with Britain—and this held good during the bloody rule of Mao Tse Tung—so that today, as I have already mentioned, any quarrels that come about are only over the share of the opium trade each is entitled to.

To advance to more modern history, the Chinese-British partnership was solidified by the Hong Kong agreement which established an equal partnership in the opium trade. This has proceeded smoothly, with an occasional ripple here and there, but while violence and death, robbery and murder marked the progression of the Colombian cocaine trade, no such baseness was allowed to disturb the heroin trade, which, as I said earlier, is once again coming into the ascendancy as we near the end of 1991.

The major problem that arose in Sino-British relations during the past 60 years concerned China's demand for a larger slice of the opium-heroin pie. This was settled when Britain agreed to hand Hong Kong over to full Chinese government control which will come into effect in 1997. Other than that, the partners retain their former equal shares of the lucrative opium trade based in Hong Kong.

The British oligarchical families of the Committee of 300 who were entrenched in Canton at the height of the opium trade left their descendants in position. Look at a list of prominent British residents in China and you will see the names of members of the Committee of 300 among them. The same holds good for Hong Kong. These plutocrats of a feudal era, that they seek to return to the world, control the gold and opium trade of which

Hong Kong is THE center. Burmese and Chinese opium poppy growers get paid in gold; they do not trust the U.S. paper $100 bill. This explains the very large volume of gold traded in the Hong Kong exchange. The Golden Triangle is no longer the largest producer of opium. That dubious title has since 1987 been shared by the Golden Crescent (Iran), Pakistan and Lebanon. These are the principle opium producers, although smaller quantities are once again coming out of Afghanistan and Turkey. The drug trade, and more especially the opium trade, could not function without the help of banks as we shall demonstrate as we proceed.

How do banks with their great air of respectability fit into the drug trade with all of its attendant filth? It is a very long and complicated story, which could be the subject of a book on its own. One way in which banks participate is by financing front companies importing the chemicals needed to process raw opium into heroin. The Hong Kong and Shanghai Bank with a branch office in London is right in the middle of such trade through a company called TEJAPAIBUL, which banks with Hong Kong and Shanghai Bank. What does this company do? It imports into Hong Kong most of the chemicals needed in the heroin refining process.

It is also a major supplier of acetic anhydride for the Golden Crescent and the Golden Triangle, Pakistan, Turkey and Lebanon. The actual financing for this trading is hived off to the Bangkok Metropolitan Bank. Thus, the secondary activities connected with processing opium, while not in the same category as the opium trade, nevertheless generates substantial income for banks. But the real income of the Hong Kong and Shanghai Bank and indeed all banks in the region is financing the actual opium trade.

It took a lot of research on my part to link the price of gold to the price of opium. I used to tell anyone who would listen, "If you want to know the price of gold find out what the price of a pound or a kilo of opium is in Hong Kong." To my critics I answered, "Take a look at what happened in 1977, a critical year for gold." The Bank of China shocked the gold pundits, and those clever forecasters who are to be found in great numbers in America, by suddenly and without warning, dumping 80 tons of gold on the market.

That depressed the price of gold in a big hurry. All the experts could say was, "We never knew China had that much gold; where could it have come from?" It came from the gold which is paid to China in the Hong Kong Gold Market for large purchases of opium. The current policy of the Chinese government toward England is the same as it was in the 18th and 19th centuries. The Chinese economy, tied to the economy of Hong Kong—and I don't mean television sets, textiles, radios, watches, pirated cassette and video tapes—I mean opium/heroin—would take a terrible beating if it were not for the opium trade it shares with Britain. The BEIC is gone but the descendants of the Council of 300 linger on in the membership of the Committee of 300.

The oldest of the oligarchical British families who were leaders in the opium trade for the past 200 years are still in it today. Take the Mathesons, for instance. This "noble" family is one of the pillars of the opium trade. When things looked a bit shaky a few years ago, the Mathesons stepped in and gave China a loan of $300 million for real estate investment. Actually it was billed as a "joint venture between the People's Republic of China and the Matheson Bank." When researching India Office papers of the 1700's I came across the name of Matheson, and it kept on cropping up everywhere—London, Peking, Dubai, Hong Kong, wherever heroin and opium are mentioned.

The problem with the drug trade is that it has become a threat to national sovereignty. Here is what the Venezuelan Ambassador to the United Nations said about this world-wide threat:

"The problem of drugs has already ceased to be dealt with simply as one of public health or a social problem. It has turned into something far more serious and far-reaching which affects our national sovereignty; a problem of national security, because it strikes at the independence of a nation. Drugs in all their manifestations of production, commercialization and consumption, denaturalizes us by injuring our ethical, religious and political life, our historic, economic, and republican values."

This is precisely the way the Bank of International Settlements and the IMF are operating. Let me say without hesitation that both these banks are nothing more than bully-boy clearing houses for the drug trade. The BIS undermines any country that the IMF wants to sink by setting up ways and means for the easy outflow of flight capital. Nor does BIS recognize nor make any distinction when it comes down to what is flight capital and what is laundered drug money.

The BIS operates on gangster lines. If a country will not submit to asset-stripping by the IMF, then it says in effect, "Right, then we will break you by means of the huge cache of narco-dollars we are holding." It is easy to understand why gold was demonetized and substituted with the paper "dollar" as the world's reserve currency. It is not as easy to blackmail a country holding gold reserves as it is one having its reserves in paper dollars.

The IMF held a meeting in Hong Kong a few years ago which was attended by a colleague of mine and he told me the seminar dealt with this very question. He informed me that the IMF agents told the meeting that they could literally cause a run on any country's currency, using narco-dollars, which would precipitate a flight of capital. Rainer-Gut, a Credit Suisse delegate and member of the Committee of 300, said he foresaw a situation where national credit and national financing would be under one umbrella organization by the turn of the century. While Rainer-Gut did not spell it out, everybody at the seminar knew exactly what he was talking about.

From Colombia to Miami, from the Golden Triangle to the Golden Gate, from Hong Kong to New York, from Bogota to Frankfurt, the drug trade, and more especially the heroin trade, is **BIG BUSINESS** and it is run from the top down by some of the most "untouchable" families in the world, and each of those families have at least one member who is on the Committee of 300. It is not a street corner business, and it takes a great deal of money and expertise to keep it flowing smoothly. The machinery under control of the Committee of 300 ensures this.

Such talents are not found on the street corners and subways of New York. To be sure the pushers and peddlers are an integral part of the trade, but only as very small part-time salesmen. I say part-time because they are caught and rivalry gets some of them shot. But what does that matter? There are plenty of replacements available.

No, it is not anything the Small Business Administration would be interested in. IT IS BIG BUSINESS, a vast empire, this dirty drug business. Of necessity, it is operated from the top down in every single country in the world. It is, in fact, the largest single enterprise in the world today, transcending all others. That it is protected from the top down is borne out by the fact that, like international terrorism, it cannot be stamped out, which should indicate to a reasonable person that some of the biggest names in royal circles, the oligarchy, the plutocracy are running it, even if it is done through intermediaries.

The main countries involved in growing poppies and the cocoa bush are Burma, Northern China, Afghanistan, Iran, Pakistan, Thailand, Lebanon, Turkey, Peru, Ecuador, Bolivia. Colombia does not grow the cocoa bush but, next to Bolivia, is the main refiner of cocaine and the chief financial center of the cocaine trade which, since General Noriega was kidnaped and imprisoned by President Bush, is being challenged by Panama for first place in money laundering and capital financing of the cocaine trade.

The heroin trade is financed by Hong Kong banks, London banks and some Middle East banks such as the British Bank of the Middle East. Lebanon is fast becoming the "Switzerland of the Middle East." Countries involved in the distribution and routing of heroin are Hong Kong, Turkey, Bulgaria, Italy, Monaco, France (Corsica and Marseilles) Lebanon and Pakistan. The United States is the largest consumer of narcotics, first place going to cocaine, which is being challenged by heroin. Western Europe and Southwest Asian countries are the biggest users of heroin. Iran has a huge heroin addict population—in excess of 2 million as of 1991.

There is not a single government that does not know precisely what is going on with regard to the drug trade, but individual members holding powerful positions are taken care of by the Committee of 300 through its world-wide network of subsidiaries. If any government member is "difficult," he or she is removed, as in the case of Pakistan's Ali Bhutto and Italy's Aldo Moro. No one is beyond the reach of this all-powerful Committee, even though Malaysia has been successful in holding out up until now. Malaysia has the strictest anti-drug laws in the world. Possession of even small amounts is punishable by the death penalty.

Like the Kintex Company of Bulgaria, most smaller countries have a direct hand in these criminal enterprises. Kintex trucks regularly ferried heroin through Western Europe in its own fleet of trucks bearing the EEC marker Triangle Internationale Routier (TIR). Trucks bearing this marker and the EEC recognition number are not supposed to be stopped at customs border posts. TIR trucks are allowed to carry only perishable items. They are supposed to be inspected in the country from whence they originated and documentation to this effect is supposed to be carried by each truck driver.

Under international treaty obligations this is what happens, thus Kintex trucks were able load their cargoes of heroin and certify it as "fresh fruit and vegetables," and then make their way through Western Europe, even entering high-security NATO bases in Northern Italy. In this manner, Bulgaria became one of the principal countries through which heroin was routed.

The only way to stop the huge amounts of heroin and

cocaine presently finding their way to markets in Europe is to end the TIR system. That will never happen. The international treaty obligations I have just mentioned were set up by the Committee of 300, using its amazing networks and control mechanisms, to facilitate passage of all manner of drugs to Western Europe. Forget perishable goods! A former DEA agent stationed in Italy told me, "TIR=DOPE."

Remember this the next time you read in the newspapers that a big haul of heroin was found in a false-bottom suitcase at Kennedy Airport, and some unlucky "mule" pays the price for his criminal activity. This kind of action is only "small potatoes," sand in the eyes of the public, to make us think our government is really doing something about the drug menace. Take for example, "The French Connection," a Nixon program embarked upon without the knowledge and consent of the Committee of 300.

The entire amount of opium/heroin seized in that massive effort is somewhat less than one quarter of what a single TIR truck carries. The Committee of 300 saw to it that Nixon paid a heavy price for a relatively small seizure of heroin. It was not the amount of heroin involved, but a matter of one whom they had helped up the ladder to the White House believing that he could now do without their help and backing, and even go against direct orders from above.

The mechanics of the heroin trade go like this: wild Thai and Burmese Hill tribesmen grow the opium poppy. At harvest time, the seed-bearing pod is cut with a razor or sharp knife. A resinous substance leaks through the cut and starts to congeal. This is raw opium. The crop of raw opium is made up into sticky roundish balls. The tribesman are paid in 1 kilo gold bars—known as 4/10ths—which are minted by Credit Suisse. These small bars are used ONLY to pay the tribesman—the normal-weight gold bars are traded on the Hong Kong market by the big buyers of raw opium or partly processed heroin. The same methods are used to pay hill tribesman in India—the Baluchis—

who have been in this business since the days of the Moguls. The "Dope Season," as it is called, sees a flood of gold traded on the Hong Kong market.

Mexico has started producing relatively small amounts of heroin called "Mexican Brown" which is much in demand by the Hollywood crowd. Here again the heroin trade is run by top government officials who have the military on their side. Some producers of "Mexican Brown" are making a million dollars a month by supplying their U.S. clients. On occasions when a few Mexican Federal police are prodded into taking action against the heroin producers, they are "taken out" by military units who seem to appear as if from nowhere.

Such an incident occurred in November 1991 at an isolated airstrip in Mexico's opium producing region. Federal narcotics agents surrounded the strip and were about to arrest people who were in the act of loading heroin when a squad of soldiers arrived. The soldiers rounded up the Federal narcotics police agents and systematically killed all of them. This action posed a serious threat to Mexican President Goltarin, who is faced with loud demands for a full-scale investigation into the murders. Goltarin is over a barrel; he can't back off from calling for an enquiry, and neither can he afford to offend the military. It is the first such crack in the tight chain of command in Mexico that stretches all the way back to the Committee of 300.

Raw opium from the Golden Triangle is pipelined to the Sicilian Mafia and the French end of the business for refining in the laboratories that infest the French coastline from Marseilles to Monte-Carlo. Nowadays, Lebanon and Turkey are turning out increasing amounts of refined heroin and a large number of laboratories have sprung up in these two countries in the past four years. Pakistan also has a number of laboratories, but it is not in the same league as France, for example.

The route taken by the raw opium carriers of the Golden Crescent goes through Iran, Turkey and Lebanon. When the Shah of Iran was in control of the country, he refused to allow

the heroin trade to continue and it was forcibly discontinued—
up until the time that he was "dealt with" by the Committee of
300. Raw opium from Turkey and Lebanon finds it way to
Corsica, from where it is shipped to Monte Carlo with the
connivance of the Grimaldi family. Pakistani laboratories, under
the guise of "military defense laboratories" are doing a bigger
share of refining than they were two years ago, but the best
refining is still done along the French Mediterranean coastline
and in Turkey. Here again, banks play a vital role in financing
these operations.

Let us stop here for a moment. Are we to believe that with all
the modern and vastly improved surveillance techniques, including satellite reconnaissance, available to law enforcement
agencies in these countries, that this vile trade cannot be pin-
pointed and stopped? How is it that law enforcement agencies
cannot go in and destroy these laboratories once they are discovered? If this IS the case, and we still cannot interdict the
heroin trade, then our anti-narcotics services ought to be known
as "The Geriatrics" and not drug enforcement agencies.

Even a child could tell our alleged "drug watchers" what to
do. Simply keep a check on all factories making acetic anhydride, THE most essential chemical component needed by laboratories to refine heroin from raw opium. THEN FOLLOW
THE TRAIL! It is as simple as that! I am reminded of Peter
Sellers in the "Pink Panther" series when I think of law enforcement efforts to locate heroin-refining laboratories. Even
someone as bumbling as the imaginary inspector would have
had no trouble in following the route taken by acetic anhydride
shipments to their final destination.

Governments could make laws that would oblige manufacturers of acetic anhydride to keep scrupulous records showing
who buys the chemical and for what purposes it is to be used.
But do not hold your breath on this one, remember Dope=Big
Business and Big Business is done by the oligarchical families
of Europe and the United States Eastern Liberal Establishment.

The drug business is not a Mafia operation, nor one run by the Colombian cocaine cartels. The noble families of Britain and America's top people are not going to advertise their role in the shop windows; they always have a layer of front men to do the dirty work.

Remember British and AMERICAN "nobility" never dirtied their hands in the China opium trade. The lords and ladies were much too clever for that, as were the American elite: the Delanos, Forbes, Appletons, Bacons, Boylestons, Perkins, Russells, Cunninghams, Shaws, Coolidges, Parkmans, Runnewells, Cabots and Codmans, by no means a complete list of families in America who grew immensely wealthy from the China opium trade.

Since this is not a book about the drug trade, I cannot of necessity, cover the subject in an in-depth manner. But its importance to the Committee of 300 must be emphasized. America is run not by 60 families but by 300 families and England is run by 100 families and, as we shall see, these families are intertwined through marriage, companies, banks, not to mention ties to the Black Nobility, Freemasonry, the Order of St. John of Jerusalem and so on. These are the people who, through their surrogates, find ways to protect huge shipments of heroin from Hong Kong, Turkey, Iran and Pakistan and ensure they reach the market places in the U.S. and Western Europe with the minimum cost of doing business.

Shipments of cocaine are sometimes interdicted and seized. That is mere window dressing. Often times the shipments seized belong to a new organization trying to break into the trade. Such competition is put out of business by informing the authorities exactly where it is going to enter the U.S. and who the owners are. The big stuff is never touched; heroin is too expensive. It is worthy of note that U.S. Drug Enforcement Agency operatives are not allowed into Hong Kong. They cannot examine any ship's manifest before it leaves the port. One wonders why, if there is so much "international cooperation" going on—what the media likes to characterize as "smashing the dope trade." Clearly the trade routes for heroin are protected by "a higher authority."

In South America, apart from Mexico, cocaine is king. The production of cocaine is very simple, unlike heroin, and great fortunes are to be made by those willing to take risks for and on behalf of the "higher ups." As in the heroin trade, interlopers are not welcome and often finish up as casualties, or victims of family feuds. In Colombia the drug mafia is a closely knit family. But such has been the bad publicity generated by the M19 guerrilla attack on the Justice Building in Bogota (M19 is the private army of the cocaine barons) and the murder of Rodrigo Lara Bonilla, a prominent prosecutor and a judge, that the "higher authority" had to rearrange matters in Colombia.

Accordingly, the Ochoas of the Medellin Cartel turned themselves in after being assured that they would not suffer any loss of fortune, harm of any kind, nor would they be extradited to the United States. A deal was struck that, provided they repatriated the bulk of their huge narco-dollar fortunes to Colombian banks, no punitive action would be taken against them. The Ochoas—Jorge, Fabio, and their top man, Pablo Escobar, would be held in private jails that resemble a luxury-class motel room, and then be sentenced to a maximum term of two years—to be served in the same motel jail. This deal is ongoing. The Ochoas have also been guaranteed the right to continue to manage their "business" from their motel-prison.

But that does not mean that the cocaine trade has come to a screeching halt. On the contrary, it has simply been transferred to the second-string Cali cartel, and it is business as usual. For some strange reason the Cali cartel, which is equal in size to the Medellin cartel, has been—at least up until now—largely ignored by the DEA. Cali differs from the Medellin cartel in that it is run by BUSINESSMEN, who eschew all forms of violence and never break agreements.

Even more significant is that Cali does virtually no business in Florida. My source told me that the Cali cartel is run by shrewd businessmen unlike any seen in the cocaine business. He believes that they were "specially appointed," but does not know by whom. "They never call attention to themselves," he said. "They do not go around importing red Ferraris like Jorge Ochoa did, attracting immediate attention, because it is forbidden to import such cars into Colombia."

Cali cartel markets are in Los Angeles, New York and Houston, which closely parallel the heroin markets. Cali has not shown any signs of moving into Florida. A former DEA operative who is a colleague of mine said recently, "These Cali people are smart. They are a different breed to the Ochoa brothers. They act like professional businessmen. They are now larger than the Medellin cartel and I think we are going to see a lot more cocaine get into the United States than ever before. The kidnaping of Manuel Noriega will facilitate an easier flow through Panama of cocaine and money, what with so many banks there. So much for President George Bush's Operation Just Cause. All it did was make life a great deal easier for Nicolas Ardito Barletta who used to be run by the Ochoa brothers and who is fixing to front for the Cali cartel."

Based on my experience with the heroin trade I believe that the Committee of 300 has stepped in and taken over full control of the South American cocaine trade. There is no other explanation for the rise of the Cali cartel which is coupled with the kidnaping of Noriega. Did Bush take his orders from London regarding Noriega? There is every indication that he was literally PUSHED into invading Panama and kidnaping Noriega, who had become a serious impediment to "trade" in Panama, especially in the banking business.

Several former intelligence agents have given me their opinions which coincide with my own. Like the Gulf War that followed in the wake of Panama, it was only after several calls from the British Ambassador in Washington that Bush finally plucked up enough courage to make his totally illegal move on

General Noriega. That he was supported by the British press and the *New York Times*, a British intelligence run newspaper, speaks volumes.

Noriega was formerly the darling of the Washington establishment. He frequently hob-knobbed with William Casey and Oliver North and even met with President George Bush on at least two occasions. Noriega was often seen at the Pentagon where he was treated like one of those Arab potentates, and the red carpet was always laid out for him at CIA headquarters in Langley, Virginia. U.S. Army Intelligence and the CIA are on record as having paid him $320,000.

Then storm clouds began to appear on the horizon at about the same time the Cali cartel was taking over the cocaine trade from the Ochoa brothers and Pablo Escobar. Led by Senator Jesse Helms, who sold out to Ariel Sharon and the Israeli Histradut Party in 1985, there suddenly began an agitation for the removal of Noriega. Jesse Helms and those of a like mind were backed up by Simon Hersh, a British intelligence agent working for the *New York Times*, which has been a British intelligence mouthpiece in the U.S. since the time that MI6 boss, Sir William Stephenson, occupied the RCA building in New York.

It is very significant that Helms should have chosen to lead the charge against Noriega. Helms is the darling of the Sharon faction in Washington and Sharon was the principal gun-runner in Central America and Colombia. Moreover, Helms has the respect of the Christian fundamentalists who believe in the maxim: "Israel, my country, right or wrong." Thus a powerful momentum was created to "get Noriega." It is evident that Noriega could well prove a serious impediment to the international drug merchants and their Committee of 300 bankers, so he had to be removed before he could do some significant damage.

Bush was pressured by his British masters to conduct an illegal search and seizure operation in Panama that resulted in the deaths of no less than 7,000 Panamanians and wanton destruction of property. Nothing to implicate Noriega as a "drug dealer" was ever found, so he was kidnaped and brought to the U.S. in one of the most blatant examples of international brigandry in history. This illegal action probably best meets the Bush philosophy: "The moral dimensions of American (read British royal family-Committee of 300) foreign policy require us to chart a moral course through a world of lesser evils. That's the real world, not black and white. Very few absolutes."

It was a "lesser evil" to kidnap Noriega, rather than have him up-end the banks in Panama working for the Committee of 300. The Noriega case is a prototype of monstrous One World Government actions waiting in the wings. An emboldened Bush came right out in the open, unafraid, because we, the people, have put on a spiritual mantle that accommodates LIES and wants no part of TRUTH. This is the world we have decided to accept. If it were not so, a firestorm of anger would have swept the country over the invasion of Panama, which would not have stopped until Bush was hounded from office. Nixon's Watergate transgressions pale into insignificance next to the many impeachable offenses committed by President Bush when he ordered the invasion of Panama to kidnap General Noriega.

The government case against Noriega is based upon perjured testimony by a group of bagmen, for the most part, already convicted and lying through their individual and collective teeth to get their own sentences lightened. Their performance would have pleased Gilbert and Sullivan immensely, were they alive today. "They made them the rulers of DEA," might be apropos instead of, "They made them the rulers of Queen's Navy," from "HMS Pinafore." It is an altogether grotesque scene to see how these con-artists are performing like not-so-well-trained seals for the U.S. Justice Department; that is if we care to insult such a nice clean animal by such an unworthy comparison.

Key dates conflict wildly, key details are altogether conspicuous by their absence, lapses of memory on crucial points all add up to the obvious fact that the government has no case against Noriega, but that does not matter; the Royal Institute for

International Affairs (RIIA) says "convict him anyway" and that is what poor Noriega can expect. One of the Justice Department's star witnesses is one Floyd Carlton Caceres, a former pilot for the Ochoa brothers. Following his arrest in 1986, Carlton tried to ease his position at the expense of Noriega.

He told his DEA interrogators that the Ochoa brothers had paid Noriega $600,000 to allow three planes loaded with cocaine to land and refuel in Panama. But once in court in Miami, it soon became apparent that what was billed as the "star witness" for the prosecution was at best damp squib. Under cross-examination the true story emerged: Far from being paid to allow the flights, Noriega wasn't even approached by the Ochoas. Worse yet, in December of 1983, Noriega had ordered that all flights to Panama from Medellin be refused permission to land in Panama. Carlton is not the only discredited witness.

One who is even a sorrier liar than Carlton is Carlos Lehder, who was a kingpin in the Medellin Cartel until he was arrested in Spain and sent to the U.S. Who gave the DEA the most vital information that Lehder was in Madrid? The DEA reluctantly concedes that they owe this important catch to Noriega. Now, however, the Justice Department is using Lehder as a witness against Noriega. If nothing else, this single witness demonstrates the wretchedness of the United States government's case against Manuel Noriega.

In return for services rendered, Lehder has been granted an easing of his sentence and far nicer quarters—a room with a view and television—and his family was given permanent residence in the U.S. Robert Merkel, a former U.S. attorney who prosecuted Lehder in 1988 told the *Washington Post*: "I don't think the government should be in the business of dealing with Carlos Lehder, period. This guy is a liar from beginning to end."

The Justice Department, purely a name which bears no resemblance to what it is supposed to stand for, has pulled out all its dirty tricks against Noriega: illegally wire-tapping his conversations with his lawyer; appointing a government lawyer to pretend he was serving Noriega but who quit in the middle of everything; freezing his bank accounts so that Noriega is unable to conduct a proper defense; kidnaping, illegal search and seizure. You name it, the government has broken more laws than Noriega has ever done—if indeed he has broken any laws at all. It is the U.S. Justice Department that is on trial tenfold more than General Noriega. The Noriega case shows the glaringly evil system that passes for "justice" in this country. The U.S "war on drugs" is on trial as is the Bush Administration's so-called drug policy. The Noriega trial, although it will end in a violent and flagrant rape of justice, will nevertheless offer some compensation to those who are not blind, deaf and dumb. It proves for once and for all that Britain is in charge of our government and it will reveal the utterly bankrupt ideology of the Bush Administration which ought to have as its motto, "No Matter What, The End Always Justifies The Means. There Are Very Few Moral Absolutes." Like the majority of politicians, for Bush to have a standard of ABSOLUTE MORALITY WOULD BE SUICIDAL. Only in this climate could we have allowed President Bush to violate at least six United States laws and DOZENS OF INTERNATIONAL AGREEMENTS in going to war against Iraq.

What we are witnessing in Colombia and Washington is a complete revision of how the cocaine trade is to be run; no more wild stuff, no more blazing guns. Let the gentlemen of the Cali cartel in pin-stripe suits conduct the business in a gentlemanly way. In short, the Committee of 300 has taken a direct hand in the cocaine trade which henceforth will go as smoothly as the heroin trade. The new government of Colombia is geared to the change in tactics and direction. It is on notice to perform according to the Committee's game plan.

There is need to mention U.S. participation in the China opium trade which began in the southern United States prior to the War Between The States. How can we tie the opium trade in with the great cotton plantations of the South? To do that, we have to start in Bengal, India, producers of the finest (if one can call such a foul substance fine) opium which was much in demand. Cotton was THE biggest trade in England, after opium sales through the BEIC.

Most of the cotton from Southern plantations was worked in the slave mills of Northern England, where women and children earned a pittance for a 16-hour day's work. The cloth mills were owned by the wealthy socialites in London, the Barings, Palmerstons, Keswicks and most of all the Jardine Mathesons who owned the Blue Star Shipping Line, on which the finished cotton cloth goods were shipped to India. They could care less about the hapless conditions endured by Her Majesty's subjects. After all, that is what they were for, and their husbands and sons were useful for fighting wars to preserve Her Majesty's far-flung empire as they had done for centuries, and latterly, in the bloody Boer War. That was British tradition, wasn't it?

Cotton cloth finished goods exported to India undercut and destroyed the long-standing Indian producers of cotton finished goods trade. Terrible privation was endured by thousands of Indians thrown out of work as a result of cheaper British goods taking over their markets. India then became utterly dependent upon Britain to earn enough currency to pay for its railroads and finished cotton goods imports. There was only one solution to India's economic woes. Produce more opium and sell it for less to the British East India Company. This was the rock upon which British trade grew and flourished. Without its opium trade, Britain would have been as bankrupt.

Did the Southern plantation owners know about the ugly secret of opium-for-cotton goods? It is unlikely that some of them didn't know what was going on. Take, for instance, the Sutherland family, one of the largest cotton plantation owners in the South. The Sutherlands were closely related to the Matheson family—Jardine Matheson—who in turn had as their business partners the Baring Brothers, founders of the famous Peninsular and Orient Navigation Line (P&O), the largest of Britain's many merchant shipping lines.

The Barings were big investors in Southern plantations as they were in the U.S. Clipper ships which plowed through the seas between Chinese ports and all the important ports along the eastern seaboard of the United States. Today the Barings run a number of very substantial financial operations in the United States. All of those names mentioned were, and their descendants still are, members of the Committee of 300.

The majority of families who go to make up the Eastern Liberal Establishment, among whom are the wealthiest to be found in this country, derived their fortunes from either the cotton trade or the opium trade and in some instances from both. Of these the Lehmans are an outstanding example. When it comes to fortunes made solely from the China opium trade, the first names that come to mind are the Astors and the Delanos. President Franklin D. Roosevelt's wife was a Delano.

John Jacob Astor made a huge fortune out of the China opium trade and then he went respectable by buying up large tracts of Manhattan real estate with his dirty money. During his lifetime Astor played a big role in the Committee of 300's deliberations. In fact, it was the Committee of 300 who chose who would be allowed to participate in the fabulously lucrative China opium trade, through its monopolist BEIC, and the beneficiaries of their largess remained forever wedded to the Committee of 300.

That is why, as we shall discover, most real estate in Manhattan belongs to various Committee members, even as it has since the days when Astor began buying it up. With the benefit of access to records that would be closed to others outside of British intelligence, I discovered that Astor had long been an asset of British intelligence in the United States. Astor's financing of Aaron Burr, the murderer of Alexander Hamilton, proves the point beyond any reasonable doubt.

John Jacob Astor's son, Waldorf Astor, had the additional honor bestowed upon him of being appointed to the Royal

Institute for International Affairs (RIIA), through which organization the Committee of 300 controls every facet of our lives in the United States. The Astor family is believed to have selected Owen Lattimore to carry on their association with the opium trade which he did through the Laura Spelman-funded Institute for Pacific Relations (IPR). It was the IPR that oversaw China's entry into the opium trade as an equal partner and not merely as a supplier. It was IPR that paved the way for the Japanese attack on Pearl Harbor. Attempts to turn the Japanese into opium addicts met with dismal failure.

By the turn of the century the oligarchical plutocrats of Britain were like overgorged vultures on the Serengeti Plain at the time of the annual Wildebeest march. Their income from the China opium trade exceeded David Rockefeller's income by SEVERAL BILLION DOLLARS PER ANNUM. Historic records made available to me in the British Museum in London and from India Office and other sources—former colleagues in well-placed positions, proves this completely.

By 1905, the Chinese government, deeply concerned about the rise in the number of opium addicts in China, tried to get help from the international community. Britain pretended to cooperate, but made no move whatsoever to abide by the 1905 protocols it had signed. Later Her Majesty's government did an about-face after showing China that it was better to join them in the opium business rather than to try and end it.

Even The Hague Convention was scoffed at by the British. Delegates to the convention had agreed that Britain must abide by the protocols it had signed, which was to drastically reduce the amount of opium sold in China and elsewhere. The British, while paying lip service, had no intention of giving up their trade in human misery, which included the so-called "pig trade."

Their servant, President George Bush, in prosecution of the cruel war of genocide waged against the Iraqi nation SOLELY for and on behalf of British interests, likewise showed his contempt by flouting the Hague Agreement on Aerial Bombardment, and a whole slew of international conventions to which the U.S. is a signatory, including ALL of the Geneva Conventions. When evidence was produced two years later, notably by the Japanese, who were growing very concerned about British smuggling of opium into their country, that opium sales had increased instead of decreased, then Her Majesty's delegate to the Fifth Hague Convention produced a set of statistics which were at variance with those provided by Japan. The British delegate turned the tables by saying that it made a very strong case for legalizing the sale of opium which would have the effect of doing away with what he called "the black market."

He suggested on behalf of Her Majesty's government that the Japanese government would then have a monopoly and full control of the trade. THIS IS PRECISELY THE SAME ARGUMENT BEING ADVANCED BY THE FRONT MEN FOR THE BRONFMANS AND OTHER BIG-TIME DOPE DEALERS—LEGALIZE COCAINE, MARIJUANA AND HEROIN, LET THE U.S GOVERNMENT HAVE THE MONOPOLY AND THEREBY STOP WASTING BILLIONS ON THE PHONY WAR ON DRUGS AND SAVE THE TAXPAYERS BILLIONS OF DOLLARS.

In the period of 1791-1894, the number of licensed opium dens in the Shanghai International Settlement rose from 87 to 663. Opium flowing into the United States was also stepped up. Sensing that they might have some problems in China with the spotlight of world concern shining upon them, the plutocrats of the Knights of St. John and the Order of the Garter, transferred some of their attention to Persia (Iran).

Lord Inchcape, who founded the biggest steamship company in the world at the turn of the 19th century, the legendary Peninsula and Orient Steam Navigation Company, was the principal mover and shaker in establishing the Hong Kong and Shanghai Bank, which remains the largest and least controlled clearinghouse bank for the opium trade, which also financed the "pig trade" with the United States.

The British had set up a scam whereby Chinese "coolies" were sent to the U.S. as so-called indentured laborers. The rapacious Harriman family's railroad needed "coolies" to push the rail connection westward to the California coast, or so they said. Strangely enough, very few Negroes were given the manual labor jobs they were used to at that time and could have done a better job than the emaciated opium addicts who arrived from China.

The problem was that there was no market for opium among the Negroes and, moreover, Lord Inchcape, son of the founder of P and O needed the "coolies" to smuggle in thousands of pounds of raw opium into North America, something the Negroes could not do. It was the same Lord Inchcape who in 1923 warned that there must be no diminishing of opium poppy cultivation in Bengal. "This most important source of revenue must be safeguarded," he told the commission allegedly investigating the production of opium gum in India.

By 1846, some 120,000 "coolies" had already arrived in the U.S. to work on Harriman's railroad pushing westward. The "pig trade" was in full profitable swing because, of this number, it was estimated by the U.S. government 115,000 were opium addicts. Once the railroad was finished, the Chinese did not go back to where they came from, but settled in San Francisco, Los Angeles, Vancouver and Portland. They created a huge cultural problem that has never ceased to exist.

It is interesting to note that Cecil John Rhodes, a Committee of 300 member who fronted for the Rothschilds in South Africa, followed the Inchcape pattern, bringing hundreds of thousand of Indian "coolies" to work on the sugar cane plantations in Natal province. Among them was Mahatma Ghandi, a Communist agitator and troublemaker. Like the Chinese coolies, they were not returned to their country of origin once their contracts expired. They, too, went on to create a massive social program, and their descendants became lawyers who spearheaded the drive to infiltrate the government on behalf of the African

National Congress.

By 1875 the Chinese "coolies" operating out of San Francisco had set up an opium supply ring that resulted in 129,000 American opium addicts. What with the known 115,000 Chinese addicts, Lord Inchcape and his family were raking in hundreds of thousands of dollars a year from this source alone which, in terms of today's dollar would represent at least a $100 million dollar income every year.

The very same British and American families who had combined to wreck the Indian textile industry in the promotion of the opium trade, and who brought African slaves to the U.S., combined to make the "pig trade" a valuable source of revenue. Later they were to combine to cause and promote the terrible War Between The States, also known as the American Civil War.

The decadent American families of the unholy partnership, thoroughly corrupted and wallowing in filthy lucre, went on to become what we know today as the Eastern Liberal Establishment whose members, under the careful guidance and direction of the Crown and subsequently its foreign policy executive arm, the Royal Institute of International Affairs (RIIA), ran this country—and still does—from top to bottom through their secret upper-level, parallel government, which is tightly meshed with the Committee of 300, the ULTIMATE secret society.

By 1923, voices were being raised against this menace that had been allowed to be imported into the United States. Believing the United States to be a free and sovereign nation, Congressman Stephen Porter, Chairman of the House of Representatives Foreign Affairs Committee, introduced a bill which called for the British to account for their opium export-import business on a country-by-country basis. The resolution set up quotas for each country, which if observed, would have reduced the opium trade by 10%. The resolution was passed into law and the bill accepted by the Congress of the United States.

But the Royal Institute of International Affairs had other ideas. Founded in 1919 in the wake of the Paris Peace Conference held at Versailles, this was one of the earliest "foreign policy" executors of the Committee of 300. Research I have done on the Congressional Records, House, show that Porter was totally unaware of the powerful forces he was up against. Porter was not even aware of the existence of the RIIA, much less that its specific purpose was to control every facet of the United States.

Apparently Congressman Porter received some kind of an intimation from the Morgan Bank on Wall Street that he should drop the whole affair. Instead, an enraged Porter took his case to the League of Nations Opium Committee. Porter's total unawareness of who he was up against is demonstrated in some of his correspondence to colleagues on the House Foreign Affairs Committee in response to open British opposition to his proposals.

Her Majesty's representative chided Porter and then, acting like a father toward an errant son, the British delegate—on instructions from the RIIA—presented Her Majesty's proposals to INCREASE opium quotas to account for an increase in the consumption of opium for medicinal purposes. According to documents that I was able to find in The Hague, Porter was at first confused, then amazed and then enraged. Joined by the Chinese delegate, Porter stormed out of the plenipotentiary session of the Committee session, leaving the field to the British.

In his absence, the British delegate got the League to rubber stamp Her Majesty's government proposals for a creation of a tame-tiger Central Narcotics Board, whose chief function was information gathering, the terms of which were purposely vague. What was to be done with the "information" was never made clear. Porter returned to the U.S. a shaken and much wiser man.

Another British intelligence asset was the fabulously rich William Bingham, into which family one of the Barings married. It was stated in papers and documents that I saw that the Baring Brothers ran the Philadelphia Quakers and owned half of the real estate of that city, all made possible because of the fortune the Baring Brothers had amassed from the China opium trade. Another beneficiary of the Committee of 300's largess was

Stephen Girard, whose descendants inherited the Girard Bank and Trust.

The names of the families, whose history is intertwined with that of Boston and who would never give us ordinary folk the time of day, were wrapped in the arms of the Committee of 300 and its vastly lucrative BEIC China opium trade. Many of the famous families became associated with the notorious Hong Kong and Shanghai Bank which is still the clearing house for billions of dollars that flow from the opium trade in China.

Such famous names as Forbes, Perkins and Hathaway appear in the records of the British East India Company. These genuine American "bluebloods" created Russell and Company, whose main trade was in opium, but also ran other shipping enterprises from China to South America and all points in between. As a reward for their services to the British Crown and the BEIC, the Committee of 300 granted them a monopoly in the slave trade in 1833.

Boston owes its celebrated past to the cotton-opium-slave trade granted to it by the Committee of 300 and it is stated in the records I was privileged to see in London that Boston's merchant families were the chief supporters of the British Crown in the United States. John Murray Forbes is mentioned as the major-domo of the "Boston Blue Bloods" in India House records and in bank records in Hong Kong.

Forbe's son was the first American allowed by the Committee of 300 to sit on the board of the most prestigious drug bank in the world—even today—the Hong Kong and Shanghai Bank. When I was in Hong Kong in the early 1960's as "an historian interested in the British East India Company," I was shown some old records, including past board members of this notorious drug bank, and sure enough, Forbes' name was among them.

The Perkins family, so illustrious that their name is still mentioned in awed whispers, were deeply involved in the nefarious filthy China opium trade. In fact Perkins the elder was one of the first Americans to be elected to the Committee of 300.

His son, Thomas Nelson Perkins, was Morgan's man in Boston, and as such also an agent for British intelligence. His unsavory— I would say disgusting—past was not in question when he richly endowed Harvard University. After all, Canton and Tientsin are a long way from Boston, and who would have cared anyway?

What helped The Perkinses a lot was that Morgan was a powerful member of the Committee of 300, which enabled Thomas N. Perkins to rapidly further his career in the China opium trade. All the Morgans and Perkinses were Freemasons, which was another tie that bound them together, for only Freemasons of highest rank have any hope of being selected by the Committee of 300. Sir Robert Hart, who for almost three decades was chief of the Imperial Chinese Customs Service (read the British Crown's number one agent in the opium trade in China) was subsequently appointed to the board of Morgan Guarantee Bank's Far Eastern Division.

Through access to the historical records in London and Hong Kong, I was able to establish that Sir Robert developed an intimate relationship with Morgan operations in the United States. It is worthy of note that Morgan interests in the opium/ heroin trade have continued in an unbroken line; witness the fact that David Newbigging is on the advisory board of Morgan's Hong Kong operation run in conjunction with Jardine Matheson.

To those who know Hong Kong, the name of Newbigging will be familiar as the most powerful name in Hong Kong. In addition to his membership of Morgan's elite bank, Newbigging doubles as an advisor to the Chinese government. Opium for missile technology, opium for gold, opium for high-tech computers—it is all the same to Newbigging. The way these banks, financial houses, trading companies and the families who run them are intertwined would perplex Sherlock Holmes, yet somehow they must be unraveled and followed if we are to understand their connections with the drug trade and their membership in the Committee of 300.

The two-track entry into the United States of alcohol and

drugs were products of the same stable occupied by the same thoroughbreds. First, prohibition had to be introduced into the United States. This was done by the British East India Company heirs who, acting upon experience gained through the well-documented China Inland Mission records found in India House, set up the Women's Christian Temperance Union, supposedly to oppose consumption of alcohol in America.

We say that history repeats itself, and in a sense, this is true, except that it repeats itself in an ever-upward spiral. Today we find that some of the largest companies, allegedly "polluting" the earth, are the largest contributors of funds to the environmentalist movement. The "big names" send forth their message. Prince Philip is one of their heroes, yet his son Prince Charles owns a million acres of forested land in Wales from which timber is regularly harvested and, in addition, Prince Charles is one of the largest owners of slum housing in London, where pollution thrives.

In the case of those who railed against the "evils of drink," we find they were financed by the Astors, the Rockefellers, the Spelmans, the Vanderbilts and the Warburgs who had a vested interest in the liquor trade. On the instructions of the Crown, Lord Beaverbrook came over from England to tell these wealthy American families that they were to invest in the WCTU. (It was the same Lord Beaverbrook who came to Washington in 1940 and ORDERED Roosevelt to get involved in Britain's war.)

Roosevelt complied by stationing a U.S. Navy flotilla in Greenland that spent the 9 months prior to Pearl Harbor hunting and attacking German U-Boats. Like his successor, George Bush, Roosevelt thought the Congress a confounded nuisance so, acting like a king—a sense he felt strongly since he is related to the British royal family—FDR never sought the permission of Congress for his illegal action. This is what the British are most fond of referring to as their "special relationship with America."

The drug trade has a connection with the murder of President John F. Kennedy, which foul deed stains the national character and will continue to do so until the perpetrators are found and brought to justice. There is proof that the Mafia was involved in this through the CIA, which brings to mind that it all started with the old Meyer Lansky network which evolved into the Irgun terrorist organization, and Lansky proved to be one of the best vehicles for peddling cultural warfare against the West.

Lansky was, through more respectable fronts, associated with the British higher-ups in bringing gambling and dope distribution to Paradise Island in the Bahamas under the cover of The Mary Carter Paint Company—a joint Lansky-British MI6 venture. Lord Sassoon was later murdered because he was skimming money and was threatening to blow the whistle if he was punished. Ray Wolfe was more presentable, representing the Bronfmans of Canada. While the Bronfmans were not privy to Churchill's massive Nova Scotia Project, they were and still are nevertheless an important asset of the British royal family in the business of dope peddling.

Sam Rothberg, close associate of Meyer Lansky, also worked with Tibor Rosenbaum and Pinchas Sapir, all king pins in the Lansky drug ring. Rosenbaum ran a drug money laundering operation out of Switzerland through a bank he established for this purpose; Banque du Credite International. The bank quickly expanded its activities and became the principal bank used by Lansky and his mobster associates for laundering money garnered from prostitution, drugs and other Mafia rackets.

It is worthy of note that Tibor Rosenbaum's bank was used by the shadowy chief of British Intelligence, Sir William Stephenson, whose right hand man, Major John Mortimer Bloomfield, a Canadian citizen, ran Division Five of the FBI throughout the Second World War. Stephenson was an early member of the 20th century Committee of 300, although Bloomfield never made it that far. As I revealed in my series of monographs on the Kennedy assassination, it was Stephenson who master-minded the operation which was run as a hands-on project by Bloomfield. Fronting for the Kennedy assassination was done through another drug-related front, Permanent Industrial Expositions (PERMINDEX), created in 1957 and centered in the World Trade Mart building in downtown New Orleans. Bloomfield just happened to be the attorney for the Bronfman family. The World Trade Mart was created by Colonel Clay Shaw and FBI Division Five station chief in New Orleans, Guy Bannister. Shaw and Bannister were close associates of Lee Harvey Oswald, accused of shooting Kennedy, who was murdered by CIA contract agent Jack Ruby before he could prove that he was not the assassin who shot President Kennedy. In spite of the Warren Commission and numerous official reports, it has NEVER been established that Oswald owned the Mannlicher rifle said to be the murder weapon (it was not) nor that he had ever fired it. The connection between the drug trade, Shaw, Bannister and Bloomfield has been established several times, and need not concern us here.

In the immediate post-WW II period, one of the most common methods used by Resorts International and other drug related companies to clean money was by courier service to a money laundering bank. Now all that has changed. Only the small fry still use such a risky method. The "big fish" conduit their money via the CHIPS system, an acronym for Clearing House International Payments System, run by a Burroughs computer system centered at the New York Clearing House. Twelve of the largest banks use this system. One of them is the Hong Kong and Shanghai Bank. Another is Credite Suisse, that oh so respectable paragon of virtue in banking—until the lid is lifted. Combined with the SWIFT system based in Virginia, dirty drug money becomes invisible. Only wanton carelessness results in the FBI getting lucky now and then, if and when it is told not to look the other way.

Only low echelon drug dealers get caught with drug money in their hands. The elite, Drexel Burnham, Credite Suisse, Hong Kong and Shanghai Bank, escape detection. But this, too, is changing with the collapse of Bank of Credit and Commerce

International (BCCI) which is likely to expose a great deal about the drug trade if ever a proper investigation is carried out.

One of the largest assets in the portfolio of the Committee of 300 companies is American Express (AMEX). Its presidents regularly occupy positions on the Committee of 300. I first got interested in Amex when I was carrying out an on-the-spot investigation that led me to the Trade Development Bank in Geneva. Later, this got me into a lot of trouble. I discovered that Trade Development Bank, then run by Edmund Safra, key man in the gold for opium trade, was supplying tons of gold to the Hong Kong market via Trade Development Bank.

Before going to Switzerland, I went to Pretoria, South Africa, where I talked with Dr. Chris Stals, at that time the deputy governor of the South African Reserve Bank which controls all bulk dealings in South African-produced gold. After several discussions over a period of a week, I was told that the bank could not supply me with the ten tons of gold that I was authorized to buy on behalf of clients I was supposed to be representing. My friends in the right places knew how to produce the documentation which passed without question.

The Reserve Bank referred me to a Swiss company whom I cannot name, because it would blow cover. I was also given the address of Trade Development Bank in Geneva. The purpose of my exercise was to find out the mechanics of how gold is moved and traded, and secondly to test bogus documents which had been prepared for me by ex-intelligence friends of mine who specialized in this kind of thing. Remember "M" in the "James Bond" series? Let me assure you that "M" does exist, only his correct initial is "C." The documents I had consisted of "buying orders" from Liechtenstein companies with supporting papers to match.

On approaching Trade Development Bank I was at first greeted cordially but, as discussions progressed with more and more suspicion until, when I felt it was no longer safe for me to visit the bank, without telling anyone at the bank I left Geneva. Later the bank was sold to American Express. American Express was briefly investigated by former Attorney General Edwin Meese, after which he was quickly removed from office and labeled "corrupt." What I found was that American Express was and still is a conduit for laundering drug money and, thus far, no one has been able to explain to me why a private company has the right to print dollars—aren't American Express travelers checks dollars? I subsequently exposed the Safra-Amex drug connections which upset a lot of people, as can be imagined.

Committee of 300 member Japhet controls Charterhouse Japhet, which in turn controls Jardine Matheson as a direct link to the Hong Kong opium trade. The Japhets are reportedly English Quakers. The Matheson family, also members of the Committee of 300, were kingpins in the China opium trade, at least up until 1943. The Mathesons have appeared in the Queen of England Honors List since the early 19th century.

The top controllers of the drug trade in the Committee of 300 have no conscience about the millions of lives they ruin each year. They are Gnostics, Cathars, members of the cult of Dionysus, Osiris, or worse. To them, "ordinary" people are there to be used for their purposes. Their high-priests, Bulwer-Lytton and Aldous Huxley, preached the gospel of drugs as a beneficial substance. To quote Huxley:

"And for private everyday use, there have always been chemical intoxicants. All the vegetable sedatives and narcotics, all the euphorics that grow on trees, the hallucinogens that ripen in berries, have been used by humans since time immemorial. And to these modifiers of conscience, modern science has added its quota of synthetics. For unrestricted use the West has permitted only alcohol and tobacco. All other chemical Doors in the Wall are labeled DOPE."

To the oligarches and plutocrats of the Committee of 300, drugs have a two-fold purpose, firstly to bring in colossal sums of money and secondly, to eventually turn a major part of the population into mindless drug zombies who will be easier to control than people who don't need drugs, as punishment for rebellion will mean withholding of supplies of heroin, cocaine, marijuana, etc. For this it is necessary to legalize drugs so that a MONOPOLY SYSTEM, which has been readied for introduction once severe economic conditions, of which the 1991 depression is the forerunner, cause drug usage to proliferate as hundreds of thousands of permanently jobless workers turn to drugs for solace.

In one of the Royal Institute of International Affairs top secret papers, the scenario is laid out as follows (in part):

"...having been failed by Christianity, and with unemployment on every hand, those who have been without jobs for five years or more will turn away from the church and seek solace in drugs. That is when full control of the drug trade must be completed in order that the governments of all countries who are under our jurisdiction will have a MONOPOLY which we will control through supply.... Drug bars will take care of the unruly and the discontent, would be revolutionaries will be turned into harmless addicts with no will of their own...."

There is ample evidence that the CIA and British intelligence, specially MI6, have already spent at least a decade working toward this goal.

The Royal Institute of International Affairs used the lifetime work of Aldous Huxley and Bulwer-Lytton as its blueprint to bring about a state where mankind will no longer have wills of their own in the One World Government-New World Order of the fast-approaching New Dark Age. Again, let us see what high priest Aldous Huxley had to say about this:

"In many societies at many levels of civilization, attempts

have been made to fuse drug intoxication with God intoxication. In ancient Greece, for example, ethyl alcohol had its place in the established religions. Dionysus, Bacchus, as he was often called, was a true divinity. Complete prohibition of chemical changes can be decreed but cannot be enforced. (THE LANGUAGE OF THE PRO-DRUG LOBBY ON CAPITOL HILL.)

"Now let us consider another type of drug—still undiscovered, but probably just around the corner—a drug making people happy in situations where they would normally feel miserable. (Is there anyone more miserable than a person who has sought and been unable to find work?) Such a drug would be a blessing, but a blessing fraught with grave social and political dangers. By making a harmless chemical euphoria freely available, a dictator (read Committee of 300) could reconcile an entire population to a state of affairs to which self-respecting human beings ought not to be reconciled."

Quite a dialectical masterpiece. What Huxley was advocating and which is official policy of the Committee of 300 and its surrogate, RIIA, can be quite simply stated as mass mind control. As I have often said, all wars are wars for the souls of mankind. Thus far it has not dawned on us that the drug trade is irregular low-intensity warfare against the whole human race of free men. Irregular warfare is the most terrible form of warfare which, while it has a beginning, has no ending.

Some will question the involvement of the British royal families, past and present, in the drug trade. To see it in print appears on the surface to be preposterous, and it is being seen in print more often these days to make it appear exactly that, preposterous. The oldest maxim in the intelligence business is, "If you want to hide something, put it where everyone can see it."

F. S. Turner's book, "BRITISH OPIUM POLICY," published in 1876, shows how the British monarchy and its hangers-on family relatives were deeply involved in the opium trade. Turner was the secretary of the Anglo Oriental Society of the Suppression of the Opium Trade. He declined to be silenced by Crown spokesperson Sir R. Temple. Turner stated that the government, and therefore the Crown, had to withdraw from the opium monopoly, "and if it takes any revenues at all, take only that which accrues from taxation honestly meant to have a restrictive force."

Turner was answered by a spokesman for the monarchy, Lord Lawrence, who fought against the BEIC losing its monopoly. "It would be desirable to get rid of the monopoly, but I myself am disinclined to be the agent of change. If it is a question of moderate loss that we could afford, I would not hesitate to undertake it." (Taken from the Calcutta Papers 1870.)

By 1874 the war against the British monarchy and the aristocracy over its deep involvement in the China opium trade was getting heated. The Society for the Suppression of the Opium Trade violently assailed the aristocracy of the day and pressed home its attacks in a fearless manner we would do well to emulate. The society said that the Treaty of Tientsin, which forced China to accept the importation of enormous amounts of opium, was a dastardly crime against the Chinese people.

There arose a mighty warrior, Joseph Grundy Alexander, a barrister by profession who, in 1866, led a strong attack on British Crown opium policy in China in which he openly mentioned the involvement of the royal family and the aristocracy. For the first time Alexander brought India, "the Jewel in the Crown," into the picture. He laid the blame squarely where it belonged, on the monarchy, the so-called aristocracy and its servants in the British government.

Under the direction of Alexander, the society committed itself to the total destruction of the cultivation of opium poppies in Bengal, India. Alexander proved to be a doughty opponent. Through his leadership, the drug aristocracy began to falter and, in the face of his open denouncements of the royal family and its hangers-on, several Members of Parliament began siding with him—Conservatives, Unionists, Labor. Alexander made it clear that the drug trade was not a party political issue; it was for all parties to join together in helping to eradicate the menace. Lord Kimberly, spokesman for the royal family and the entrenched oligarchists, threatened that any attempts to interfere with what he called "the commerce of the nation will run into serious opposition from the cabinet." Alexander and his society pressed on in the face of innumerable threats and finally parliament agreed to appoint a Royal Commission to enquire into the opium trade, with Lord Kimberly, who was Secretary of India, as its chairman. A more inappropriate person to head the commission could not have been found. It was akin to Dulles being appointed to the Warren Commission.

In his first statement, Lord Kimberly made it clear that he would rather resign from his august position than consent to a resolution that would surrender Indian Opium Revenues. It is worthy of note that "Indian Opium Revenue" implied money shared by the nation. Like the idea that the people of South Africa share in the enormous profits from the sale of gold and diamonds, this was just not the case. Indian opium revenues went straight into the royal coffers and the pockets of the nobility and the oligarchists and plutocrats, and made them billionaires.

Rowntree's book, "THE IMPERIAL DRUG TRADE" gives a fascinating account of how Prime Minister Gladstone and his fellow plutocrats lied, cheated, twisted and turned to keep the astonishing truth of the involvement of the British monarchy in the opium trade from being exposed. Rowntree's book is a treasure house of information on the deep involvement of the British royal family and the lords and ladies of England and the huge fortunes they accumulated from the misery of the Chinese opium addicts.

Lord Kimberly, secretary of the commission of inquiry, was

himself deeply involved in the opium trade so he did everything in his power to close the proceedings to all who sought the truth. Finally, under a great deal of pressure from the public, the Royal Commission was forced to open the door to this inquiry just a crack, so that it became apparent that the highest in the land were running the opium trade and receiving huge benefits from it. But the door was quickly slammed shut again, and the Royal Commission called no expert witnesses, thereafter sitting for an absurdly short period of time. The commission was nothing but a farce and a cover-up, such as we have become accustomed to in 20th century America.

The Eastern Liberal Establishment families of the United States were just as deeply involved in the China opium trade as were the British, indeed they still are. Witness recent history when James Earl Carter toppled the Shah of Iran. Why was the Shah deposed and then murdered by the United States government? In a word, because of DRUGS. The Shah had clamped down and virtually put an end to the immensely lucrative opium trade being conducted out of Iran by the British. At the time that the Shah took over in Iran, there were already one million opium/heroin addicts.

This the British would not tolerate, so they sent the United States to do their dirty work for them in terms of the "special relationship" between the two countries. When Khomeini took over the U.S. Embassy in Teheran, arms sales by the United States, which had begun with the Shah, were not discontinued. Why not? Had the United States done so, Khomeini would have canceled the British monopoly of the opium trade in his country. To prove the point, after 1984, Khomeini's liberal attitude toward opium had increased the number of addicts to 2 million, according to United Nations and World Health Organization statistics.

Both President Carter and his successor, Ronald Reagan, willingly and with full knowledge of what was at stake, went on supplying arms to Iran even while American hostages languished in captivity. In 1980 I wrote a monograph under the title, "What

Really Happened in Iran," which set out the facts. The arms trade with Iran was sealed at a meeting between Cyrus Vance, a servant of the Committee of 300, and Dr. Hashemi, which resulted in the U.S. Air Force beginning an immediate airlift of arms to Iran, carried on even at the height of the hostage crisis. The arms came from U.S. Army stockpiles in Germany and some were even flown directly from the United States with refueling stops at the Azores.

With the advent of Khomeini, who was put in power in Iran by the Committee of 300, opium production skyrocketed. By 1984 Iran's opium production exceeded 650 metric tons of opium per annum. What Carter and Reagan did was ensure that there was no further interference in the opium trade and they carried out the mandate given to them by the oligarchical families in Britain in this connection. Iran presently rivals the Golden Triangle in the volume of opium produced.

The Shah was not the only victim of the Committee of 300. William Buckley, CIA station chief in Beirut, in all his lack of experience on who is behind the opium trade, began conducting investigations in Iran, Lebanon and even spent time in Pakistan. From Islamabad, Buckley began sending back damning reports to the CIA in Langley about the burgeoning opium trade in the Golden Crescent and Pakistan. The U.S. Embassy in Islamabad was firebombed, but Buckley escaped the mob attack and returned to Washington because his cover was blown by forces unknown.

Then a very strange thing happened. Contrary to all procedures laid down by the CIA when an agent's cover has been blown, Buckley was sent back to Beirut. Buckley was in effect sentenced to death by the CIA in order to silence him, and this time the sentence was carried out. William Buckley was kidnaped by agents of the Committee of 300. Under brutal interrogation by General Mohammed el Khouili of Syrian intelligence to force him to disclose the names of all field officers of the DEA in these countries, he was brutally murdered. His efforts to expose the huge opium trade developing out of Pakistan, Lebanon and Iran cost Buckley his life.

If the remaining free men in this world believe that singlehandedly or in small groups they can smash the drug trade, they are sorely mistaken. They could cut off the tentacles of the opium and cocaine trade here and there, but never the head. The crowned cobras of Europe and their Eastern Liberal Establishment family will not tolerate it. The war on drugs which the Bush administration is allegedly fighting, but which it is not, is for TOTAL legalization of ALL types and classes of drugs. Such drugs are not solely a social aberration, but a full-scale attempt to gain control of the minds of the people of this planet, or as the "Aquarian Conspiracy" authors put it, "to bring about radical changes in the United States." THIS IS THE PRINCIPAL TASK OF THE COMMITTEE OF 300, THE ULTIMATE SECRET SOCIETY.

Nothing has changed in the opium-heroin-cocaine trade. It is still run by the same "upper class" families in Britain and the United States. It is still a fabulously profitable trade where what seem to be big losses through seizures by the authorities are written off in paneled boardrooms in New York, Hong Kong and London over port and cigars as "merely the cost of doing business, old boy."

British colonial capitalism has always been the mainstay of the oligarchical feudal system of privilege in England and remains so to the present day. When the poor, untutored pastoral people in South Africa who became known as the Boers fell into the bloodstained hands of the British aristocracy in 1899, they had no idea that the revoltingly cruel war so relentlessly pursued by Queen Victoria, was financed by the incredible amounts of money which came from the "instant fortunes" of the BEIC opium trade in China into the pockets of the plutocrats.

Committee of 300 members Cecil John Rhodes, Barney Barnato and Alfred Beit instigated and engineered the war. Rhodes was the principle agent for the Rothschilds, whose banks were awash in cash flowing in from the opium trade. These robbers, thieves and liars—Rhodes, Barnato, Oppenheimer, Joel and Beit—dispossessed the South African Boers of their birthright, the gold and diamonds that lay beneath their soil. The South African Boers received nothing out of the BILLIONS UPON BILLIONS of dollars derived from the sale of THEIR gold and diamonds.

The Committee of 300 quickly took full control of these vast treasures, control which it even now maintains through one of its members, Sir Harry Oppenheimer. The average South African receives $100 per annum per capita from the gold and diamond industry. The BILLIONS which flow out annually go to the bankers of the Committee of 300. It is one of the most foul and vile stories of greed, theft and the murder of a nation ever recorded in the annals of history.

How could the British Crown have succeeded in pulling off this stunning fraud of gigantic proportion? To accomplish such a Herculean task requires skilled organizing with devoted agents-in-place to carry out the daily instructions passed down from the conspirators' hierarchy. The first step was a press propaganda campaign portraying the Boers as uncivilized barbarians, only slightly human, who were denying British citizens the right to vote in the Boer Republic. Then, demands were made on Paul Kruger, leader of the Transvaal Republic, which of course could not be met. After that, a series of incidents were staged to provoke the Boers into retaliation, but that didn't work either. Then came the infamous Jameson Raid where a certain Jameson led a party of several hundred armed men in an attack on the Transvaal. War followed immediately thereafter.

Queen Victoria mounted the largest and best equipped army that the world had ever seen at that time (1898). Victoria thought the war would be over in two weeks, since the Boers had no standing army and no trained militia and would be no match for her 400,000 soldiers drawn from the ranks of Britain's underclasses. The Boers never numbered more than 80,000 farmers and their sons—some were as young as fourteen—Rudyard Kipling also thought the war would be over in less than a week.

Instead, with rifle in one hand and the Bible in the other, the Boers held out for three years. "We went to South Africa thinking the war would be over in a week," said Kipling. "Instead, the Boers taught us no end of a lesson." That same "lesson" could be taught to the Committee of 300 today if we could but muster 80,000 leaders, good men and true to lead this nation in battle against the gargantuan monster threatening to devour everything our Constitution stands for.

After the war ended in 1902, the British Crown had to consolidate its grip on the unimaginable fortune of gold and diamonds that lay beneath the barren veldt of the Boer Republics of Transvaal and Orange Free State. This was done through the Round Table of the legend of King Arthur and his Knights. The Round Table is strictly a British MI6 intelligence operation established by the Committee of 300 which, together with the Rhodes Scholarship program, is a dagger in the heartland of America.

The Round Table was established in South Africa by Cecil Rhodes and funded by the English Rothschild family. Its purpose was to train business leaders loyal to the British Crown who would secure the vast gold and diamond treasures for the British Crown. South Africans had their birthright stolen from them in a coup so massive and all pervading that it was apparent only a central unified command could have pulled it off. That unified command was the Committee of 300.

That this was accomplished is not in dispute. By the early 1930's, the British Crown had a stranglehold on the biggest supplies of gold and diamonds ever found in the world. NOW THE COMMITTEE OF 300 HAD AT ITS DISPOSAL BOTH THE VAST FORTUNE COMING FROM THE DRUG TRADE AND THE EQUALLY VAST FORTUNE OF THE MINERAL AND METAL WEALTH OF SOUTH AFRICA. Financial control of the world was complete.

The Round Table played a pivotal role in the coup. The express purpose of the Round Table, after swallowing up South Africa, was to blunt the benefits to the United States of the American War of Independence, and once more bring the United States under British control. Organizing ability was essential for such an enterprise and it was provided by Lord Alfred Milner, protege of the London Rothschild family. Using Scottish Rite Freemason principles in selecting members of Round Table, those chosen underwent a period of intense training at Cambridge and Oxford Universities under the watchful eyes of John Ruskin, a self-confessed "old school communist," and T. H. Green, an operative of MI6.

It was Green, the son of a Christian evangelical cleric, who spawned Rhodes, Milner, John Wheeler Bennet, A. D. Lindsay, George Bernard Shaw and Hjalmar Schacht, Hitler's finance minister. I pause here to remind readers that the Round Table is only ONE SECTOR of this vast and all-encompassing Committee of 300. Yet the Round Table itself consists of a maze of companies, institutions, banks and educational establishments, which in itself would take qualified insurance actuaries a year to sort out.

Round Tablers fanned out throughout the world to take control of fiscal and monetary policies and political leadership in all countries where they operated. In South Africa, General Smuts, who had fought against the British in the Boer War, was "turned" and became a leading British intelligence, military and political agent who espoused the cause of the British Crown. In the United States, in later years, the task of boring away at the United States from the inside fell to William Yandell Elliot, the man who spawned Henry Kissinger and who was responsible for his meteoric rise to power as chief U.S. advisor to the Committee of 300.

William Yandell Elliot was "an American at Oxford," who had already served the Committee of 300 well, which is a prerequisite for higher office in the service of the committee.

After graduating from Vanderbilt University in 1917, Elliot was drafted by the Rothschild-Warburg banking network. He worked at the Federal Reserve Bank in San Francisco and rose to be a director. From there he acted as a Warburg-Rothschild intelligence officer, reporting on the important areas of the United States he was overseeing. Elliot's "Freemason" talent spotters recommended him for a Rhodes Scholarship and, in 1923, he went to Balliol College at Oxford University whose "dreaming spires" hid a network of intrigue and future traitors to the West.

Balliol College was, and still is, the center of recruiting for the Round Table. After a thorough brainwashing conducted by the Tavistock Institute of Human Relations representative, A. D. Lindsay, who had succeeded Master of Balliol T. H. Green, Elliot was received into the Round Table and sent to The Royal Institute of International Affairs to be given his assignment, which was that he return to the United States to become a leader in the academic community.

The Round Table's driving philosophy was to have Round Tablers in positions to formulate and carry out social policies through social institutions whereby what Ruskin called "the masses" could be manipulated. Members infiltrated the highest levels of banking after undergoing a course at the Tavistock Institute. The course was drawn up by Lord Leconsfield, an intimate of the British royal family, and later run by Robert Brand who went on to manage Lazard Freres. The Royal Institute of International Affairs was and remains totally interfaced with the British monarchy.

Some of the spinoffs of the Round Table are the Bilderbergers, set up and run by Duncan Sandys, a prominent politician and son-in-law of the late Winston Churchill, the Ditchley Foundation, a secret banker's club which I exposed in my 1983 work, "International Banker's Conspiracy: The Ditchley Foundation," the Trilateral Commission, the Atlantic Council of the United States and the Aspen Institute for Humanistic Studies, whose well-hidden, behind the scenes founder was Lord Bullock of the

RIIA for whom Robert Anderson fronted.

The way in which Henry Kissinger, the RIIA's chief asset in the United States, came to power is a story of the triumph of the institution of the British monarchy over the Republic of the United States of America. It is a tale of horror, too long to be included here. Nevertheless, it would be remiss of me if I did not mention just a few of the highlights of Kissinger's rise to fame, fortune and power.

After a stint in the United States Army, beginning with the job of driving General Fritz Kraemer around war-torn Germany, thanks to the Oppenheimer family Kissinger was picked to attend Wilton Park for further training. At the time he held the rank of private first class. In 1952 Kissinger was sent to the Tavistock Institute where R. V. Dicks took him in hand and turned him inside out. Thereafter there was no holding Kissinger back. He was later drafted to serve under George Franklin and Hamilton Fish of the Council on Foreign Relations' New York office.

It is believed that the official nuclear policy adopted by the United States was delivered to Kissinger during his stay at Tavistock and further shaped by his participation in "Nuclear Weapons and Foreign Policy," a Round Table seminar which brought forth the doctrine known as "flexible response," a total irrationality, which became known by the acronym MAD.

Thanks to William Yandell Elliot and under the tutelage of John Wheeler Bennett, top intelligence director of the Round Table and chief of MI6 field operations in the United States, Kissinger became Elliot's "favorite son" as he explained in his book, "The Pragmatic Revolt in Politics." Kissinger was co-opted into the Round Table to push monetarist policies he studied at Harvard International Seminars.

Kissinger avidly absorbed Elliot's teachings and was no longer recognizable as the man General Kraemer once described as "my little Jew-boy driver." Kissinger was inculcated with the spirit of the Master of Balliol, becoming an ardent disciple of decadent British aristocracy. Adopting the philosophies of

Toynbee, chief intelligence director for MI6 at the Royal Institute of International Affairs, Kissinger used its papers to write his undergraduate "dissertation."

By the mid 1960's Kissinger had proved his worth to the Round Table and the RIIA, and thus to the British monarchy. As a reward and a test of what he had learned, Kissinger was placed in charge of a small group consisting of James Schlessinger, Alexander Haig and Daniel Ellsberg. The Round Table was using to conduct a series of experiments. Cooperating with this group was the Institute of Policy Studies chief theoretician, Noam Chomsky.

Haig, like Kissinger, worked for General Kraemer, albeit not as a driver, and the general found a number of varied openings in the Department of Defense for his protege. Once Kissinger was installed as National Security Advisor, Kraemer got Haig the job as his deputy. Ellsberg, Haig, and Kissinger then set in motion the RIIA's Watergate plan to oust President Nixon for disobeying direct instructions. Haig played the lead role in brainwashing and confusing President Nixon, and in effect it was Kissinger who ran the White House during the softening up of the President. As I mentioned in 1984, Haig was the White House go-between known as "Deep Throat," passing information to the *Washington Post* team of Woodward and Bernstein.

The Watergating of Nixon was the biggest coup yet pulled off by the Round Table as an agency and an arm of the RIIA. All the tangled threads led back to the Round Table; from there to the RIIA, and right back to the Queen of England. The humiliation of Nixon was an object lesson and a warning to future Presidents of the United States not to imagine they could go against the Committee of 300 and win. Kennedy was brutally murdered in full view of the American people for the same reason; Nixon was not considered worthy enough to suffer the same fate as John F. Kennedy.

But whatever the method used, the Committee of 300 made

sure that all would-be aspirants for the White House got the message: "Nobody is beyond our reach." That this message remains just as forceful as it was when Kennedy was murdered and Nixon hounded out of office, is evidenced by the character of President George Bush, whose eagerness to please his masters should be cause for grave concern among those who worry about the future of the United States.

The purpose of the exercise was made clear in the Pentagon Papers episode and the drafting of Schlessinger into the Nixon Administration to act as a spoiler in the defense establishment and a counterforce to the development of atomic energy, which role Schlessinger carried out from the shelter of his position in the Atomic Energy Commission, one of the key factors in deindustrializing the United States in the planned Club of Rome Post Industrial-Zero-growth strategies. From this beginning we can trace the roots of the 1991 recession/depression which has thus far cost the jobs of 30 million Americans.

It is virtually impossible to penetrate the Committee of 300 and the oligarchical families that go to make it up. The camouflage they pull over themselves as protective covering is very hard to rip off. This fact should be noted by every freedom-loving American: The Committee of 300 dictates what passes for United States foreign and domestic policies and has done so for over 200 years. Nowhere was this more strikingly portrayed than when a cocky President Truman had the wind knocked out of him by Churchill ramrodding the so-called "Truman Doctrine" down the throat of the little man from Independence, Missouri.

Some of their former members, whose descendants filled vacancies caused by death, and present members include Sir Mark Turner, Gerald Villiers, Samuel Montague, the Inchcapes, Keswicks, Peases, Schroeders, Airlies, Churchills, Frasers, Lazars and Jardine Mathesons. The full list of members is presented elsewhere in this book; these people on the Committee OR-DERED President Wilson to go to war against Germany in the First World War; this Committee ordered Roosevelt to engineer the Japanese attack on Pearl Harbor with the object of getting the United States into the Second World War.

These people, this Committee, ordered this nation to war in Korea, Vietnam and the Persian Gulf. The plain truth is that the United States has fought in 5 wars this century for and on behalf of the infamous Committee of 300. It seems that, apart from just a few, no one has stopped to ask, "WHY ARE WE FIGHTING THESE WARS?" The big drum of "patriotism," martial music and waving flags and yellow ribbons, it seems, caused a great nation to become bereft of its senses.

On the 50th anniversary of Pearl Harbor, a new "hate Japan" campaign is being waged, not by the Institute of Pacific Relations (IPR), but in the most direct and brazen manner by the Bush Administration and the Congress. The object is the same as it was when Roosevelt inspired the attack on Pearl Harbor, paint the Japanese as aggressors and wage economic war, then ready our forces for the next phase—armed aggression against Japan.

This is already in the works; it is only a matter of time before more of our sons and daughters are sent off to be slaughtered in the service of the feudal lords of the Committee of 300. We ought to shout from the housetops, "It is not for freedom nor for love of country that we are going to die, but for a system of tyranny that will shortly envelope the entire world."

So tight is the grip of this organization on Britain that 95% of British citizens have, since the 1700's, been forced to accept as their share, less than 20% of the national wealth of the country. This is what the oligarchical feudal lords of England like to call "democracy." These nice, proper English gentlemen are, in reality, utterly ruthless—what they did in India, Sudan, Egypt, Iraq, Iran and Turkey will be repeated in every country under the New World Order-One World Government. They will use every nation and its wealth to protect their privileged way of life. It is this class of British aristocracy whose fortunes are inextricably woven and intertwined with the drug trade, the gold, diamond and arms trades, banking, commerce and industry, oil, the news media and entertainment industry.

Apart from the rank and file of the Labour Party (but not its leaders), the majority of British political leaders are descendants of titled families, the titles being hereditary and handed down from father to eldest son. This system ensures that no "outsiders" aspire to political power in England. Nevertheless, some aliens have been able to squeeze their way in.

Take the case of Lord Halifax, former British Ambassador to Washington and the man who delivered Committee of 300 orders to our government during the Second World War. Halifax's son, Charles Wood, married a Miss Primrose, a blood relative of Lord Rothschild. Behind such names as Lord Swaythling is hidden the name of Montague, director of the Bank of England and adviser and confidant of the majority stockholder of the Shell Oil Company, Queen Elizabeth II. All are members of the Committee of 300. Some of the old barriers have been broken down. Title is today not the only criteria for admission to the Club of Rome.

It is appropriate to provide an overview of what the Committee of 300 hopes to achieve, what its aims and objectives are, before we proceed to its vast, far flung interlocking interfacing of banks, insurance companies, corporations, etc. The following information has taken years of investigative research to put together from hundreds of documents and sources of mine who gave me access to some of the papers in which the details are hidden.

The Committee of 300 consists of certain individuals specialists in their own fields, including cultus diabolicus, mind altering drugs, and specialists in murder by poison, intelligence, banking, and every facet of commercial activity. It will be necessary to mention former members since deceased, because of their former roles and because their places were given to family members or new members considered worthy of the honor.

Included in the membership are the old families of the European Black Nobility, the American Eastern Liberal Establishment (in Freemason hierarchy and the Order of Skull and

Bones), the Illuminati, or as it is known by the Committee, "MORIAH CONQUERING WIND," the Mumma Group, The National and World Council of Churches, the Circle of Initiates, the Nine Unknown Men, Lucis Trust, Jesuit Liberation Theologists, The Order of the Elders of Zion, the Nasi Princes, International Monetary Fund (IMF), the Bank of International Settlements (BIS), the United Nations (U.N.), the Central, British Quator Coronati, Italian P2 Masonry—especially those in the Vatican hierarchy—the Central Intelligence Agency, Tavistock Institute selected personnel, various members of leading foundations and insurance companies named in the lists that follow, the Hong Kong and Shanghai Bank, the Milner Group-Round Table, Cini Foundation, German Marshall Fund, Ditchley Foundation, NATO, Club of Rome, Environmentalists, The Order of St. John of Jerusalem, One World Government Church, Socialist International, Black Order, Thule Society, Anenherbe-Rosicrucianists, The Great Superior Ones and literally HUNDREDS of other organizations.

What then are we looking at? A loosely-knit gathering of people with weird ideas? Certainly not. In the Committee of 300, which has a 150-year history, we have some of the most brilliant intellects assembled to form a completely totalitarian, absolutely controlled "new" society—only it isn't new, having drawn most of its ideas from the Clubs of Cultus Diabolicus. It strives toward a One World Government rather well described by one of its late members, H. G. Wells, in his work commissioned by the Committee which Wells boldly called: "THE OPEN CONSPIRACY— PLANS FOR A WORLD REVOLUTION."

It was a bold statement of intent, but not really so bold since nobody believed Wells except the Great Superior Ones, the Anenherbes and those who were what we would call "insiders" today. Here is an extract of what Wells proposed:

"The Open Conspiracy will appear first, I believe as a conscious organization of intelligent, and in some cases wealthy men, as a movement having distinct social and political aims, confessedly ignoring most of the existing apparatus of political control, or using it only as an incidental implement in the stages, a mere movement of a number of people in a certain direction, who will presently discover, with a sort of a surprise, the common object toward which they are all moving. In all sorts of ways, they will be influencing and controlling the ostensible government."

Like George Orwell's *1984*, Wells' account is a mass-appeal for a One World Government. Summarized, the intent and purpose of the Committee of 300 is to bring to pass the following conditions:

A One World Government and one-unit monetary system, under permanent non-elected hereditary oligarchists who self-select from among their numbers in the form of a feudal system as it was in the Middle Ages. In this One World entity, population will be limited by restrictions on the number of children per family, diseases, wars, famines, until 1 billion people who are useful to the ruling class, in areas which will be strictly and clearly defined, remain as the total world population.

There will be no middle class, only rulers and servants. All laws will be uniform under a legal system of world courts practicing the same unified code of laws, backed up by a One World Government police force and a One World unified military to enforce laws in all former countries where no national boundaries shall exist. The system will be on the basis of a welfare state; those who are obedient and subservient to the One World Government will be rewarded with the means to live; those who are rebellious will simply be starved to death or be declared outlaws, thus a target for anyone who wishes to kill them. Privately owned firearms or weapons of any kind will be prohibited.

Only one religion will be allowed and that will be in the form of a One World Government Church, which has been in existence since 1920 as we shall see. Satanism, Luciferianism and Witchcraft shall be recognized as legitimate One World Government curricula with no private or church schools. All Christian churches have already been subverted and Christianity will be a thing of the past in the One World Government.

To induce a state where there is no individual freedom or any concept of liberty surviving, there shall be no such thing as republicanism, sovereignty or rights residing with the people. National pride and racial identity shall be stamped out and in the transition phase it shall be subject to the severest penalties to even mention one's racial origin.

Each person shall be fully indoctrinated that he or she is a creature of the One World Government with an identification number clearly marked on their person so as to be readily accessible, which identifying number shall be in the master file of the NATO computer in Brussels, Belgium, subject to instant retrieval by any agency of the One World Government at any time. The master files of the CIA, FBI, state and local police agencies, IRS, FEMA, Social Security shall be vastly expanded and form the basis of personal records of all individuals in the United States.

Marriage shall be outlawed and there shall be no family life as we know it. Children will be removed from their parents at an early age and brought up by wards as state property. Such an experiment was carried out in East Germany under Erich Honnecker when children were take away from parents considered by the state to be disloyal citizens. Women will be degraded through the continued process of "women's liberation" movements. Free sex shall be mandatory.

Failure to comply at least once by the age of 20 shall be punishable by severe reprisals against her person. Self-abortion shall be taught and practiced after two children are born to a woman; such records shall be contained in the personal file of each woman in the One World Government's regional computers. If a woman falls pregnant after she has previously given birth to two children, she shall be forcibly removed to an abortion clinic for such an abortion and sterilization to be carried out.

Pornography shall be promoted and be compulsory showing in every theater of cinema, including homosexual and lesbian pornography. The use of "recreational" drugs shall be compulsory, with each person allotted drug quotas which can be purchased at One World Government stores throughout the world. Mind control drugs will be expanded and usage become compulsory. Such mind control drugs shall be given in food and/or water supplies without the knowledge and/or consent of the people. Drug bars shall be set up, run by One World Government employees, where the slave-class shall be able to spend their free time. In this manner the non-elite masses will be reduced to the level and behavior of controlled animals with no will of their own and easily regimented and controlled.

The economic system shall be based upon the ruling oligarchical class allowing just enough foods and services to be produced to keep the mass slave labor camps going. All wealth shall be aggregated in the hands of the elite members of the Committee of 300. Each individual shall be indoctrinated to understand that he or she is totally dependent upon the state for survival. The world shall be ruled by Committee of 300 Executive Decrees which become instant law. Boris Yeltsin is using Committee of 300 decrees to impose the Committee's will on Russia as a trial run. Courts of punishment and not courts of justice shall exist.

Industry is to be totally destroyed along with nuclear powered energy systems. Only the Committee of 300 members and their elitists shall have the right to any of the earth's resources. Agriculture shall be solely in the hands of the Committee of 300 with food production strictly controlled. As these measures begin to take effect, large populations in the cities shall be forcibly removed to remote areas and those who refuse to go shall be exterminated in the manner of the One World Government experiment carried out by Pol Pot in Cambodia.

Euthanasia for the terminally ill and the aged shall be compulsory. No cities shall be larger than a predetermined number as described in the work of Kalgeri. Essential workers will be moved to other cities if the one they are in becomes overpopulated. Other non-essential workers will be chosen at random and sent to underpopulated cities to fill "quotas."

At least 4 billion "useless eaters" shall be eliminated by the year 2050 by means of limited wars, organized epidemics of fatal rapid-acting diseases and starvation. Energy, food and water shall be kept at subsistence levels for the non-elite, starting with the White populations of Western Europe and North America and then spreading to other races. The population of Canada, Western Europe and the United States will be decimated more rapidly than on other continents, until the world's population reaches a manageable level of 1 billion, of which 500 million will consist of Chinese and Japanese races, selected because they are people who have been regimented for centuries and who are accustomed to obeying authority without question.

From time to time there shall be artificially contrived food and water shortages and medical care to remind the masses that their very existence depends on the goodwill of the Committee of 300.

After the destruction of housing, auto, steel and heavy goods industries, there shall be limited housing, and industries of any kind allowed to remain shall be under the direction of NATO's Club of Rome as shall all scientific and space exploration development, limited to the elite under the control of the Committee of 300. Space weapons of all former nations shall be destroyed along with nuclear weapons.

All essential and non-essential pharmaceutical products, doctors, dentists and health care workers will be registered in the central computer data bank and no medicine or medical care will be prescribed without express permission of regional controllers responsible for each city, town and village.

The United States will be flooded by peoples of alien cultures who will eventually overwhelm White America, people with no concept of what the United States Constitution stands for and who will, in consequence, do nothing to defend it, and in whose minds the concept of liberty and justice is so weak as to matter little. FOOD and shelter shall be the main concern.

No central bank save the Bank of International Settlement and the World Bank shall be allowed to operate. Private banks will be outlawed. Remuneration for work performed shall be under a uniform predetermined scale throughout the One World Government. There shall be no wage disputes allowed, nor any diversion from the standard uniform scales of pay laid down by the One World Government. Those who break the law will be instantly executed.

There shall be no cash or coinage in the hands of the non-elite. All transactions shall be carried out by means of a debit card which shall bear the identification number of the holder. Any person who in any way infringes the rules and regulations of the Committee of 300 shall have the use of his or her card suspended for varying times according to the nature and severity of the infringement.

Such persons will find, when they go to make purchases, that their card is blacklisted and they will not be able to obtain services of any kind. Attempts to trade "old" coins, that is to say silver coins of previous and now defunct nations, shall be treated as a capital crime subject to the death penalty. All such coinage shall be required to be surrendered within a given time along with guns, rifles, explosives and automobiles. Only the elite and One World Government high-ranking functionaries will be allowed private transport, weapons, coinage and automobiles.

If the offense is a serious one, the card will be seized at the checking point where it is presented. Thereafter that person shall not be able to obtain food, water, shelter and employment, medical services, and shall be officially listed as an outlaw. Large bands of outlaws will thus be created and they will live in regions that best afford subsistence, subject to being hunted down and shot on sight. Persons assisting outlaws in any way whatsoever, shall likewise be shot. Outlaws who fail to surrender to the police or military after a declared period of time, shall have a former family member selected at random to serve prison terms.in their stead.

Rival factions and groups such as Arabs and Jews and African tribes shall have differences magnified and allowed to wage wars of extermination against each other under the eyes of NATO and U.N. observers. The same tactics will be used in Central and South America. These wars of attrition shall take place BEFORE the take-over of the One World Government and shall be engineered on every continent where large groups of people with ethnic and religious differences live, such as the Sikhs, Moslem Pakistanis and the Hindu Indians. Ethnic and religious differences shall be magnified and exacerbated and violent conflict as a means of "settling" their differences shall be encouraged and fostered.

All information services and print media shall be under the control of the One World Government. Regular brainwashing control measures shall be passed off as "entertainment" in the manner in which it was practiced and became a fine art in the United States. Youths removed from "disloyal parents," shall receive special education designed to brutalize them. Youth of both sexes shall receive training to qualify as prison guards for the One World labor camp system.

It is obvious from the foregoing that much work remains to be done before the dawning of the New World Order can occur. The Committee of 300 has long ago perfected plans to destabilize civilization as we know it, some of which plans were made known by Zbignew Brzezinski in his classic work "THE TECHNOTRONIC ERA" and the works of Aurellio Peccei who founded the Club of Rome, especially in his book, "THE CHASM AHEAD."

In "THE CHASM AHEAD," Peccei spelled out Committee of 300 plans to tame man, whom he called "THE ENEMY."

Peccei quoted what Felix Dzerzinski once said to Sydney Reilly at the height of the Red Terror when millions of Russians were being murdered: "Why should I concern myself with how many die? Even the Christian Bible says what is man that God should be mindful of him? For me men are nothing but a brain at one end and a shit factory at the other."

It was from this brutish view of man that Emmanuel The Christ came to rescue the world. Sydney Reilly was the MI6 operative sent to watch over Dzerzinski's activities. Reilly was allegedly shot by his friend Felix while attempting to flee Russia. The elaborate plot was devised when certain members of the British parliament raised a hue and cry and began to loudly demand an accounting of Reilly's activities in Russia, which threatened to expose the role of the Committee of 300 in gaining control of the Baku oilfields and its major role in assisting Lenin and Trotsky during the Bolshevik Revolution. Rather than have the truth dragged out of Reilly, MI6 thought it expedient to stage his death. Reilly lived out his days in utter luxury in a Russian villa usually reserved for the Bolshevik elite.

Arguing that chaos would ensue unless the "Atlantic Alliance," a euphemism for the Committee of 300 ruled post industrial America, Peccei proposed a Malthusian triaging on a global scale. He envisioned a collision between the scientific-technological-military apparatus of the Soviet Union and the Western world. Thus the Warsaw Pact countries were to be offered a convergence with the West in a One World Government to run global affairs on the foundations of crisis management and global planning.

Events unfolding in what was formerly the USSR and the emergence of several independent states in a loose federation in Russia, is exactly what was envisaged by Peccei and the Club of Rome and this is clearly spelled out in both the books I have mentioned. A USSR thus divided will be easier to cope with than a strong, united Soviet nation. Plans that were laid down by the Committee of 300 for a One World Government, which included the prospect of a divided Russia, are now approaching a point of rapid escalation. Events in Russia at the close of 1991 are all the more dramatic when viewed against the 1960 long-range planning by the Committee of 300.

In Western Europe the people are working toward a federation of states within a one government framework with a single currency. From there the EEC system will be transferred bit by bit to the United States and Canada. The United Nations is being slowly but surely transformed into a rubber stamp of One World Government, with policies dictated to it by the United States as we saw in the case of the Gulf War.

Precisely the same thing is happening with the British Parliament. Discussion on Britain's participation in the Gulf War was kept to a ridiculously minimal level and belatedly took place only during a motion to adjourn the House. This has never happened before in the ancient history of parliament, where so important a decision had to be made and so little time was allowed for discussion. One of the most noteworthy events in parliamentary history has gone virtually unnoticed.

We are close to the point where the United States will send its military forces to settle any and all disputes brought before the United Nations. Departing Secretary General Perez de Cuellar, heavily laden with bribe money, was the most compliant U.N. leader in history in granting demands of the United States without discussion. His successor will be even more inclined to go along with whatever the U.S. government places before him. This is an important step along the road to a One World Government.

The International Court of Justice at The Hague will be used in increasing measure in the next two years to settle legal arguments of all types. It is of course the prototype for a One World Government legal system that will supplant all others. As for central banks, essential in the planning of the New World Order, this is already very much a fait-accompli with the Bank of International Settlements dominating the scene at the close of 1991. Private banks are fast disappearing in preparation for the

Big Ten banks that will control banking the world over under the guidance of BIS and the IMF. Welfare states abound in Europe, and the United States is fast becoming the largest welfare state in the world. Once people come to depend on government for their subsistence, it will be very hard to wean them away from it as we saw in the results of the last mid-term election held in the United States, where 98% of incumbents were returned to Washington to enjoy the good life in spite of their utterly deplorable records. The abolition of privately owned firearms is already in force in three quarters of the world. Only in the United States can the populace still own guns of all types, but that legal right is being chipped away at an alarming rate by local and state laws which violate the Constitutional right of all citizens to bear arms. Private gun ownership will have become a thing of the past in the United States by the year 2010.

SIMILARLY, EDUCATION IS BEING ERODED AT AN ALARMING RATE. PRIVATE SCHOOLS ARE BEING FORCED TO CLOSE BY A VARIETY OF LEGAL STRATA-GEMS AND LACK OF FUNDING. The standard of education in the United States has already sunk to such a deplorable level that today it can barely be classified as education at all. This is according to plan; as I described earlier, the One World Government does not want our youth to be properly educated.

Destruction of national identity proceeds apace. It is no longer a good thing to be patriotic—unless it is in the cause of some One World Government project such as the war of genocide being waged against the nation of Iraq, or the impending destruction of Libya. Racial pride is now frowned upon and deemed to be an illegal act in many parts of the world, IN-CLUDING THE UNITED STATES, BRITAIN, WESTERN EUROPE AND CANADA, ALL COUNTRIES HAVING THE LARGEST CONCENTRATIONS OF THE WHITE RACE.

Led by the secret societies in America, destruction of republican forms of government has proceeded apace since the close of WW II. A list of such governments destroyed by the U.S. is long, and it is difficult for the non-informed to accept that a government of a country allegedly wedded to republicanism under a unique constitution would engage in such conduct, but the facts speak for themselves.

This is a goal which was set over a century ago by the Committee of 300. The United States has led the attacks on such governments and continues to do so even as the United States republican base is being steadily undermined. Starting with James Earl Carter's legal counsel, Lloyd Cutler, a committee of constitutional lawyers has been working to change the U.S. Congress into a non-representative parliamentary system. Work has been in progress since 1979 on the blueprint for such a change, and because of his devotion to the cause, Cutler was made a member of the Committee of 300. The final draft for a parliamentary type of government is to be presented to the Committee of 300 at the end of 1993.

In the new parliamentary system, members will not be responsible to their constituents, but to parliamentary whips and will vote the way they are told to vote. Thus, by judicial and bureaucratic subversion will the Constitution vanish as will individual liberty. Preplanned degrading of man through licentious sexual practices will be stepped up. New sexually degenerate cults are even now being set up by the British Crown— working through the SIS and MI6 services. As we already know, all cults operating in the world today are the product of British intelligence acting for the oligarchical rulers.

We may think this phase of creating a whole new cult which specializes in sexual degenerate behavior is still far off, but my information is that it is due to be stepped up in 1992. By 1994 it will be quite commonplace to have "live shows" in the most prestigious clubs and places of entertainment. This type of "entertainment" is already in the process of having its image cleaned and brightened.

Soon the big names in Hollywood and the entertainment

world will be recommending this or that club as a "must" for live sex shows. Lesbianism and homosexuality will not be featured. This new socially acceptable "entertainment" will consist of heterosexual displays and will be written up in reviews as one finds in today's newspapers about shows on Broadway, or the latest hit movie.

An unprecedented assault on moral values will go into high gear in 1992. Pornography will no longer be called "pornography," but adult sex entertainment. Sloganeering will take the form of "why hide it when everybody does it. Let's take away the image that public displays of sex are ugly and dirty." No more will those who care for this type of unbridled sexual lust have to go to seedy porno parlours. Instead, the upper-class supper clubs and places favored by the rich and famous will make public sexual displays a highly "artistic" form of entertainment. Worse yet, some church "leaders" will even recommend it.

The voluminous all-pervading and enormous social psychiatry apparatus put in place by the Tavistock Institute and its huge web of related capabilities has been under the control of one single entity, and that entity is still in control as we enter 1992. That single entity, the conspirators' hierarchy, is called THE COMMITTEE OF 300. It is a power structure and a power center that operates far beyond the reach of any single world leader or any government, including the United States government and its Presidents—as the late John F. Kennedy found out. The Kennedy murder was an operation of the Committee of 300 and we shall return to that.

The Committee of 300 is the ultimate secret society made up of an untouchable ruling class, which includes the Queen of England, the Queen of the Netherlands, the Queen of Denmark and the royal families of Europe. These aristocrats decided at the death of Queen Victoria, the matriarch of the Venetian Black Guelphs that, in order to gain world-wide control, it would be necessary for its aristocratic members to "go into business" with the non-aristocratic but extremely powerful leaders of corporate business on a global scale, and so the doors to ultimate power were opened to what the Queen of England likes to refer to as "the commoners."

From my days in the intelligence business I know that heads of foreign governments refer to this all-powerful body as "The Magicians." Stalin coined his own phrase to describe them: "The Dark Forces," and President Eisenhower, who was never able to get beyond the "hofjuden" (court Jew) grade, referred to it in a colossal understatement as "the military-industrial complex." Stalin kept the USSR heavily armed with conventional and nuclear forces because he did not trust what he called "the family." His ingrained mistrust and fear of the Committee of 300 proved to be well-founded.

Popular entertainment, especially the medium of movie making, was used to bring discredit upon those who tried to warn of this most dangerous threat to individual liberty and freedom of mankind. Freedom is a God-given law which man has constantly sought to subvert and undermine; yet the yearning for freedom by each individual is so great that up to now, no system has been able to tear that feeling from the heart of man. The experiments that have gone on in the USSR, Britain and the USA, to blunt and dull man's yearnings for freedom, have thus far proved to be unsuccessful.

But with the coming of the New World Order-One World Government, far-reaching experiments will be stepped up to drive man's God-given yearning for freedom out of his mind, body and soul. What we are already experiencing is but nothing, a mere bagatelle, when compared with what is to come. Attacking the soul is the thrust of a host of experiments being readied, and I regret to say that institutions in the United States will play a leading role in the terrible experiments which have already been carried out on local small-scale levels at such places as Bethesda Naval Hospital and Vacaville prison in California.

The movies we have seen thus far include the James Bond

series, the "Assassination Bureau," the "Matarese Circle" and so on. They were make-believe movies, designed to hide the truth that such organizations do exist and on a far greater scale than even Hollywood's fertile idea-men could dream up. Yet the Assassination Bureau is absolutely real. It exists in Europe and the United States solely to do the bidding of the Committee of 300 to carry out high-level assassinations where all other remedies have failed. It was PERMINDEX which ran the Kennedy assassination under the direction of Sir William Stephenson, for years the Queen of England's number one "pest control" operative.

Clay Shaw, a contract agent of the CIA, ran PERMINDEX out of the Trade Mart Center in New Orleans. Former New Orleans District Attorney Jim Garrison came very close to cracking the Kennedy assassination plot up to the level of Clay Shaw until Garrison was "dealt with" and Shaw was found not guilty of involvement in the Kennedy assassination plot. The fact that Shaw was eliminated in the manner of Jack Ruby, another CIA contract agent—both died of induced quick-acting cancer—speaks volumes that Garrison was on the right track.

A second assassination bureau is located in Switzerland and was until recently run by a shadowy figure of whom no photographs existed after 1941. The operations were and probably still are financed by the Oltramaire family—Swiss Black Nobility, owners of the Lombard—Odier Bank of Geneva, a Committee of 300 operation. The primary contact man was Jacques Soustelle—this according to U.S. Army-G2 intelligence files.

This group was also closely allied with Allen Dulles and Jean de Menil, an important member of the Committee of 300 and a very prominent name in the oil industry in Texas. Army-G2 records show that the group was heavily involved in the arms trade in the Middle East, but more than that, the assassination bureau made no less than 30 attempts to assassinate General de Gaulle, in which Jacques Soustelle was directly involved. The same Soustelle was the contact man for the

Sendero Luminosa-Shining Pathway guerrilla group protecting the Committee's Peruvian cocaine producers.

When all of the best that the assassination bureau could do had failed, thanks to the excellent work done by DGSE (French intelligence-formerly SDECE) the job was assigned to MI6—Military Intelligence Department Six, and also known as Secret Intelligence Service (SIS), under the code name "Jackal." SDECE employed clever young graduates and was not infiltrated by MI6 or the KGB to any measurable extent. Its record in tracking down foreign agents made it the envy of the secret services of every nation, and it was this group that followed "Jackal" to his final destination and then killed him before he could fire on General de Gaulle's motorcade.

It was the SDECE who uncovered a Soviet mole in the cabinet of De Gaulle, who also happened to be a liaison man with the CIA in Langley. In order to discredit the SDECE, Allen Dulles, who hated De Gaulle, (the feeling was mutual) had one of its agents, Roger De Louette, caught with $12 million worth of heroin in his possession. After a great deal of expert "interrogation," De Louette "confessed" but was unable to say why he was smuggling drugs into the United States. The whole thing stank to high heaven of a set-up.

Based upon an examination of SDECE methods in protecting De Gaulle, especially in motorcades, the FBI, Secret Service and the CIA knew exactly how to strip President Kennedy of his security and make it easy for the three PERMINDEX shooters to murder him in Dealey Plaza in November 1963.

Another example of FACT disguised as fiction is the Leon Uris novel, "TOPAZ." In "TOPAZ" we find a factual account of the activities of Thyraud de Vosjoli, the very KGB agent uncovered by SDECE and denounced as the KGB's liaison man with the CIA. There are many fictionalized accounts of the MOSSAD's activities, nearly all of which are based on fact.

The MOSSAD is also known as "The Institute." Many would-be writers make nonsensical statements about it, especially one writer who is much in favor with the Christian right wing, which is accepted as truth. One can pardon the offender because he has no intelligence training, but that does not stop him from dropping "Mossad names" all over the place. Such disinformation exercises are routinely run against American right wing patriotic groups. Originally the MOSSAD consisted of 3 groups, the Bureau of Military Intelligence, the Political Department of the Foreign Office and the Department of Security (Sherut Habitachon). David Ben Gurion, a member of the Committee of 300, received some considerable help from MI6 in putting it together.

But it was not a success, and in 1951 Sir William Stephenson of MI6 restructured it into a single unit as an arm of the Political Department of the Israeli Foreign Office, with a special operations group for espionage and "black job" operations. British intelligence gave further assistance in training and equipping for servicing the Sarayet Maktal, also known as the General Staff Reconnaissance unit, in the format of Britain's Special Air Service (SAS). This service unit of the MOSSAD is never mentioned by name and is known simply as "The Guys."

"The Guys" are merely an extension of British intelligence's SAS unit who continually train and update them in new methods. It was "The Guys" who killed the leaders of the P.L.O. and kidnaped Adolph Eichmann. "The Guys," and indeed ALL MOSSAD agents, operate on a war-time footing. The MOSSAD has a tremendous advantage over other intelligence services in that every country in the world has a large Jewish community.

By studying social and criminal records, the MOSSAD is able to pick agents among local Jews it can have a hold over AND MAKE THEM WORK FOR IT WITHOUT PAY. The MOSSAD also has the advantage of having access to the records of all U.S. law enforcement agencies and U.S. intelligence services. The Office of Naval Intelligence (ONI) ELINT services the Mossad at no cost to Israel. Citizens of the United States would be shocked, angered and dismayed if ever it was discovered just how much the MOSSAD knows about the lives of millions of Americans in every walk of life, even those who are not political in any way.

The first head of the MOSSAD, Reuben Shiloach, was made a member of the Committee of 300, but it is not known whether his successor enjoyed the same privilege. Chances are that he does. The MOSSAD has a skillful disinformation service. The amount of disinformation it feeds to the American "market" is embarrassing, but even more embarrassing is how it is swallowed hook, line and sinker and all.

What we are actually witnessing in the microcosm of the MOSSAD is the extent of control exercised by the "Olympians" over the intelligence services, entertainment, publishing, opinion-making (polls) and the television "news" media on a global scale. Ted Turner was recently given a seat on the Committee of 300 in recognition for his "news" (making) CNN broadcasts. The Committee has the power and the means to tell the people of this world ANYTHING, and it will be believed by the vast majority.

On every occasion that a researcher happens upon this astounding central control group, he is either successfully bought off, or else he undergoes some "speciality training" at the Tavistock Institute after which he becomes a contributor to more fiction, of the James Bond type, i.e., he is derailed and well rewarded. If such a person as John F. Kennedy should stumble onto the truth about who directs world events, and cannot be bought, he is assassinated.

In the case of John F. Kennedy, the assassination was carried out with great attendant publicity and with the utmost brutality to serve as a warning to world leaders not to get out of line. Pope John Paul I was quietly murdered because he was getting close to the Committee of 300 through Freemasons in the Vatican hierarchy. His successor, Pope John Paul II, was publicly humiliated as a warning to cease and desist—which he has done. As we shall see, certain Vatican leaders are today seated on the Committee of 300.

It is easy to put serious researchers off the track of the Committee of 300 because Britain's MI6 (SAS) promotes a wide variety of kookery such as the New Age, Yogaism, Zen Buddhism, Witchcraft, Delphic Priesthood of Apollo (Aristotle was a member) and hundreds of small "cults" of all kinds. A group of "retired" British intelligence agents who stayed on the track labeled the conspirators' hierarchy "Force X," and declared that it possesses a super-intelligence service that has corrupted the KGB, the Vatican Intelligence, the CIA, the ONI, DGSE, U.S. military intelligence, the State Department intelligence service and even the most secret of all U.S. intelligence agencies, the Office of National Reconnaissance.

The existence of the National Reconnaissance Office (NRO) was known to only a handful of people outside of the Committee of 300, until Truman stumbled upon it quite by accident. Churchill had a hand in setting up the NRO and he was reportedly livid when Truman discovered its existence. Churchill, more than any other servant of the Committee of 300, considered Truman His-Little-Man from Independence "without any independence at all." This referred to Truman's every move being controlled by Freemasonry. Even today, NRO's annual budget is not known to the Congress of the United States, and it is responsible to only a selected few in Congress. But it is a creature of the Committee of 300 to whom its reports are routinely sent every few hours.

Thus the fictionalized spoofs one sees about the various branches and arms of control of the Committee were designed to take suspicion away from the real thing, but we should never doubt that the real thing does indeed exist. Take another example of what I mean, the book "THE DAY OF THE JACKAL," from which a highly successful movie was created.

The events related in the book are factual. Although for obvious reasons the names of some of the players and the locales were changed, but the thrust of the story, that a single MI6 operative was assigned to get rid of General Charles De

Gaulle, is absolutely correct. General De Gaulle had become unmanageable, refusing to cooperate with the Committee—whose existence he knew very well since he had been invited to join it—came to a climax when De Gaulle withdrew France from NATO and immediately began building his own nuclear force—the so-called "force de frappe."

This so angered the Committee that De Gaulle's assassination was ordered. But the French secret intelligence service was able to intercept "Jackal's" plans and keep De Gaulle safe. In the light of the record of MI6, which I might add is the Committee of 300's main resource when it comes to intelligence, the work done by French intelligence borders on the miraculous.

Military Intelligence Department Six dates back to Sir Francis Walsingham, paymaster of Queen Elizabeth I for dirty tricks operations. Over hundreds of years, MI6 has established a record which no other intelligence agency can come near to duplicating. MI6 agents have gathered information from the four corners of the earth and have carried out secret operations that would astound even the most knowledgeable if ever they were to be made public, which is why it rates as the Master service of the Committee of 300.

Officially, MI6 does not exist, its budget comes out of the Queen's purse and "private funds," and is reported to be in a range of $350-$500 million per annum, but no one knows for sure what the exact amount is. In its present form MI6 dates back to 1911, when it was under the leadership of Sir Mansfield Cumming, a captain in the Royal Navy, who was always identified by the letter "C," from which "M" of James Bond fame is taken.

No official record of MI6's failures and successes exist—it is that secret, although the Burgess-Maclean-Blake-Blunt disasters did great damage to the morale of MI6 officers. Unlike other services, future members are recruited from universities and other areas of learning by highly skilled "talent scouts" as we saw in the case of Rhodes Scholars inducted into the Round Table. One of the requirements is an ability to speak foreign languages. Candidates undergo a rigorous "blooding."

With the backing of such a formidable force, the Committee of 300 had little fear from ever being exposed, and this will go on for decades. What makes the Committee incredible is the *incredible* secrecy that prevails. None of the news media has ever made mention of this conspiratorial hierarchy; therefore, as is to be expected, people doubt its existence.

The Committee of 300 is for the most part under the control of the British monarch, in this case, Elizabeth II. Queen Victoria is believed to have been quite paranoid about keeping it secret and went to great lengths to cover up MASONIC writings left at the scene of "Jack the Ripper" murders which alluded to the Committee of 300's connections with "experiments" carried out by a family member who was also a highly-placed member of the Scottish Rite of Freemasonry. The Committee of 300 is filled with members of British aristocracy which has corporate interests and associates in every country of the world, including the USSR.

The Committee's structure is as follows:

The Tavistock Institute at Sussex University and London sites is owned and controlled by the Royal Institute for International Affairs whose "hofjuden" in America is Henry Kissinger. The EAGLE STAR GROUP, which changed its name to the STAR GROUP after the close of the Second World War, is composed of a group of major international companies involved in overlapping and interfaced areas (1) Insurance, (2) Banking, (3) Real Estate, (4) Entertainment, (5) High technology, including cybernetics, electronic communications, etc.

Banking, while not the mainstay, is vitally important, especially in the areas where banks act as clearing houses and money launderers of drug money. The main "big name banks" are The Bank of England, the Federal Reserve Banks, Bank of International Settlements, the World Bank and the Hong Kong and Shanghai Bank. American Express Bank is a means of recycling drug dollars. Each of these banks is affiliated with and/or controls hundreds of thousands of large and small banks throughout the world.

Banks large and small in the thousands are in the Committee of 300 network, including Banca Commerciale d'Italia, Banca Privata, Banco Ambrosiano, the Netherlands Bank, Barclays Bank, Banco del Colombia, Banco de Ibero-America. Of special interest is Banca del la Svizzeria Italiana (BSI)—since it handles flight capital investments to and from the United States—primarily in dollars and U.S. bonds—located and isolated in "neutral" Lugano, the flight capital center for the Venetian Black Nobility. Lugano is not in Italy or in Switzerland, and is a kind of a twilight zone for shady flight capital operations. George Ball, who owns a large block of stock in BSI, is a prominent "insider" and the bank's U.S. representative.

BCCI, BNL, Banco Mercantil de Mexico, Banco Nacional de Panama, Bangkok Metropolitan Bank, Bank Leumi, Bank Hapoalim, Standard Bank, Bank of Geneva, Bank of Ireland, Bank of Scotland, Bank of Montreal, Bank of Nova Scotia, Banque Paris et Pays Bas, British Bank of the Middle East and the Royal Bank of Canada to name but a very small number in a huge list of "speciality" banks.

The Oppenheimers of South Africa are much bigger "heavyweights" than the Rockefellers. For instance, in 1981 Harry Oppenheimer, chairman of the giant Anglo American Corporation that controls gold and diamond mining, sales and distribution in the world, stated that he was about to launch into the North American banking market. Oppenheimer promptly invested $10 billion in a specially created vehicle for the purpose of buying into big banks in the U.S., among which was Citicorp. Oppenheimer's investment vehicle was called Minorco, which set up shop in Bermuda, a British royal family preserve. On the board of Minorco was to be found Walter Wriston of Citicorp and Robert Clare, its chief counsel.

The only other company to rival Oppenheimer in the field of precious metals and minerals was Consolidated Gold Fields of

South Africa, but Oppenheimer took control of it with a 28% stake—the largest single stockholder. Thus gold, diamonds, platinum, titanium, tantalite, copper, iron ore, uranium and 52 other metals and minerals, many of them of absolutely vital strategic value to United States, passed into the hands of the Committee of 300.

Thus was the vision of one of the earlier South African members of the Committee of 300, Cecil John Rhodes, fully realized, a vision which started with the spilling of the blood of thousands upon thousands of White farmers and their families in South Africa, whom history records as the "Boers." While the United States stood by with folded hands as did the rest of the world, this small nation was subjected to the most vicious war of genocide in history. The United States will be subjected to the same treatment by the Committee of 300 when our turn comes, and it will not be long in coming.

Insurance companies play a key role in the business of the Committee of 300. Among these are found such top insurance companies as Assicurazioni Generali of Venice and Riunione Adriatica di Sicurta, the largest and second largest insurance companies in the world, who keep their bank accounts at Bank of International Settlements in Swiss gold francs. Both control a multiplicity of investment banks whose turnover in stocks on Wall Street double that of U.S. investors.

Prominent on the board of these two insurance giants are Committee of 300 members: the Giustiniani family, Black Nobility of Rome and Venice who trace their lineage to the Emperor Justianian; Sir Jocelyn Hambro of Hambros (Merchant) Bank; Pierpaolo Luzzatti Fequiz, whose lineage dates back six centuries to the most ancient Luzzatos, the Black Nobility of Venice, and Umberto Ortolani of the ancient Black Nobility family of the same name.

Other old Venetian Black Nobility Committee of 300 members and board members of ASG and RAS are the Doria family, the financiers of the Spanish Hapsburgs, Elie de Rothschild of the

French Rothschild family, Baron August von Finck (Finck, the second richest man in Germany is now deceased), Franco Orsini Bonacassi of the ancient Orsini Black Nobility that traces its lineage to an ancient Roman senator of the same name, the Alba family whose lineage dates back to the great Duke of Alba, and Baron Pierre Lambert, a cousin of the Belgian Rothschild family.

The English companies controlled by the British royal family are Eagle Star, Prudential Assurance Company, the Prudential Insurance Company, which own and control most American insurers, including Allstate Insurance. At the head of the list is Eagle Star, probably the most powerful "front" for Military Intelligence Department Six (MI6). Eagle Star, although nowhere near as large as Assicurazioni Generale, is perhaps equally important simply because it is owned by members of the Queen of England's family and, as titular head of the Committee of 300, Eagle Star makes a tremendous impact.

Eagle Star is more than a major "front" for MI6, it is also a front for major British banks, including Hill-Samuels, N. M. Rothschild and Sons (one of the gold price "fixers" who meet daily in London), and Barclays Bank (one of the funders of the African National Congress-ANC). It can be said with a great degree of accuracy that the most powerful British oligarchical families created Eagle Star as a vehicle for "black operations" against those who oppose Committee of 300 policies.

Unlike the CIA, British law makes it a serious crime to name MI6 officials, so the following is but a partial list of "top brass" of MI6, who are (or were) also members of the Committee of 300:

>   Lord Hartley Shawcross.
>   Sir Brian Edward Mountain.
>   Sir Kenneth Keith.
>   Sir Kenneth Strong.
>   Sir William Stephenson.
>   Sir William Wiseman.

All of the foregoing are (or were) heavily involved in key Committee of 300 companies which interface with literally thousands of companies engaged in every branch of commercial activity as we shall see.

Some of these companies include Rank Organization, Xerox Corporation, ITT, IBM, RCA, CBS, NBC, BBC and CBC in communications, Raytheon, Textron, Bendix, Atlantic Richfield, British Petroleum, Royal Dutch Shell, Marine Midland Bank, Lehman Brothers, Kuhn Loeb, General Electric, Westinghouse Corporation, United Fruit Company and a great many more.

MI6 ran a large number of these companies through British intelligence stationed in the RCA building in New York, which was the headquarters of its chief officer, Sir William Stephenson. Radio Corporation of America (RCA) was formed by G.E., Westinghouse, Morgan Guarantee and Trust (acting for the British crown), and United Fruit, back in 1919 as a British intelligence center. RCA's first president was J.P. Morgan's Owen Young, after whom the Young Plan was named. In 1929 David Sarnoff was appointed to run RCA. Sarnoff had acted as an assistant to Young at the 1919 Paris Peace Conference where a fallen Germany was stabbed in the back by the victorious "allies."

A network of Wall Street banks and brokerage houses takes care of the stock market for the Committee, and prominent among these are Blyth, Eastman Dillon, the Morgan groups, Lazard Freres and Kuhn Loeb Rhodes. Nothing happens on Wall Street that is not controlled by the Bank of England, whose instructions are relayed through the Morgan groups and then put into action through key brokerage houses whose top executives are ultimately responsible for carrying out Committee directives.

Before it overstepped the limits laid down by Morgan Guarantee, Drexel Burnham Lambert was a favorite of the Committee of 300. In 1981 almost every major brokerage house on Wall Street had sold out to the Committee, Phibro merging with Salomon Brothers. Phibro is the business arm of the Oppenheimers of Anglo American Corporation. By this control mechanism, the Committee of 300 ensures that its members and their far-flung business corporations turned their investments on

Wall Street over at a rate of double that of the "non-insider" foreign investors.

Remember, some of the richest families in the world live in Europe, so it is natural that they should have a preponderance of members on the Committee. The Von Thurn und Taxis family who once owned the German postal franchise, make David Rockefeller look like a very poor relation. The Von Thurn und Taxis dynasty dates back 300 years and generation after generation of family members have had seats on the Committee which they occupy to this day. We have already mentioned by name many of the most wealthy Venetian Black Nobility members of the Committee of 300 and other names will be added as we come across them in their various fields of endeavor. Now we shall include some American members of the Committee of 300 and try to trace their affiliations and connections to the British Crown.

How can these facts be verified? Actually, some of them cannot be verified because the information comes straight out of intelligence files, but with a lot of legwork, there are many sources which can verify at least part of the facts. The work would involve a diligent search of Dun and Bradstreet Reference Book of Corporations, Standard and Poors, British and American "Who's Who" with long hours of hard work in cross-referencing names with their corporate affiliations.

Committee of 300 corporations, banks, and insurance companies operate under the unified command covering every conceivable matter of strategy and cohesive action. The Committee is the ONLY organized power hierarchy in the world transcending all governments and individuals, however powerful and secure they may feel themselves to be. This covers finance, defense matters and political parties of all colors and types.

There is no entity the Committee cannot reach and control, and that includes organized religions of the world. This then, is the all powerful OLYMPIAN GROUP whose power base is in London and the City of London's financial centers with its grip on minerals, metals and precious gems, cocaine, opium and pharmaceutical drugs, rentier-financier bankers, cult promoters and founders of rock music. The British Crown is the control point from which all things radiate. As the saying goes, "They have a finger in every pie."

It is obvious that the communications field is tightly controlled. Going back to RCA, we find that its directorate is composed of British-American establishment figures who feature prominently in other organizations such as the CFR, NATO, the Club of Rome, the Trilateral Commission, Freemasonry, Skull and Bones, Bilderbergers, Round Table, Milner Society and the Jesuits-Aristotle Society. Among them was David Sarnoff who moved to London at the same time Sir William Stephenson moved into the RCA building in New York.

All three major television networks came as spinoffs from RCA, especially the National Broadcasting Company (NBC) which was first, closely followed by the American Broadcasting Company (ABC) in 1951. The third big television network was Columbia Broadcasting System (CBS) which, like its sister companies was, and still is, dominated by British intelligence. William Paley was trained in mass brainwashing techniques at the Tavistock Institute prior to being passed as qualified to head CBS.

Thus, if we the people of the United States but knew it, all our major television networks are subject to British oversight, and information they provide first goes to London for clearance. It is interesting to note that the Tavistock intelligence paper written by Stanford Research Institute, commonly named "The Aquarian Conspiracy" was funded by donations from all three major television networks.

All three major networks are represented on the Committee of 300 and are affiliated with the giant of the mass communication business, the Xerox Corporation of Rochester, New York, whose Robert M. Beck holds a seat on the Committee. Beck is also a director of the Prudential Life Insurance Company, which is a subsidiary of the London Prudential Assurance Company Limited.

Others on the board of Xerox are Howard Clark of the American Express Company, one of the main conduits for moving drug money through "travelers checks," former Secretary of the Treasury, William Simon, and Sol Linowitz, who negotiated the Panama Canal Treaties for the Committee. Linowitz is important to the Committee by virtue of his long standing expertise in laundering drug money through Marine Midland and the Hong Kong and Shanghai Bank.

Another Xerox board member is Robert Sproull, who is of real interest because, as president of the University of Rochester, he allowed the Tavistock Institute, working through the CIA, to use the university's facilities for the 20-year MK-Ultra LSD experiments. Some 85 other universities in the U.S. also allowed their facilities to be misused in this manner. As giant-sized as Xerox is, it is dwarfed by the Rank Organisation, a London-based conglomerate fully controlled by members of Queen Elizabeth's immediate family.

Notable members of the board of Rank Organisation who are also members of the Committee of 300 are the following:

Lord Helsby, chairman of the drug money clearing house, Midland Bank. Helsby's other positions include a directorship in the giant Imperial Group and the Industrial and Commercial Finance Corporation.

Sir Arnold France, a director of Tube Investments who runs the London underground train service. France is also a director of the BANK OF ENGLAND which has so much control over the Federal Reserve Banks.

Sir Dennis Mountain, chairman of the mighty Eagle Star group and a director of English Property Corp, one of the rentier-financier companies of the British royal family. One such member is the Honorable Angus Ogilvie, "Prince of Companies," who is married to Her Royal Highness Princess Alexandria, sister of the Duke of Kent, leader of the Scottish Rite of Freemasonry and who takes the place of the Queen when she is outside of Britain. Ogilvie is a director of the Bank of England

and chairman of the giant LONRHO conglomerate. It was LONRHO that ended the rule of Ian Smith in Rhodesia so that he could be replaced by Robert Mugabe. At stake was Rhodesia's chrome mines which produce the finest high-grade chrome ore in the world.

Cyril Hamilton, chairman of the Standard and Chartered Bank (the old Lord Milner-Cecil Rhodes bank) and a board member of the Bank of England. Hamilton is also on the board of the Xerox Corporation, the Malta International Banking Corporation (A Knights of Malta bank), a director of the Standard Bank of South Africa—the largest bank in that country, and a director of the Banque Belge d'Afrique.

Lord O'Brien of Lotherby, past president of the British Bankers Association, director of Morgan Grenfell—a powerful bank, director of Prudential Assurance, director of J. P.Morgan, director of the Bank of England, a board member of the Bank of International Settlements, a director of the giant Unilever conglomerate.

Sir Reay Geddes, chairman of the giant Dunlop and Pirelli tyre companies, director of the Midland and International Banks, director of the Bank of England. Note how many of these powerful men are directors of the Bank of England which makes control of American fiscal policies simple.

Many of these organizations and institutions, companies and banks are so interfaced and interlocked as to make it an almost impossible task to sort them out. On RCA's board sits Thornton Bradshaw, president of Atlantic Richfield and a member of NATO, World Wildlife Fund, the Club of Rome, The Aspen Institute for Humanistic Studies, the Council on Foreign Relations. Bradshaw is also chairman of NBC. The most important function of RCA remains its service to British intelligence.

It is not generally known how powerful was the role played by the Committee of 300 in stopping the investigation into the CIA which Senator McCarthy almost succeeded in pulling off. Had McCarthy been successful, it is very likely that President John F. Kennedy would be alive today.

When McCarthy said he was going to summon William Bundy to appear before his commission of enquiry, panic swept Washington and London. Bundy, had he been called to testify, would most probably have cracked and opened the door to the "special relations" that existed between British oligarchical circles and their cousins in the United States Government.

Such a possibility could not be entertained. The Royal Institute of International Affairs was called in to put an end to McCarthy. The RIIA chose Allen Dulles, a man who was totally enamored of decadent British society, to attack McCarthy head on. Dulles put Patrick Lyman and Richard Helms in charge of the McCarthy case. Helms was later rewarded for his services against McCarthy by being made head of the CIA.

General Mark Clark, a member of the CFR and a well-liked military man in London circles, was appointed by General Eisenhower to turn back McCarthy's full-fledged attack on the CIA. McCarthy was preempted when Clark announced that a special committee was to be appointed to examine the agency. Clark, on instructions from the RIIA, recommended a Congressional watchdog committee to "periodically examine the work of government intelligence agencies." The whole thing was a super tragedy for America and a victory for the British, who feared that McCarthy would accidentally stumble onto the Committee of 300 and its control over every aspect of United States affairs.

Lehman Brothers-Kuhn Loeb's former chairman, Peter G. Peterson, served under former MI6 chief Sir William Wiseman and as such was no stranger to British royalty. Peterson is tied in with Aspen Institute, yet another arm of British intelligence.

John R. Petty is president and chairman of the Marine Midland Bank—a bank whose drug trade connections have been well established long before it was taken over by the Hong Kong and Shanghai Bank, probably the number one bank in the opium trade, a position it has held since 1814.

But the best proof I can offer of the existence of the Committee of 300 is the Rank Organization which, in conjunction with Eagle Star, IS THE BRITISH CROWN. It is also the black operations center of MI6 (SIS). Between them, these two Committee of 300 companies control Her Majesty's Dominion of Canada, using the "hofjuden" Bronfman family to carry out their orders.

Trizec Holdings, ostensibly owned by the Bronfman family, is in reality the main asset of the Queen of England's in Canada. The entire Southeast Asian opium trade interfaces with the Bronfman empire and is one of the means whereby heroin is brought to America. In a sense, Canada is like Switzerland, pristine snow-covered landscapes, big cities, a place of great beauty, but underneath lies a deep layer of filth and dirt arising from its massive heroin trade.

The Bronfman family are "cut-outs," what is known in MI6 as "front men"—controlled from London by MI6 "deskmen," intelligence jargon for controllers at headquarters. Edgar Bronfman, the family leader, was sent to "Moscow Center"— cover name for the KGB headquarters at 2 Dzerzhinsky Square, Moscow, on a large number of occasions.

At a low level, Bronfman was probably very useful as a contact man with Moscow. Bronfman was never at any stage a contract agent for MI6 and so never carried the title "Paroles," a key intelligence word for mutual identification between agents, which greatly disappointed the eager Bronfman family head. At one stage when it was thought that some of the family were acting suspiciously, "watchers"—intelligence jargon for intelligence officers keeping persons under surveillance, were put on the Bronfman family, but found only that one of the Bronfmans had been bragging to a United States "cousin" (the word MI6 uses for the C.I.A.) who was unaware of the role of Edgar Bronfman. This was quickly corrected.

Two Eagle Star directors, who were also the two top MI6 operatives, took control of the Bronfman family about six months after the war ended. Sir Kenneth Keith and Sir Kenneth Strong, whom we have already met, legitimized the Bronfman family by setting up Trizec Holdings. There is no one in the world who can do a better job of "fronting," through companies, than MI6.

Yet, like Switzerland, there is a dirty side to Canada that has been well-hidden from view by the Committee of 300 under cover of the Official Secrets Act, a carbon-copy of the British law passed in 1913. Drugs, dirty money laundering, crime and racketeering are all covered by their infamous Act.

Not known to many is that, if charged under the Official Secrets Act, which can be interpreted any way the Crown agents choose, persons could face the death penalty. As I have said so many times since 1980, Canada is not a nation like South Africa, or Holland or Belgium; it always was, and remains tied to the Queen of England's apron strings. Canada, we find, is always first in carrying out Queen Elizabeth's wishes. Canadian troops have fought in every one of Her Majesty's wars, including the Boer War (1899-1903).

Like its American counterpart, the Canadian Institute of International Affairs is a child of the Royal Institute for International Affairs (RIIA) and runs Canadian politics. Its members have filled the position of Secretary of State ever since it was founded in 1925. The Institute for Pacific Relations, the body that fostered the attack on Pearl Harbor, was welcomed in Canada after Owen Lattimore and his fellow members had their treasonous activities exposed in 1947 and left the United States before they could be charged.

The Canadian Institute for International Affairs is connected with the Rank Organization through Sir Kenneth Strong, who was second in charge of MI6 at the end of the Second World War. As a member of the Order of St. John of Jerusalem, Strong is the number two man in Canada for Rank and the British Crown's commercial interests. He is on the board of one of the most prolific drug banks in the world after the Hong Kong and Shanghai Bank, the Bank of Nova Scotia, through which proceeds of the Canadian heroin trade are handled.

First in line is Sir Brian Edward Mountain, the ranking member of the Knights of the Order of St. John of Jerusalem. It is well to remember that, when the British Crown wanted the United States to enter the Second World War, it sent Lord Beaverbrook and Sir Brian Mountain to meet with President Roosevelt to deliver the Crown's orders in this regard. Roosevelt complied by ordering the United States Navy to operate out of a base in Greenland, from where attacks on German submarines were carried out nine months before Pearl Harbor. This was done without the knowledge and consent of the Congress.

Another big name in the Rank-Canadian interfacing was Sir Kenneth Keith, a director of Canada's equivalent of the Hong Kong and Shanghai Bank, the Bank of Nova Scotia, dripping in drug money laundering. He was also on the board of Britain's oldest and most venerable newspaper institution, the *London Times* and the *Sunday Times*. For over 100 years the *"Times"* has been the Crown's voice on foreign affairs, finance matters and political life in England.

Like so many Committee of 300 members, Sir Kenneth circulated between MI6 and the opium supply chain of command in Hong Kong and China, ostensibly on business for the Canadian Institute for International Affairs, of which he was a member. Furthermore, as a director of the Hill Samuel banking house, his presence in China and Hong Kong could be explained without any problem. One of his closest associates outside of MI6 circles was Sir Philip de Zuleta, the Committee of 300's direct controller of all British prime ministers, both Conservative and Labor. Sir Kenneth Strong tied in all the spokes of the drug wheel, including terrorism, production of opium, the gold markets, dirty money laundering and banking to its central core, the British Crown.

At the top of British Crown control of Canada was Walter Gordon. A former member of the Queen's hands-on oversight committee, also known as the Privy Council, Gordon sponsored the Institute for Pacific Relations via the Canadian Institute of

International Affairs. As a former minister of finance, Gordon was able to place Committee of 300 selected accountants and lawyers inside the three main chartered banks: the Bank of Nova Scotia, the Canadian Imperial Bank and the Toronto Dominion Bank.

Through these three "Crown banks" a network of Committee of 300 agents responsible to Gordon oversaw the world's second largest dirty drug money laundering operation, with a direct open door to China. Before his death, Gordon controlled James Endicott, Chester Ronning and Paul Linn, identified by MI6 as Canada's top "China specialists." All three men worked closely with Chou-En-lai, who once told Gamal Abdul Nasser that he would do to Britain and the USA what they had done to China, i.e., turn them into nations of heroin addicts. Chou-En-lai made good on his promise, starting with American GI's in Vietnam. Other close collaborators in the Canadian heroin drug ring were John D. Gilmer and John Robert Nicholson, both members of the Order of the Knights of St. John of Jerusalem.

Lord Hartley Shawcross, who is believed to report directly to Queen Elizabeth II, was on the board of the Royal Institute for International Affairs and chancellor of Sussex University where the notorious Tavistock Institute for Human Relations is located, with extensive connections in Canada.

As part of Rank's United States operation, no other single company has been more successful for Rank than the Corning Group, owners of the Metropolitan Life Insurance Company and the New York Life Insurance Company. Committee of 300 members, Amory Houghton and his brother James Houghton, have long served the British Crown through the above named insurance companies, and Corning Glass, Dow Corning and Corning International. Both sit on the board of IBM and Citicorp. James Houghton is a director of the Princeton Institute for Advanced Studies, a director of the J. Pierpont Morgan Library, a stronghold of the RIIA and the CFR, and he is also a director of CBS.

It was the Houghton brothers who donated hundreds of acres known as Wye Plantation in Maryland to the British Crown's Aspen Institute. Also on the Corning Glass board sits the Bishop of the Archdiocese of the Anglican (Episcopalian) Church of Boston. All this gives the group its much-vaunted air of respectability, which insurance company executives must carry, and as we shall see, in addition to James Houghton, Keith Funston and John Harper, both on Corning's board, run the Metropolitan Life Insurance Company.

The MASSIVE gridding and interfacing of just this one single unit of the Committee of 300 will give us a good indication of the vast power at the disposal of the conspirators' hierarchy, before which all knees are bowed, including the knee of the President of the United States, whomever that happens to be.

What is important to note is how this American company, one of HUNDREDS, is interfaced with British intelligence, with Canada, the Far East and South Africa, not to mention its gridding of corporate officials and directors reaching into every aspect of business and politics in the United States.

While Metropolitan Life Insurance Company does not begin to compare with the Committee of 300's giant Assicurazioni Generale, it is nevertheless a good indicator of how the Houghtons' power extends right across the business spectrum of the U.S. and Canada. Starting with R. H. Macy, (whose floor walkers no longer wear red carnations to honour the company's affiliation with Communism), the Royal Bank of Canada, National and Westminster Bank, Intertel (a virulent and vile private intelligence agency), Canadian Pacific, The Reader's Digest, RCA, AT&T, the Harvard Business School, W. R. Grace Shipping Company, Ralston Purina Company, U.S. Steel, Irving Trust, Consolidated Edison of New York and ABC, the Houghtons' power grid extends as far as the Hong Kong and Shanghai Bank.

Another successful Rank company in the United States is the Reliance Insurance Group. As an integral part of the Strategic Bombing Survey, Reliance established the initial structural base for brainwashing, opinion-making, polling, survey and the systems analysis used by the Tavistock Institute in the United States. The Reliance Insurance Company, based in Philadelphia, set up the corporate structure which enabled the Strategic Bombing Survey to be turned against the people of the United Sates who, although unaware of it, have been subjected to savage psychological warfare for the past 45 years.

A key operative in this assault on the United States was David Bialkin of the Committee of 300 law firm, Wilkie, Farr and Gallagher. Bialkin ran the Anti-Defamation League (ADL) for many years. The ADL is a British intelligence operation founded in the U.S. by MI6 and run by Saul Steinberg and Eric Trist of Tavistock. Saul Steinberg is the U.S. representative and business partner of the Jacob de Rothschild family of London.

Reliance Corporation is home for Carl Lindner who succeeded Eli Black when he "fell" from a 44th floor window of a New York skyscraper. Reliance Company interfaces with the powerful United Fruit Company of Boston and New Orleans run by Max Fisher who, before he was sheepdipped, was a well-known Detroit underworld figure. United Fruit Company has long been a conveyer of heroin and cocaine into the U.S. under the expertise of Mishulam Riklis of Rapid American Corporation who masterminds shipments from Canada to the U.S. Remember, all this is under the aegis of a single company, gridding and interfacing with a myriad of smaller companies and operations to give the Committee of 300 full control of a multiplicity of operations, each one carefully interlocked in the grid.

Reliance Group is a spinoff of the parent company whose function it is to brainwash the American people through a network of pollsters and opinion makers and relies on Operations Research for direct links with the Tavistock Institute. Another associate company is Leasco, which is closely interfaced with AT&T, Disclosure Incorporated, Western Union International, Imbucon Ltd and Yankelovich, Skelly and White.

Daniel Yankelovich is the emperor of the polling-opinion

making corporate structure in the United States, a vast apparatus which provides "public opinions on social, economic and political matters of substance," to quote Edward Bernays. It was this vast apparatus that turned the majority of Americans, who had never even heard of Saddam Hussein and vaguely knew that Iraq was a country somewhere in the Middle East, into a people howling for his blood and the extermination of Iraq as a nation.

Yankelovich utilized to the full all knowledge gained during the Second World War. As a second-generation warrior, Yankelovich has no equal, which is why ABC polls conducted by his company are always in the forefront of "public opinion." The population of the United States was targeted in the same manner of German worker housing by attacking the sense of reality. This technique is, of course, standard training for certain intelligence groups, which includes the CIA.

Yankelovich's task was to destroy traditional American values and replace them with New Age-Age of Aquarius values. As the Committee of 300's most senior public opinion maker, no one can doubt that Yankelovich has done a superb job.

Probably the best way to explain what methods are used and what results are expected to be achieved is to quote John Naisbitt's work as explained in his "Trend Report." Naisbitt has acted as advisor to Lyndon Johnson, Eastman Kodak, IBM, American Express, the Center for Policy Study, Chase Manhattan, General Motors, Louis Harris Polls, the White House, Institute of Life Insurance, the American Red Cross, Mobil Oil, B.P. and a host of Committee of 300 companies and institutions. His methodology, derived from MI6 Tavistock procedures, is of course not unique:

"I will briefly outline our methodology. In developing *Trend Report* for our clients we rely mostly on a system of monitoring local events and behavior. We are over-whelmingly impressed with the extent to which this is a bottom-up society, so we monitor what is going on locally, rather than what is going on in Washington or

New York. Things start in Los Angeles, in Tampa, in Hartford, in Wichita, Portland, San Diego and Denver. It is a very much 'from the bottom-up' society.

"The tracking concept employed in determining these trends has its roots in WW II. During the war, intelligence experts sought to find a method for obtaining information on enemy nations that public opinion polls would normally have provided. Under the leadership of Paul Lazarsfeld and Harold Laswell, a method was developed for monitoring what was going on in these societies that involved doing a content analysis of the daily press.

"Although this method of monitoring public thinking continues to be the choice of the intelligence community—the nation annually spends millions of dollars doing newspaper content analyses in all parts of the world.... The reason this system of monitoring changes in society works so well is that 'news holes' in newspapers is a closed system. For economic reasons the amount of space devoted to news in a newspaper doesn't change over time.

"So when something new is introduced into that news hole, something or a combination of things has to go out or be omitted. The principle involved here is classified as a forced choice within a closed system. In this forced situation societies add new preoccupations and forget old ones. We keep track of the ones that are added and the ones that are given up.

"Evidently, societies are like human beings. I do not know what the number is, but a person can only keep so many problems and concerns in his head at any one time. If new problems or concerns are added, some existing ones must be given up. We keep track of what Americans have given up and have taken up.

"The United States is rapidly shifting from a mass industrial society to an information society and the final impact will be more profound than the 19th century shift from an agricultural to an industrial society. Starting in 1979, the number one occupation in the U.S. became clerking, replacing laborer and farmer. In this latter statement is a brief history of the United States."

It is not by chance that Naisbitt is a member of the Club of Rome and, as such, a "senior staffer" of the Committee of 300. He is also one of the senior vice presidents of Yankelovich, Skelly and White. What Naisbitt is doing is not forecasting trends but MAKING them. We have seen how the industrial base of the United States has been destroyed, starting with the steel industry. In 1982 I wrote a work I called "Death of the Steel Industry," in which I stated that by the mid-1990's, steel production in the U.S. will have declined to a point of no return, and that the auto and housing industries would go the same way.

All this has come to pass, and what we are witnessing today is not an economic recession due not only to unsound economic policies, but the deliberately planned destruction of our industrial base—and along with it the destruction of America's unique middle class—the backbone of the country—which depends on a progressive industrial expansion for growth and for steady employment.

This is one of the reasons why the recession, which started in earnest in January of 1991, has turned into a depression from which the United States as we knew it in the 1960's-1970's will most probably never reappear. The economy will not come out of the depression of 1991 until at least 1995-1996, at which time the United States will have become an entirely different society from the one it was when the recession began.

Opinion makers have played no small part in this war on the United States; we need to examine the role of the Committee of 300 in bringing about these far-reaching changes and how the social engineers have used central systems analyses to keep public opinion from expressing anything other than the policies of the invisible government. How and where did it all begin?

From documents covering the First World War that I was able to gather and examine in the War Office in Whitehall, London, it appears that the Royal Institute for International Affairs was commissioned by the Committee of 300 to do a study of manipulating war information. This task was given to Lord Northcliffe and Lord Rothmere and Arnold Toynbee, who was MI6's agent at the RIIA. Lord Rothmere's family owned a newspaper which was used to support various government positions, so it was thought that the paper could change public perceptions, especially among the ranks of growing opposition to the war.

The project was housed in Wellington House, named after the Duke of Wellesly. American specialists drafted to help Lords Rothmere and Northcliffe included Edward Bernays and Walter Lippman. The group held "brain storming" sessions to work out techniques for mobilizing mass support for the war, especially among the working class people whose sons were expected to go to the slaughter fields of Flanders in record numbers.

Using Lord Rothmere's newspaper, new manipulative techniques were tried out and, after a period of about 6 months, it was apparent that they were a success. What the researchers discovered was that only a very small group of people understood the process of reasoning and the ability to observe the problem as opposed to passing an opinion on it. This, said Lord Rothmere, was the way in which 87% of the British public approached the war, and that the same principle applied not only to the war, but to every conceivable problem in society in general.

In this manner, irrationality was elevated to a high level of public consciousness. The manipulators then played upon this to undermine and distract the grasp of reality governing any given situation and, the more complex the problems of a modern industrial society became, the easier it became to bring greater and greater distractions to bear so that what we ended up with was that the absolutely inconsequential opinions of masses of people, created by skilled manipulators, assumed the position of scientific fact.

Having literally stumbled upon so profound a conclusion, the manipulators put it to one test after another during the war, so that in spite of hundreds of thousands of the youth of Britain being slaughtered on the battlefields of France, there was virtually no opposition to the bloody war. Records of the time show that by 1917, just before the United States entered the war, 94% of the British working class bearing the brunt of the war did not have the faintest idea what they were fighting for, other than the image created by the media manipulators that the Germans were a horrible race, bent upon destroying their monarch and their country, and who had to be wiped off the face of the earth.

Certainly nothing has changed because, in 1991, we had the exact same situation created by the news media which allowed President Bush to flagrantly violate the Constitution in waging a war of genocide against the nation of Iraq with the full consent of 87% of the American people. Woodrow Wilson can be credited—if that is the proper expression to use—of jumping on the public opinion manipulators' band wagon and using it to further the causes whispered in his ear by his controller, Colonel House.

On instructions from President Wilson, or rather Colonel House, the Creel Commission was created and, as far as can be ascertained, the Creel Commission was the first organization in the United States to use the RIIA techniques and methodology for polling and mass propaganda. The psychological warfare experiments perfected at Wellington House were used in the Second World War with equal success, and have been in continuous use in the massive psychological war against the United States which began in 1946. The methods did not change, only the target. Now it was not German worker housing but the middle class of the United States that became the focus of the attack.

As so often happens, the conspirators could not contain their glee. After WW II, in 1922 to be precise, Lippmann detailed the work done by the RIIA in a book he called "PUBLIC OPINION":

> "Public opinion deals with indirect, unseen and puzzling facts, and there is nothing obvious about them. The situations to which public opinion refers are known only as opinions, pictures inside heads of human beings, pictures of themselves, of others, of their needs, purposes and relationships, are their public opinions. These pictures which are acted upon by groups of people, or by individuals acting in the name of groups are PUBLIC OPINION with capital letters. The picture inside the head often misleads men in their dealings with the world outside of their heads."

No wonder Lippmann was chosen to make the people of the United States "like" the Beatles when they arrived on our shores and were thrust upon an unsuspecting country. Combined with the propaganda sent forth night and day from radio and television, it was only a comparatively short time before The Beatles became "popular." The technique of radio stations allegedly receiving hundreds of requests from imaginary listeners for Beatlemusic, led to charts and ratings for first, the "top ten" and gradually escalated until, by 1992, it has expanded to "the top 40 on the charts."

In 1928, Lippmann's compatriot Edward Bernays wrote a book called "CRYSTALLIZING PUBLIC OPINION" and in 1928 a second book of his was published entitled simply "PROPAGANDA." In it Bernays described his experiences at Wellington House. Bernays was a close friend of Master Manipulator H.G. Wells, whose many quasi-novels were used by

Bernays to help formulate mass mind control techniques. Welis was not shy about his role as a leader in changing lower class society, mainly because he was a close friend of members of the British royal family, and spent a great deal of time with some of the most highly placed politicians of the day, men like Sir Edward Grey, Lord Haldane, Robert Cecil of the Jewish Cecil family that had controlled the British monarchy since a Cecil became the private secretary and lover of Queen Elizabeth I, Leo Amery, Halford Mackinder of MI6 and later head of the London School of Economics, whose pupil Bruce Lockhart would become MI6 controller of Lenin and Trotsky during the Bolshevik Revolution, and even the great man himself, Lord Alfred Milner.

One of Wells' favorite watering holes was the prestigious St. Ermins Hotel, meeting place of the Coefficient Club, a club to which certified gentlemen only were admitted and where they met once a month. All of the men mentioned above were members and also members of the Souls Club. Wells claimed that any nation could be defeated, not by direct confrontation but by understanding the human mind—what he called, "the mental hinterlands hidden behind the persona."

With such a powerful backer, Bernays felt confident enough to launch his "PROPAGANDA":

"As civilization becomes more complex, **AND AS THE NEED FOR INVISIBLE GOVERNMENT HAS BEEN INCREASINGLY DEMONSTRATED** (emphasis added-JC), the technical means have been invented and developed **BY WHICH PUBLIC OPINION MAY BE REGIMENTED** (emphasis added-JC). With printing press and newspaper, the telephone, telegraph, radio and airplanes, ideas can be spread rapidly, and even instantaneously, across the whole of America." Bernays had not yet seen how much better television, which was to follow, would do the job.

"The conscious and intelligent manipulation of organized habits and opinions of the masses is an important element in a democratic society. Those who manipulate this unseen mechanism of society constitute an **INVISIBLE GOVERNMENT WHICH IS THE TRUE RULING POWER IN OUR COUNTRY.**" To back up his position, Bernays quoted H. G. Wells' article published in the *New York Times* in which Wells enthusiastically backed the idea of modern means of communication "opening up a new world of political processes which will allow the common design to be documented and sustained against perversion and betrayal" (of the invisible government).

To continue with the revelations contained in "PROPAGANDA":

"We are governed, our minds are moulded, our tastes formed, our ideas suggested, largely by men we have never heard of. What ever attitude one chooses to take toward this condition, it remains a fact that in almost every act of our daily lives, whether in the sphere of politics or business, our social conduct or our ethical thinking, we are dominated by a relatively small number of persons, a trifling fraction of our hundred and twenty million, who understand the mental processes and social patterns of the masses. It is they who pull the wires which control the public mind, and who harness old social forces and contrive new ways **TO BIND AND GUIDE THE WORLD**" (emphasis added-JC).

Bernays was not bold enough to tell the world who the "THEY" are who "pull the wires which control the public mind...," but in this book we shall make up for his intentional oversight by disclosing the existence of that "relatively small number of persons," the Committee of 300. Bernays was roundly applauded for his work by the CFR whose members voted to place him in charge of CBS. William Paley became his "undergraduate" and eventually replaced Bernays, having acquired a thorough knowledge of the new-science science of public opinion making, which made CBS the leader of the field, a role which CBS television and radio has never relinquished.

Political and financial control by the "relatively small number," as Bernays called them, is exercised through a number of secret societies, most notably the Scottish Rite of Freemasonry, and perhaps even more importantly, through the Venerable Order of the Knights of St. John of Jerusalem, an ancient order consisting of the British monarch's hand-picked executives chosen for their expertise in areas vital to the continued control of the Committee.

In my work "The Order of St. John of Jerusalem" published in 1986, I described The Order in the following manner:

"...It is therefore not a secret society, except where its purposes have been perverted in the inner councils like the Order of the Garter, which is a prostituted oligarchical creation of the British royal family, which makes a mockery of what the Sovereign Order of St. John of Jerusalem stands for.

"As an example, we find the atheist Lord Peter Carrington, who pretends to be an Anglican Christian, but who is a member of the Order of Osiris and other demonic sects, including Freemasonry, installed as a Knight of the Garter at St. George's Chapel, Windsor Castle, by Her Majesty, Queen Elizabeth II of England, of the Black Nobility Guelphs, also head of the Anglican Church, which she thoroughly despises."

Carrington was selected by the Committee of 300 to bring

down the government of Rhodesia, sign over the mineral wealth of Angola and South West Africa to City of London control, wreck the Argentine and turn NATO into a leftwing political organization beholden to the Committee of 300.

Another strange face we see attaching itself to the Holy Christian Order of St. John of Jerusalem, and I use the word stranger as it is used in the original Hebrew of the Old Testament to denote the lineage of an individual, is that of Major Louis Mortimer Bloomfield, the man who helped plan the murder of John F. Kennedy. We see photos of this "strange" man wearing with pride the Cross of Malta, the same cross worn on the sleeve of the Knights of the Order of the Garter.

We have been so brainwashed that we believe the British royal family is just a nice, harmless and colorful institution, and fail to realize just how corrupt and therefore highly dangerous is this institution called the British Monarchy. The Knights of the Order of the Garter are the INNERMOST circle of the most corrupt public servants who have utterly betrayed the trust placed in them by their nation, their people.

The Knights of the Order of the Garter are the leaders of the Committee of 300, Queen Elizabeth II's most trusted "privy council." When I did my research on the Order of St. John of Jerusalem some years ago, I went to Oxford to talk with one of the Masters who is a specialist on ancient and modern British traditions. He told me that the Knights of the Garter are the inner sanctum, the elite of the elite of Her Majesty's Most Venerable Order of St. John of Jerusalem. Let me say this is not the original order founded by the true Christian warrior, Peter Gerard, but is typical of many fine institutions that are taken over and destroyed from the inside, while yet appearing to the uninitiated to be the original.

From Oxford I went to the Victoria and Albert Museum and gained access to the papers of Lord Palmerston, one of the founders of the Opium Dynasty in China. Palmerston, like so many of his kind, was not only a Freemason, but a dedicated servant of Gnosticism.... Like the present 'royal family,' Palmerston made a pretense of being a Christian but was in fact a servant of Satan. Many satanists became leaders of British aristocracy and made immense fortunes out of the China opium trade. I learned from the papers in the museum named after Victoria that she changed the name of the Order of St. John of Jerusalem in 1885 in order to break away from the Catholic connection of the Order's founder, Peter Gerard, and renamed it the "Protestant Most Venerable Order of Jerusalem." Membership was open to every oligarchical family that had made its fortune in the China opium trade and every thoroughly decadent family received a place in the 'new order.'

Many of these venerable gentlemen were responsible for overseeing the prohibition era in the United States from Canada, where several of its members supplied the whisky ferried to the United States. Notable among this group was Committee of 300 member Earl Haig, who gave his whisky franchise to old Joe Kennedy. Both prohibition and the distilleries who met the demand for alcohol were creations of the British Crown acting through the Committeemen of 300. It was an experiment which became the forerunner of today's drug trade, and the lessons learned from the prohibition era are being applied to the soon to be legalized drug trade.

Canada is the route most used by Far East heroin suppliers. The British Monarchy sees to it that this information never becomes public. Using her powers, Queen Elizabeth rules over Canada through the Governor-General (one wonders how modern Canadians can accept such an archaic arrangement?), who is the Queen's PERSONAL representative, and on down the line to the Privy Council (yet another archaic hang-over from colonialist days) and the Knights of St. John Of Jerusalem, who control Canadian commerce in all of its facets.

Opposition to British rule is suppressed. Canada has some of the most restrictive laws in the world, including so-called "hate crime" laws imposed upon the country by Jewish members of the House of Lords in England. At present there are four major trials in various stages in Canada involving persons charged with "hate crimes." These are the Finta, Keegstra, Zundel and Ross cases. Anyone who dares to try and show proof of Jewish control of Canada (which the Bronfmans exercise), is immediately arrested and charged with so-called "hate crimes." This will give us some idea of the vastness of the reach of the Committee of 300 which quite literally sits on top of everything in this world.

Testifying to the truth of this statement is the fact that the Committee of 300 set up the International Institute for Strategic Studies (IISS) under the auspices of the Round Table. This institute is the vehicle for MI6-Tavistock black propaganda and wet jobs (an intelligence cover name denoting an operation where bloodshed is required), nuclear and terrorist, which goes to the world's press for dissemination, as well as to governments and military establishments.

Membership of IISS includes representatives of 87 major wire services and press associations as well as 138 senior editors and columnists drawn from international newspapers and magazines. Now you know where your favorite columnist gets all of his information and opinions from. Remember Jack Anderson, Tom Wicker, Sam Donaldson, John Chancellor, Mary McGrory, Seymour Hersh, Flora Lewis and Anthony Lewis, et al? The information provided by IISS, especially scenarios like those prepared to blacken President Hussein and to justify the coming attack on Libya and condemn the PLO are all specially tailor-made for the occasion. The Mai Lai massacre story published by Seymour Hersh came straight out of IISS, just in case we wrongly suppose that men like Hersh do their own research work.

The International Institute for Strategic Studies is nothing more than a higher echelon opinion-maker as defined by Lippmann and Bernays. Instead of writing books, newspapers report opinions presented by chosen columnists, and IISS was formed to be a coordinating center for not only creating opinions, but to get those opinions and scenarios out much faster and to a greater audience than could be reached by a book, for example. IISS is a good example of the gridding and interfacing of Committee of 300 institutions. The idea of bringing IISS into being arose at the 1957 Bilderberger meeting. It will be recalled that the Bilderberger Conference is a creation of MI6 under the direction of the Royal Institute of International Affairs. The idea came from Alastair Buchan, son of Lord Tweedsmuir. Buchan was chairman at the time, and a board member of the RIIA and a member of the Round Table reportedly very close to the British royal family. This was the same conference that welcomed Labour Party leader Dennis Healey to its ranks. Others in attendance were Francois Duchene, whose mentor, Jean Monet Duchenes, ran the Trilateral Commission under the tutelage of H. V. Dicks from Tavistock's Columbus Center.

Among the governing council of this gigantic propaganda opinion-making apparat is included the following:

Frank Kitson, a one time controller of The IRA PROVISIONALS, the man who started the Mau-Mau insurgency in Kenya.

Lazard Freres, represented by Robert Ellsworth.

N. M. Rothschild, represented by John Loudon.

Paul Nitze, representative of Schroeder Bank. Nitze has played a very prominent and substantial role in matters of Arms Control agreements, which have AL-WAYS been under the direction of the RIIA.

C. L. Sulzberger of the *New York Times.*

Stansfield Turner, a former director of the CIA.

Peter Calvocoressi, representing Penguin Books.

Royal Institute for International Affairs, represented by Andrew Schoenberg.

Columnists and Reporters, represented by Flora Lewis, Drew Middleton, Anthony Lewis, Max Frankel.

Daniel Ellsberg.

Henry Kissinger.

Robert Bowie, a former director of the CIA's National Intelligence Estimates.

Flowing from the 1957 Bilderberger meeting, Kissinger was instructed to open a Round Table office in Manhattan, the nucleus of which consisted of Haig, Ellsberg, Halperin, Schlessinger, McNamara and the McBundy brothers. Kissinger was directed to fill all executive positions in the Nixon administration with Round Tablers, loyal to the RIIA and therefore to the Queen of England. It was no accident that Kissinger chose President Nixon's old hangout, the Hotel Pierre, as his center of operations.

The significance of the Round Table-Kissinger operation was thus: On orders of the RIIA chairman Andrew Schoeberg, a block was placed on all agencies involved in intelligence, preventing them from giving information to President Nixon. This meant Kissinger and his staff were getting ALL INTELLIGENCE, FOREIGN AND DOMESTIC, LAW ENFORCEMENT INFORMATION, INCLUDING FBI DIVISION 5, before any of it was released to the President. This made certain that all MI6-controlled terrorist operations in the U.S. would have no chance of being leaked. This was Halperin's bailiwick.

By working this methodology, Kissinger at once established hegemony over the Nixon presidency, and after Nixon was disgraced by the Kissinger group and hounded from office, Kissinger emerged with unprecedented powers such as have not been equaled before or since Watergate. Some of these seldom enumerated powers included the following:

Kissinger ordered National Security Decision Memorandum No. I to be drafted by Halperin, who got the actual wording directly from the RIIA through Round Table circles. The memorandum appointed Kissinger as the supreme U.S. authority, chairman of the Verification Panel. All SALT negotiations were directed from here, using Paul Nitze, Paul Warnke and a nest of traitors inside the Arms Control mission at Geneva.

In addition, Kissinger was appointed to The Vietnam Special

Studies Group, which oversaw and made evaluations of all reports, civilian and military, including intelligence reports, coming out of Vietnam. Kissinger also demanded and got oversight of the "40 Committee," a super-secret agency that has the task of deciding when and where to initiate covert activities and then monitors the progress of operations it sets in motion.

Meantime Kissinger ordered a blizzard of wire-taps by the FBI, even on his closest assistants, so as to give the impression that he was on top of everything. Most of his circle were told that wiretaps on them were in force. This nearly backfired when an MI6 operative by the name of Henry Brandon was ordered wiretapped, but was not informed by Kissinger. Brandon was doubling as a reporter for the *London Times* and Kissinger very nearly got thrown out because nobody does this to the *London Times*.

The full story of the Ellsberg break-in and the subsequent Watergating of Nixon is too long to be included here. Suffice to say, Kissinger had control of Ellsberg from the day that Ellsberg was recruited while at Cambridge. Ellsberg had always been a hardliner in favor of the Vietnam War, but was gradually "converted" to a radical leftist activist. His "conversion" was only a shade less miraculous than St. Paul's Damascus Road experience.

The entire spectrum of the new left in the United States was the work of British intelligence MI6 acting through Round Table assets and the Institute for Policy Studies (IPS). Just as it did with all countries with a republican base, whose policies had to be changed, IPS played a leading role, even as it does today in South Africa and South Korea. Much of IPS's activities are explained in my work "IPS Revisited" published in 1990.

IPS had one main function, that being to sow discord and spread disinformation resulting in chaos. One such program, aimed at America's youth, centered on drugs. Through a series of IPS fronts, acts like the stoning of Nixon's motorcade and a large number of bombings, a climate of deception was effectively created which led a majority of Americans to believe that the United States was under threat from the KGB, the GRU and

Cuban DGI. The word went out that a lot of these imaginary agents had close ties to the Democrats through George McGovern. It was in fact, a model disinformation campaign for which MI6 is justly famous.

Haldeman, Ehrlichman and Nixon's closest aides had no clue as to what was happening, hence a flurry of statements emanating from the White House that East Germany, The Soviet Union, North Korea and Cuba were training terrorists and funding their operations in the United States. I doubt whether Nixon knew very much about IPS, let alone suspected what it was doing to his presidency. We suffered the same kind of disinformation during the Gulf War when the word went out that terrorists of all stripes were about to invade the United States and blow up everything in sight.

President Nixon was literally left in the dark. He didn't even know that David Young, a Kissinger pupil, was working in the basement of the White House, supervising "leaks." Young was a graduate of Oxford and a long-time Kissinger associate through Round Table assets such as the law firm of Milbank Tweed. President Nixon was no match for the forces arrayed against him under the direction of MI6 on behalf of the Royal Institute for International Affairs and hence the British royal family.

About the only thing that Nixon was guilty of, in so far as Watergate is concerned, was his ignorance of what was going on all around him. When James McCord "confessed" to Judge John Sirica, Nixon should have been on to it like a flash that McCord was playing a double game. He ought to have challenged Kissinger about his relationship with McCord there and then. That would have thrown a spanner in the works and derailed the whole MI6-Watergate operation.

Nixon did not abuse his presidential powers. His crime was not defending the Constitution of the United States of America and not charging Mrs. Katherine Meyer Graham and Ben Bradley with conspiracy to commit insurrection. Mrs. Katherine Meyer Graham's pedigree is of the most doubtful kind, as

"Jessica Fletcher" of "Murder She Wrote" would soon have discovered. But even knowing that, Mrs. Graham's controllers in the Round Table would have fought hard to keep the lid on things. The role of the *Washington Post* was to keep the pot boiling by one "revelation" after another, thereby engendering a climate of public distrust of President Nixon, even when there was not one shred of evidence to support wrongdoing by him. Yet it shows the immense power of the press, as Lippman and Bernays had quite properly anticipated, in that Mrs. Graham, long suspected of the murder of her husband, Philip L. Graham—officially classed as "suicide"—should have retained any credibility at all. Other traitors who should have been indicted for insurrection and treason were Kissinger, Haig, Halperin, Ellsberg, Young, McCord, Joseph Califano and Chomsky of IPS and those CIA operatives who went to McCord's house and burned all of his papers. Again, it is worth repeating that Watergate, like many other operations we do not have the space to include here, demonstrated the COMPLETE CONTROL exercised over the United States by the Committee of 300.

While Nixon kept company with people like Earl Warren and some Mafia dons who had built Warren's house, that does not mean that he should have been disgraced over the Watergate Affair. My dislike of Nixon stems from his willingness to sign the infamous ABM Treaty in 1972 and his all-too-cozy relationship with Leonid Brezhnev. One of the sorriest slip-ups of the Minority Council was its abject failure to expose the dirty role played by INTERTEL, the Corning Group's ugly private intelligence agency whom we have already met, who "leaked" a lot of Watergate material to Edward Kennedy. Private intelligence agencies like INTERTEL have no right to exist in the United States. They are a MENACE to our right to privacy and an insult to all free men everywhere.

Blame must also fall on those who were supposed to protect President Nixon from the kind of steelmesh net that was thrown around him to isolate him. The intelligence personnel around

Nixon were a poor lot who had no knowledge of just how thorough British intelligence operations are; indeed, they had no inkling that Watergate was a British intelligence operation in its entirety. The Watergate plot was a coup-d'etat against the United States of America, as was the murder of John F. Kennedy. Although this fact is not recognized as such today, I am confident that when all the secret papers are finally opened, history will record that two coup-d'etats, one against Kennedy and one against Nixon, did indeed take place, and which in their wake brought the most violent rape and assault on the institutions upon which the Republic of the United States stands.

The individual who most deserves the title of traitor and who is most guilty of sedition is General Alexander Haig. This desk-man office-colonel whose paper-shuffling career did not include commanding any troops in battle, was suddenly thrust upon the scene by the invisible upper-level parallel government. President Nixon once described him as a man who had to ask Kissinger's permission to go to the bathroom.

Haig was a product of the Round Table. He was noticed by Round Tabler Joseph Califano, one of Her Majesty's most trusted Round Tablers in the United States. Joseph Califano, legal council of the Democratic National Convention, had actually interviewed Alfred Baldwin, one of the plumbers A MONTH BEFORE THE BURGLARY TOOK PLACE. Califano was stupid enough to write a memorandum on his interview with Baldwin, in which he gave details of information on McCord's background and why McCord had selected Baldwin to be on the "team."

Even more damaging, Califano's memorandum contained full details of transcripts of wiretaps of conversations between Nixon and the reelection committee, all this BEFORE the break-in occurred. Califano should have been indicted on a score of federal offenses; instead he got away cleanly with his criminal activity. Sanctimonious Sam Ervin refused to allow Fred Thompson, Minority Council, to introduce this highly damaging evidence at the Watergate hearings—on the spurious grounds that it was "too speculative."

On Round Table orders, Kissinger had Haig promoted from colonel to four-star general in the most meteoric rise ever recorded in the annals of United States military history, in the course of which Haig was leap-frogged over 280 senior U.S. Army generals and high-ranking officers.

During Haig's "promotion," and as a result of it, 25 senior generals were forced to resign. As a reward for his treachery toward President Nixon, AND THE UNITED STATES, Haig was subsequently given the plum job of Commanding General of the North Atlantic Treaty Organization forces (NATO), although he was THE LEAST QUALIFIED COMMANDER EVER TO HOLD THAT POSITION. Here again he was leap-frogged over 400 senior generals from NATO countries and the United States.

When the news of his appointment reached the Soviet Armed Forces High Command, Marshall Orgakov recalled his three top Warsaw Pact generals from Poland and East Germany, and there was much merrymaking, clinking of glasses and quaffing of champagne until well into the night. All through Haig's tenure as commander of NATO forces the professional elite cadre of the Soviet Armed Forces, men who have never been anything else but professional soldiers, held Haig in the utmost contempt and openly referred to him as the "office manager of NATO." They knew that Haig owed his appointment to the RIIA and not to the United States military.

But before his military promotion took him out of Washington, let it be known that Alexander Haig, in conjunction with Kissinger, all but destroyed the office of the President of the United States and its government. The chaos left by Kissinger and Haig in the wake of Watergate has never been chronicled to the best of my knowledge. On the insistence of the RIIA, Haig virtually took over the management of the Government of the United States after the April 1973 coup d'etat. Bringing 100 Round Table agents chosen from the Brookings Institution,

Institute of Policy Studies and the Council on Foreign Relations, Haig filled the top one hundred posts in Washington with men who, like himself, were beholden to a foreign power. In the ensuing debacle, the Nixon Administration was torn asunder, and the United States along with it.

Thrusting aside the pious platitudes and posturings of defending the Constitution, Senator Sam Ervin did more to change the United States than anything President Nixon was alleged to have done, and the United States has not yet recovered from the near-mortal wound of Watergate, a Committee of 300 sponsored operation conducted by the Royal Institute for International Affairs, the Round Table and "hands on" MI6 officers based in the United States.

The way President Nixon was first isolated, surrounded by traitors and then confused, followed to the letter the Tavistock method of gaining full control of a person according to the methodology laid down by Tavistock's chief theoretician, Dr. Kurt Lewin. I have already given details of Lewin's methodology elsewhere in this book, but in view of the text-book case of President Richard M.Nixon, I think it is worth repeating·

"One of the main techniques for breaking morale through a strategy of terror consists in exactly this tactic—keep the person hazy as to where he stands and just what he may expect. In addition, if frequent vacillations between severe disciplinary measures and promises of good treatment together with the spreading of contradictory news, make the cognitive structure of this situation utterly unclear, then the individual may cease even to know a particular plan would lead toward or away from his goal. Under these conditions even those individuals who have definite goals and are ready to take risks are paralyzed by severe inner conflict in regard to what to do."

Kissinger and Haig followed Tavistock training manuals to

the letter. The result was a distraught, confused, frightened and demoralized President Nixon, whose only course of action—he was told by Haig—was to resign. In 1983 I wrote two works, "The Tavistock Institute: Sinister and Deadly" and "The Tavistock Institute: Britain's Control of U.S. Policy," based upon Tavistock secret manuals which had fallen into my hands. Tavistock Institute's methods and actions are spelled out in these two works.

So successfully were Tavistock methods applied to unseat President Nixon that the people of this nation fully believed the calumny of lies, distortions and set-piece contrived situations mounted by the conspirator as truth, when in fact Watergate was a diabolical lie from end to end. It is important to stress this because we have certainly not seen the last of Watergate-type operations.

What were the alleged impeachable offenses committed by President Nixon, and the so-called "smoking gun" evidence which was supposed to back up the charges? First, the "smoking gun." This piece of FICTION was created by Kissinger and Haig around the June 23rd tape, which Haig coerced Nixon into surrendering to Leon Jaworski.

Haig spent hours convincing President Nixon that this tape would sink him, because it proved "beyond any doubt" that Nixon was guilty of serious wrong doing and a co-conspirator in the Watergate break-in. President Nixon's first response was to tell Haig, "It's utter nonsense to make such a big deal of this," but Haig chipped away until Nixon became convinced that he could not make a successful defense before the Senate, based solely on this particular June 23rd tape!

How had Haig accomplished his mission? Acting out a scenario prepared for him by his Round Table controllers, Haig had an unedited transcript of the "smoking gun" tape typed by his staff. In reality there was nothing in the tape that President Nixon could not have explained. Sensing this, Haig then circulated his unauthorized unedited transcript of the tape among Nixon's staunchest supporters in the House and Senate and the Republican Party high command. Peppered with "smoking gun" and "devastating," and coming from Nixon's trusted aide, the transcript had the effect of a falcon hitting a flock of pigeons; Nixon's supporters panicked and ran for cover.

Following up his sedition and insurrection, Haig summoned to his office Congressman Charles Wiggins, a staunch Nixon supporter who had agreed to lead the fight in the House to head off impeachment proceedings. In a bare-faced blatant lie, Wiggins was informed by Haig, "The fight is lost." After that Wiggins lost all interest in defending Nixon, believing that Nixon himself had agreed to give up. Haig then dealt with Senator Griffin, a leading supporter of the president in the Senate in the same way. AS A RESULT OF HAIG'S SEDITIOUS, TREASONOUS ACTIVITIES, SENATOR GRIFFIN IMMEDIATELY WROTE A LETTER TO PRESIDENT NIXON CALLING UPON HIM TO RESIGN.

THREE MONTHS EARLIER, Round Table controlled Institute for Policy Studies, child of James Warburg, founder and a fellow, Marcus Raskin, delivered EXACTLY the same ultimatum that President Nixon resign, using the British intelligence propaganda journal, *The New York Times* of May 25th to deliver the ultimatum. The Watergate tragedy was a step in the irreversible transition to barbarism which is enveloping the United States, and which is leading us into the One World Government-New World Order. The United States is now at the same place that Italy found itself when Aldo Moro tried to rescue it from created instability.

With what wrongdoing was Nixon charged? John Doar, whose brutish character was well-suited to his task of bringing so-called articles of impeachment against the president, was the author and finisher of one of the most far-reaching ILLEGAL domestic surveillance counterintelligence operations ever run in the United States.

Heading the Interdepartmental Intelligence Unit (IDIU), Doar garnered information from every conceivable agency of the federal government, including the Internal Revenue Service.

The program was linked to the Institute for Policy Studies. One of the highlights of John Doar's career was to provide the CIA—which is forbidden by law to engage in domestic surveillance, with 10,000-12,000 names of citizens he suspected as political dissidents, for further investigation.

On July 18th, 1974, this great upholder of the law, with measured pomposity, delivered the "charges" against President Nixon, which episode was nationally televised. THERE WAS NOT A SINGLE PIECE OF EVIDENCE THAT NIXON HAD DONE ANYTHING IMPEACHABLE; indeed, Doar's pathetic litany of Nixon's alleged "crimes" were so trivial that it is a wonder the proceedings went beyond this point. Income tax fiddling, unauthorized bombing of Cambodia and a vague "abuse of power" charge that would never have stuck in a court of law, was the best that Doar could do. The United States was as unstable as it would ever be when President Nixon resigned on August 8th, 1974.

Nowhere more so than in our economic and fiscal policies. In 1983 the international bankers met in Williamsburg, Virginia to work out a strategy to prepare the United States for a total disintegration of its banking system. This planned event was to stampede the U.S. Senate into accepting control of our monetary and fiscal policies by the International Monetary Fund (IMF). Dennis Weatherstone of Morgan Guarantee on Wall Street stated that he was convinced this was the only way for the United States to save itself.

The proposal was endorsed by the Ditchley Group which had its beginning in May of 1982 at Ditchley Park in London. On January 10th-11th, 1983, this alien group met in Washington D.C., in violation of the Sherman Anti-Trust Act and the Clayton Act, and conspired to overthrow the sovereignty of the United States of America in its monetary and financial freedom. The United States Attorney General knew of the meeting and its purpose. Instead of charging members of the group with conspiracy to commit a federal crime, he simply looked the other way.

Under the abovementioned acts, proof of a conspiracy is all that is needed for a felony conviction, and there was ample evidence that a conspiracy did indeed take place. But as the Ditchley Foundation had met at the request of the Royal Institute for International Affairs and was hosted by the Round Table, no one in the Justice Department had the courage to take action as required by those who had sworn to uphold the laws of the United States.

The Ditchley Plan to usurp control of the fiscal and monetary policies of the United States was the brainchild of Sir Harold Lever, a strong backer of Zionism and a close confidant of members of the British royal family and a member of the Committee of 300. Sir Harold Lever was a director of the giant UNILEVER conglomerate, an important Committee of 300 company. Lever's plan called for the IMF's influence to be broadened so that it could influence central banks of all nations, including the U.S. and guide them into the hands of a One World Government bank.

This was considered a vital step in bringing about a situation where the IMF would become the supreme arbiter of world banking. The ultra-secret January meeting was preceded by an earlier meeting in October 1982, and was attended by representatives of 36 of the world's top banks who met at the New York Vista Hotel. Security for the October 26th-27th seminar was as tight as anything ever seen in the Big Apple. This earlier Ditchley Group meeting also violated United States law.

Addressing the meeting, Sir Harold Lever said it was essential that national sovereignty as an archaic hang-over must be ended before the year 2000. "The United States will soon have to realize that it will be no better than any Third World country when the IMF takes control," said Sir Harold. It was later reported to the delegates that plans to appoint the IMF as the controller of United States fiscal policies were being readied to bring before the United States Senate by the year 2000.

Rimmer de Vries, speaking for Morgan Guarantee, said it

was high time that the United States became a member of the Bank of International Settlements. "There must be a reconsideration of U.S. hesitancy over the past 50 years," De Vries declared. Some British and German bankers, fearing possible violations of U.S. law, said that the Ditchley Group is nothing but a committee to iron out exchange rate problems. Felix Rohatyn also spoke of the great need to change U.S. banking laws so that the IMF could play a greater role in this country. Rohatyn headed Lazard Freres, a Club of Rome bank and part of the Eagle Star Group which we have already met.

Round Tablers William Ogden and Werner Stang spoke enthusiastically in support of surrendering U.S. fiscal sovereignty to the International Monetary Fund and the Bank of International Settlements. Delegates representing the Alpha banking Group, a P2 Freemasonry bank, said the United States must be forced to surrender to "the higher authority of a world bank," before any progress toward the New World Order could be made.

On January 8th, 1983, before their big meeting on January 10th-11th, Hans Vogel, a leading Club of Rome member, was received at the White House. President Ronald Reagan had invited George Schultz, Caspar Weinberger, George Kennan and Lane Kirkland to be present at his meeting with Vogel, who explained to President Reagan what the aims and objectives of the Ditchley Group were. From that day, President Reagan did an about face and worked with the Committee of 300's various agencies to advance the International Monetary Fund and the Bank of International Settlements as the authority on U.S. domestic and foreign monetary policies.

The invisible government of the Committee of 300 has put tremendous pressure on America to change its ways—for the worse. America is the last bastion of freedom and unless our freedoms are taken away from us, progress toward a One World Government will be considerably slowed. Such an undertaking as a One World Government is a massive one, requiring a great deal of skill, organizing abilities, control of governments and their policies. The only organization that could possibly have undertaken this mammoth task with any hope of success is the Committee of 300, and we have seen just how far it has come toward total success.

Above all, the battle is a spiritual one. Unfortunately, the Christian churches have become little more than social clubs run by the infinitely evil World Council of Churches (WCC), whose beginnings lie not in Moscow but in the City of London, as we see from the chart at the end of the book which gives the structure of the One World Government Church. This body was set up in the 1920's to serve as a vehicle for One World Government policies, and stands as a monument to the long-range planning capabilities of the Committee of 300.

Another corrupt body similar in structure and design to the WCC is the Union of Concerned Scientists, set up by the Trilateral Commission, and funded by the Carnegie Endowment Fund, the Ford Foundation and Aspen Institute. This is the group that has led the fight to prevent the United States from mounting an effective deterrent against Soviet Cosmospheres, space-based laser beam weapons which can destroy selected targets in the United States or elsewhere from outer space.

The United States SDI program was designed to counter the threat posed by Soviet Cosmospheres, a threat which still exists in spite of the assurances that "communism is dead." Soviet spokesman Georgi Arbatov told a meeting of the Union of Concerned Scientists that it is important for them to oppose the SDI program, because if the SDI program became operational, "it will be a military catastrophe." Year after year the Union of Concerned Scientists has opposed every budget which included funding for the vital SDI program, until by the end of 1991, there is not even enough money to fund further research still required, let alone place the system in orbit. The Union of Concerned Scientists is run by the Royal Institute for International Affairs and is heavily infiltrated with MI6 British intelligence agents.

There is not one single aspect of life in America that is not watched over, steered in the "right" direction, manipulated, and controlled by the invisible government of the Committee of 300. There is not one elected official or political leader that is not subject to its rule. No one thus far has got away with defying our secret rulers, who do not hesitate to make "a horrible example" of anyone, including the President of the United States of America.

From 1776 when Jeremy Bentham and William Petty, the Earl of Shelburne, fresh from the triumph of the French Revolution which they planned and ran, were drafted by the British Crown to bring their combined experience to bear against the colonists, to 1812 when the British sacked and burned Washington, destroying secret documents that would have exposed the treason being worked against the young United States of America, to the Watergating of President Nixon and assassination of President Kennedy, the hand of the Committee of 300 is clearly visible. This book is an attempt to open the eyes of the American people to this terrible truth: We are not an independent nation, nor can we ever be, as long as we are ruled by an invisible government, the Committee of 300.

Past and Present Institutions/ Organizations and Those Directly Under Influence of the Committee of 300

Academy for Contemporary Problems.
Africa Fund.
Agency of International Development.
Albert Previn Foundation.
Alliance Israelite Universalle.
American Civil Liberties Union.

American Council of Race Relations.
American Defense Society.
American Press Institute.
American Protective League.
Anti-Defamation League.
Arab Bureau.
Arab Higher Committee.
ARCA Foundation.
Armour Research Foundation.
Arms Control and Foreign Policy Caucus.
Arthur D. Little, Inc.
Asian Research Institute.
Aspen Institute.
Association for Humanistic Psychology.
Augmentation Research Center.
Baron De Hirsh Fund.
Battelle Memorial Institute.
Berger National Foundation.
Berlin Center for Future Research.
Bilderbergers.
Black Order.
Boycott Japanese Goods Conference.
British Newfoundland Corporation.
British Royal Society.
Brotherhood of Cooperative Commonwealth.
Bureau of International Revolutionary Propaganda.
Canadian Jewish Congress.
Cathedral of St. John the Divine, New York.
Center for Advanced Studies in the Behavioral Sciences.
Center for Constitutional Rights.
Center for Cuban Studies.
Center for Democratic Institutions.
Center for International Policy.
Center for the Study of Responsive Law.
Christian Socialist League.

Cini Foundation.
Club of Rome.
Cominform.
Committee for the Next Thirty Years.
Committee of Fourteen.
Committee on National Morale.
Committee to Frame A World Constitution.
Communist League.
Congress of Industrial Organizations.
Council on Foreign Relations.
David Sassoon Company.
De Beers Consolidated Mines.
Democratic League of Brussels.
East India Committee of 300.
Economic and Social Control (ECOSOC).
Environmental Fund.
Environmetrics Inc.
Esalen Institute.
Fabian Society.
Federation of American Zionists.
Fellowship for a Christian Social Order.
Fellowship of Reconciliation.
Ford Foundation.
Fordham University Institution Educational Research.
Foundation for National Progress.
Garland Fund.
German Marshall Fund.
Governing Body of the Israelite Religious Community.
Gulf South Research Institute.
Haganah.
Harvard University.
Hells Fire Club.
Horace Mann League.
Hudson Guild.
Hudson Institute.

Hudson Bay Company.
Imperial College University of London.
Industrial Christian Fellowship.
Institute for Brain Research.
Institute for Pacific Relations.
Institute for Policy Studies.
Institute for Social Research.
Institute for the Future.
Institute for World Order.
Institute on Drugs, Crime and Justice.
Inter-Alpha.
Inter-American Social Development Institute.
International Institute for Strategic Studies.
Interreligious Peace Colloquium.
Irgun.
Knights of Malta.
League of Nations.
Logistics Management Institute.
London Board of Deputies of British Jews.
London School of Economics.
Mary Carter Paint Company.
Massachusetts Institute of Technology.
Mellon Institute.
Metaphysical Society.
Milner Group.
Mocatto Metals.
Mont Pelerin Society.
NAACP.
National Action Research on Military/Industrial Complex.
National Center for Productivity Institute.
National Council of Churches.
National Opinion Research Center.
National Training Laboratories.
New Democratic Coalition.
New World Foundation.

New York Rand Institute.
NORML.
North Atlantic Treaty Organization (NATO).
Odd Fellows.
Order of St. John of Jerusalem.
Order of The Golden Dawn.
OXFAM.
Oxford Univac.
Pacific Studies Center.
Palisades Foundation.
Peninsula and Orient Navigation Company.
PERMINDEX.
Princeton University.
Rand Corporation.
Rand School of Social Sciences.
Research Triangle Institution.
Rhodes Scholarship Committee.
Rio Tinto Zinc Company.
Riverside Church Disarmament Program.
Round Table.
Royal Institute for International Affairs.
Russell Sage Foundation.
San Francisco Foundation.
Sharps Pixley Ward.
Social Science Research Council.
Socialist International.
Socialist Party of the United States.
Society for Promotion of Study of Religions.
Society of Heaven (TRIADS).
Soviet State Committee for Science and Technology.
Stanford Research Institute.
Stockholm International Peace Research Institute.
Sun Yat Sen Society.
Systems Development Corporation.
Tavistock Institute of Human Relations.

Tempo Corporation.
The High Twelve International.
The Public Agenda Foundation.
The Quality of Life Institute.
Theosophist Society.
Thule Society.
Transatlantic Council.
Trilateral Commission.
U.S. Association of the Club of Rome.
U.S. Institute for Peace.
Union of Concerned Scientists.
UNITAR.
University of Pennsylvania Wharton School.
Warburg, James P. and Family.
Western Training Laboratories.
Wilton Park.
Women's Christian Temperance Union.
Wong Hong Hon Company.
Work in America Institute.
World Council of Churches.

SPECIAL FOUNDATIONS AND INTEREST GROUPS

Arab Bureau.
Aristotelian Society.
Asian Research Institute.
Bertrand Russell Peace Foundation.
British American Canadian Corporation.
Brotherhood of Eternal Love.
Cambridge Apostles.
Canadian Histadrut Campaign.
Canadian Pacific Ltd.
Caribbean-Central American Action Group.
China Everbright Holdings Ltd.
Chinese People's Institute of Foreign Affairs.

Council of South America.
Endangered Peoples' Society.
English Property Corporation Ltd.
Hospice Inc.
International Brotherhood of Teamsters.
International Red Cross.
Jerusalem Foundation, Canada.
Kissinger Associates.
Kowloon Chamber of Commerce.
Organization of American States.
Overseas Chinese Affairs Committee.
Radio Corporation of America (RCA).
Royal Police of Hong Kong.
YMCA.

BANKS

American Express.
Banca de la Svizzera d'Italia.
Banca Andioino.
Banca d'America d'Italia.
Banca Nazionale del Lavoro.
Banca Privata.
Banco Ambrosiano.
Banco Caribe.
Banco Commercial Mexicana.
Banco Consolidato.
Banco d'Espana.
Banco de Colombia.
Banco de Commercio.
Banco de Iberio-America.
Banco de la Nacion.
Banco del Estada.
Banco Internacional.
Banco Latino.

Banco Mercantile de Mexico.
Banco Nacional de Cuba.
Banco Nacional de Panama and 54 smaller Panamanian banks.
Bangkok Commercial d' Italian.
Bangkok Metropolitan Bank.
Bank al Meshreq.
Bank America.
Bank for International Settlements.
Bank Hapoalim.
Bank Leu.
Bank Leumi.
Bank of Bangkok.
Bank of Boston.
Bank of Canada.
Bank of Credit and Commerce International.
Bank of East Asia.
Bank of England.
Bank of Escambia.
Bank of Geneva.
Bank of Ireland.
Bank of London and Mexico.
Bank of Montreal.
Bank of Norfolk.
Bank of Nova Scotia.
Bank Ohio.
Banque Bruxelles-Lambert.
Banque Commerciale Arabes.
Banque du Credit International.
Banque e Paris et Pays-Bas.
Banque Francais et Italienn por l' Amerique du Sud.
Banque Louis Dreyfus e Paris.
Banque Privee.
Banques Sud Ameris.
Barclays Bank.

Baring Brothers Bank.
Barnett Banks.
Baseler Handeslbank.
Basel Committee on Bank Supervision.
BCCI.*
Canadian Imperial Bank of Commerce.
Centrust Bank.
Chartered Bank.
Charterhouse Japhet Bank.
Chase Manhattan Bank.
Chemical Bank.
Citibank.
Citizens and Southern Bank of Atlanta.
City National Bank of Miami.
Claridon Bank.
Cleveland National City Bank.
Corporate Bank and Trust Company.
Credit and Commerce American Holdings.
Credit and Commerce Holdings, Netherlands Antilles.
Credit Suisse.
Crocker National Bank.
de' Neuflize, Schlumberger, Mallet Bank.
Dresdener Bank.
Dusseldorf Global Bank.
First American Bank of Georgia.
First American Bank of New York.
First American Bank of Pensacola.
First American Bank of Virginia.
First American Banking Corp.
First Empire Bank.
First Fidelity Bank.
First National Bank of Boston.
First National City Bank.
Florida National Bank.
Foreign Trade Bank.

Franklin National Bank.
Hambros Bank.
Hong Kong and Shanghai Banking Corporation.
Independence Bank of Encino.
Israeli Discount Bank.
Litex Bank.
Ljubljanska Bank.
Lloyds Bank.
Marine Midland Bank.
Midland Bank.
Morgan Bank.
Morgan Et Cie.
Morgan Grenfell Bank.
Narodny Bank.
National Bank of Cleveland.
National Bank of Florida.
National Westminister Bank.
Orion Bank.
Paravicini Bank Ltd.
Republic National Bank.
Royal Bank of Canada.
Schroeder Bank.
Seligman Bank.
Shanghai Commercial Bank.
Soong Bank.
Standard and Chartered Bank.
Standard Bank.
Swiss Bank Corporation.
Swiss Israel Trade bank.
Trade Development Bank.
Unibank.
Union Bank of Israel.
Union Bank of Switzerland.
Vanying Bank.
White Weld Bank.

World Bank.
World Commerce Bank of Nassau.
World Trade Bank.
Wozchod Handelsbank.

Note: With the exception of the Basel Committee on Banking, each of the above mentioned banks have been, and may still be, involved in the drug, diamond, gold and weapons trade.

* BCCI. This bank has been indicted on several charges of being heavily involved in drug money laundering throughout the world. Its structure girds every operation of the Committee of 300. Of interest is its corporate structure. Middle East Interests, 35% of stock held by:

Ruling Family of Bahrain.
Ruling Family of Sharjah.
Ruling Family of Dhubai.
Ruling Family of Saudi Arabia.
Ruling Family of Iran.
Group of Middle East Businessmen.
BCCI Cayman Islands 41%.
Bank of America 24%.

BCCI Cayman Islands and BCCI Luxembourg established Agency offices in Miami, Boca Raton, Tampa, New York, San Francisco and Los Angeles.

LEGAL ASSOCIATIONS AND LAWYERS
American Bar Association.
Clifford and Warnke.
Coudert Brothers.
Cravaith, Swain and Moore.
Wilkie, Farr and Gallagher.

Accountants/Auditors

Price, Waterhouse.

Tavistock Institutions in the United States

FLOW LABORATORIES
Gets contracts from the National Institute of Health.

MERLE THOMAS CORPORATION
Gets contracts from the U.S. Navy, analyzes data from satellites.

WALDEN RESEARCH
Does work in the field of pollution control.

PLANNING RESEARCH CORPORATION, ARTHUR D. LITTLE, G.E. "TEMPO," OPERATIONS RESEARCH INC.
Part of approximately 350 firms who conduct research and conduct surveys, make recommendations to government.

They are part of what President Eisenhower called "a possible danger to public policy that could itself become captive of a scientific-technological elite."

BROOKINGS INSTITUTION
Dedicates its work to what it calls a "national agenda." Wrote President Hoover's program, President Roosevelt's "New Deal," the Kennedy Administration's "New Frontiers" program (deviation from it cost John F. Kennedy his life), and President Johnson's "Great Society." Brookings has been telling the United States Government how to conduct its affairs for the past 70 years and is still doing so on behalf of the Committee of 300.

HUDSON INSTITUTE

Under the direction of Herman Khan, this institution has done more to shape the way Americans react to political and social events, think, vote and generally conduct themselves than perhaps any except the BIG FIVE. Hudson specializes in defense policy research and relations with the USSR. Most of its military work is classified as SECRET. (One idea during the Vietnam War was to build a moat around Saigon.) Some of its earlier papers were entitled "Stability and Tranquility Among Older Nations," and "Analytical Summary of U.S. National Security Policy Issues."

Hudson prides itself on its diversity; it helped NASA with its space programs and helped to promote new youth fashions and ideas, youth rebellion and alienation for the Committee of 300, ostensibly funded by Coca Cola. Hudson may be quite properly classified as one of the Committee of 300's BRAIN-WASHING establishments. Some of its nuclear war scenarios make for very interesting reading and, if they can be obtained, I would recommend "The 6 Basic Thermonuclear Threats" and "Possible Outcomes of Thermonuclear War" and one of its more frightening papers entitled "Israeli-Arab Nuclear War."

Hudson also does corporate advising for Committee of 300 companies, Rank, Xerox, General Electric, IBM and General Motors, to name but a few of them, but its really big client remains the U.S. Department of Defense which includes matters of civil defense, national security, military policy and arms control. To date it has not got into "wet NASA," that is to say, the National Oceanographic Agency.

NATIONAL TRAINING LABORATORIES

NTL is also known as the International Institute for Applied Behavioral Sciences. This institute is definitely a brainwashing center based on Kurt Lewin principles which include so-called T-Groups (training groups), artificial stress training whereby participants suddenly find themselves immersed in defending themselves against vicious accusations. NTL takes in the National Education Association, the largest teacher-group in the United States.

While officially decrying "racism," it is interesting to note that NTL, working with NEA, produced a paper proposing education vouchers which would separate the hard-to-teach children from the brighter ones, and funding would be allocated according to the number of difficult children who would be separated from those who progressed at a normal rate. The proposal was not taken up.

UNIVERSITY OF PENNSYLVANIA, WHARTON SCHOOL OF FINANCE & COMMERCE

Founded by Eric Trist, one of the "brain trusts" of Tavistock, Wharton has become one of the more important Tavistock institutions in the U.S. in so far as "Behavioral Research" is concerned. Wharton attracts clients such as the U.S. Department of Labor—which it teaches how to produce "cooked" statistics at the Wharton Econometric Forecasting Associates Incorporated. This method is very much in demand as we come to the close of 1991 with millions more out of work than is reflected in USDL statistics.

Wharton's ECONOMETRIC MODELING is used by every major Committee of 300 company in the United States, Western Europe and by the International Monetary Fund, the United Nations and the World Bank. Wharton has produced such noteworthy persons as George Schultz and Alan Greenspan.

INSTITUTE FOR SOCIAL RESEARCH

This is the institute set up by "brain trusters" from Tavistock: Rensis Likert, Dorwin Cartwright and Ronald Lippert. Among its studies are "The Human Meaning of Social Change," "Youth in Transition" and "How Americans View Their Mental Health." Among the institute's clients are The Ford Foundation, U.S. Department of Defense, U.S. Postal Service and the U.S. Department of Justice.

INSTITUTE FOR THE FUTURE

This is not a typical Tavistock institution in that it is funded by the Ford Foundation, yet it draws its long-range forecasting methodology from the mother of all think tanks. Institute for the Future projects what it believes to be changes that will be taking place in time frames of fifty years. The institute is supposed to be able to forecast socioeconomic trends and to blow the whistle on any departures from what it has laid down as normal. Institute for the Future believes it is possible and normal to intervene now and give decisions for the future. So-called "Delphi Panels" decide what is normal and what is not, and prepare position papers to "steer" government in the right direction to head off such groups as "people creating civil disorder." (This could be patriotic groups demanding abolition of graduated taxes, or demanding that their right to bear arms is not infringed.)

The institute recommends actions such as liberalizing abortion laws, drug usage and that cars entering an urban area pay tolls, teaching birth control in public schools, requiring registration of firearms, making the use of drugs a non-criminal offense, legalizing homosexuality, paying students for scholastic achievements, making zoning controls a preserve of the state, offering bonuses for family planning and last, but by no means least, a Pol Pot Cambodia-style proposal that new communities be established in rural areas. As will be observed, many of the Institute for the Future's goals have already been more than fully realized.

INSTITUTE FOR POLICY STUDIES (IPS)

One of the "Big Three," IPS has shaped and reshaped United States policies, foreign and domestic, since it was founded by James P. Warburg and the Rothschild entities in the United States, bolstered by Bertrand Russell and the British Socialists through its networks in America which include the League for Industrial Democracy in which Leonard Woodcock played a leading, if behind-the-scenes role. Local lead players in the League for

Industrial Democracy included "conservative" Jeane Kirkpatrick, Irwin Suall (of the ADL), Eugene Rostow (Arms Control negotiator), Lane Kirkland (Labor leader), and Albert Shanker.

For record purposes only, IPS was incorporated in 1963 by Marcus Raskin and Richard Barnett, both highly-trained Tavistock Institute graduates. Most of the funding came from Rothschild associates in America like the James Warburg Family, the Stern Family Foundation and the Samuel Rubin Foundation. Samuel Rubin was a registered member of the Communist Party who stole the Faberge name (Faberge was "Jeweler of the Imperial Russian Court") and made a fortune out of the Faberge name.

The objectives of IPS came from an agenda laid down for it by the British Round Table, which agenda in turn came from Tavistock Institute, one of the most notable being to create the "New Left" as a grass roots movement in the U.S. IPS was to engender strife and unrest and spread chaos like a wildfire out of control, proliferate the "ideals" of left wing nihilistic socialism, support unrestricted use of drugs of all types, and be the "big stick" with which to beat the United States political establishment.

Barnett and Raskin controlled such diverse elements as the Black Panthers, Daniel Ellsberg, National Security Council staff member Halperin, The Weathermen Underground, the Venceramos and the campaign staff of candidate George McGovern. No scheme was too big for IPS and its controllers to take on and manage.

Take the plot to "kidnap" Kissinger, which was in the hands of Eqbal Ahmed, a British MI6 intelligence agent of Pakistani origin, laundered through "TROTS" (Trotskyite terrorists based in London). The "plot" was "discovered" by the FBI so that it could not go too far. Ahmed went on to become the director of one of IPS's most influential agencies, The Transnational Institute which, chameleon-like, changed from its former name, Institute of Race Relations, when intelligence agents of BOSS (Bureau of State Security) in South Africa unmasked the fact that it was tied directly to Rhodes Scholarship-Harry Oppenheimer and Anglo-American-British mining interests in South Africa. BOSS also discredited the South Africa Foundation at the same time.

Through its many powerful lobbying groups on Capitol Hill, IPS relentlessly used its "big stick" to beat Congress. IPS has a network of lobbyists, all supposedly operating independently but in actual fact acting cohesively, so that Congressmen are pummeled from all sides by seemingly different and varied lobbyists. In this way, IPS was, and is still, able to successfully sway individual Representatives and Senators to vote for "the trend, the way things are going." By using key pointmen on Capitol Hill, IPS was able to break into the very infrastructure of our legislative system and the way it works.

To give only a single concrete example of what I am talking about: in 1975, an IPS point man persuaded representative John Conyers (D-Michigan) and forty-seven members of the House to request IPS to prepare a budget study that would oppose the budget being prepared by President Gerald Ford. Although not adopted, the request was reinstated in 1976, 1977, and 1978, gathering sponsors as it went.

Then in 1978, fifty-six Congressmen signed their names to sponsor an IPS budget study. This was prepared by Marcus Raskin. Raskin's budget called for a fifty percent cut in the Defense Budget, a socialist housing program "that would compete with and steadily replace private housing and mortgage markets," a national health service, "radical changes in the educational system that would disrupt capitalist control over the distribution of knowledge," and several other radical ideas.

The influence of IPS on Arms Control negotiations was a major factor in getting Nixon to sign the treasonous ABM Treaty in 1972, which left the United States virtually defenseless against ICBM attack for almost 10 years. IPS became, and remains to this day, one of the most prestigious "think tanks" controlling foreign policy decisions, which we, the people, foolishly believe are those of our law makers.

By sponsoring militant activism at home and with links to revolutionaries abroad, by engineering such victories as "The Pentagon Papers," besieging the corporate structure, bridging the credibility gap between underground movements and acceptable political activism, by penetrating religious organizations and using them to sow discord in America, such as radical racial politics under the guise of religion, using the establishment media to spread IPS ideas, and then supporting them, IPS has lived up to the role which it was founded to play.

STANFORD RESEARCH INSTITUTE

Jesse Hobson, the first president of Stanford Research Institute, in a 1952 speech made it clear what lines the institute was to follow. Stanford can be described as one of the "jewels" in Tavistock's Crown in its rule over the United States. Founded in 1946 immediately after the close of WW II, it was presided over by Charles A. Anderson, with emphasis on mind control research and "future sciences." Included under the Stanford umbrella was Charles F. Kettering Foundation which developed the "Changing Images of Man" upon which the Aquarian Conspiracy rests.

Some of Stanford's major clients and contracts were at first centered around the defense establishment but, as Stanford grew, so did the diversity of its services:

Applications of Behavioral Sciences to Research Management.

Office of Science and Technology.

SRI Business Intelligence Program.

U.S. Department of Defense Directorate of Defense Research and Engineering.

U.S. Department of Defense Office of Aerospace Research.

Among corporations seeking Stanford's services were Wells Fargo Bank, Bechtel Corporation, Hewlett Packard, Bank of America, McDonnell-Douglas Corporation, Blyth, Eastman

Dillon and TRW Company. One of Stanford's more secret projects was extensive work on chemical and bacteriological warfare (CAB) weapons.

Stanford Research is plugged into at least 200 smaller "think tanks" doing research into every facet of life in America. This is known as ARPA networking and represents the emergence of probably the most far-reaching effort to control the environment of every individual in the country. At present Stanford's computers are linked with 2500 "sister" research consoles which include the Central Intelligence Agency (CIA), Bell Telephone Laboratories, U.S. Army Intelligence, the Office of Naval Intelligence (ONI), RAND, MIT, Harvard and UCLA. Stanford plays a key role in that it is the "library," cataloging all ARPA documentation.

"Other agencies"—and one can use one's imagination here, are allowed to search through SRI's "library" for key words, phrases, look through sources and update their own master files with those of Stanford Research Center. The Pentagon, for instance, uses SRI's "master files" extensively, and there is little doubt that other U.S. Government agencies do the same. Pentagon "command and control" problems are worked out by Stanford.

While ostensibly these apply only to weapons and soldiers, there is absolutely no guarantee that the same research could not, and will not, be turned to civilian applications. Stanford is known to be willing to do anything for anyone, and it is my belief that if ever SRI were to be fully exposed, the hostility which would arise from revelations as to what it actually does would most probably force SRI to close.

MASSACHUSETTS INSTITUTE OF TECHNOLOGY, ALFRED P. SLOAN SCHOOL OF MANAGEMENT

This major institute is not generally recognized as being a part of Tavistock U.S.A. Most people look upon it as a purely American institution, but that is far from being the case. MIT-Alfred Sloan can be roughly divided into the following groups:

Contemporary Technology.
Industrial Relations.
Lewin Group Psychology.
NASA-ERC Computer Research Laboratories.
Office of Naval Research Group, Psychology.
Systems Dynamics. Forrestor and Meadows wrote The
    Club of Rome's "Limits of Growth" zero growth
    study.
Some of MIT's clients include the following:
American Management Association.
American Red Cross.
Committee for Economic Development.
GTE.
Institute for Defense Analysis (IDA).
NASA.
National Academy of Sciences.
National Council of Churches.
Sylvania.
TRW.
U.S. Army.
U.S. Department of State.
U.S. Navy.
U.S. Treasury.
Volkswagen Company.

So vast is the reach of IDA that it would take hundreds of pages to describe the activities in which it is engaged, and IDA is fully described in my book on the role played by Institutions and Foundations in committing treason against the United States of America, which will be published early in 1992.

RAND RESEARCH AND DEVELOPMENT CORPORATION

Without a doubt, RAND is THE think tank most beholden to Tavistock Institute and certainly the RIIA's most prestigious vehicle for control of United States policies at every level.

Specific RAND policies that became operative include our ICBM program, prime analyses for U.S. foreign policy making, instigator of space programs, U.S. nuclear policies, corporate analyses, hundreds of projects for the military, the Central Intelligence Agency (CIA) in relation to the use of mind altering drugs like peyote, LSD (the covert MK-Ultra operation which lasted for 20 years).

Some of RAND's clients include the following:
American Telephone and Telegraph Company (AT&T).
Chase Manhattan Bank.
International Business Machines (IBM).
National Science Foundation.
Republican Party.
TRW.
U.S. Air Force.
U.S. Department of Energy.
U.S. Department of Health.

There are literally THOUSANDS of highly important companies, government institutions and organizations that make use of RAND's services, and to list them all would be an impossible task. Among RAND's "specialities" is a study group that predicts the timing and the direction of a thermonuclear war, plus working out the many scenarios based upon its findings. RAND was once accused of being commissioned by the USSR to work out terms of surrender of the United States Government, an accusation that went all the way to the United States Senate, where it was taken up by Senator Symington and subsequently fell victim to articles of scorn poured out by the establishment press. BRAINWASHING remains the primary function of RAND.

To summarize, the major Tavistock institutions in the United States engaged in brainwashing at all levels, including government, the military, business, religious organizations and education are the following:
Brookings Institution.
Hudson Institute.

Institute for Policy Studies.
Massachusetts Institute of Technology.
National Training Laboratories.
Rand Research and Development Corporation.
Stanford Research Institute.
Wharton School at University of Pennsylvania.

It is estimated by sources of mine that the total number of people employed by these institutions is in the region of 50,000 with funding close to $10 billion dollars.

Some major world-wide Committee of 300 institutions and organizations are as follows:

Americans for a Safe Israel.
Biblical Archaeology Review.
Bilderbergers.
British Petroleum.
Canadian Institute of Foreign Relations.
Christian Fundamentalism.
Council on Foreign Relations, New York.
Egyptian Exploration Society.
Imperial Chemical Industries.
International Institute for Strategic Studies.
Order of Skull and Bones.
Palestine Exploration Fund.
Poor Knights of the Templars.
Royal Dutch Shell Company.
Socialist International.
South Africa Foundation.
Tavistock Institute of Human Relations.
Temple Mount Foundation.
The Atheist Club.
The Fourth State of Consciousness Club.
The Hermetic Order of the Golden Dawn.
The Milner Group.
The Nasi Princes.
The Order of Magna Mater.

The Order of the Divine Disorder.
The RIIA.
The Round Table.
Trilateral Commission.
Universal Freemasonry.
Universal Zionism.
Vickers Armament Company.
Warren Commission.
Watergate Committee.
Wilton Park.
World Council of Churches.

PAST AND PRESENT MEMBERS OF THE COMMITTEE OF 300

Abergavemy, Marquis of.
Acheson, Dean.
Adeane, Lord Michael.
Agnelli, Giovanni.
Alba, Duke of.
Aldington, Lord.
Aleman, Miguel.
Allibone, Professor T. E.
Alsop Family Designate.
Amory, Houghton.
Anderson, Charles A.
Anderson, Robert O.
Andreas, Dwayne.
Asquith, Lord.
Astor, John Jacob and successor, Waldorf.
Aurangzeb, Descendants of.
Austin, Paul.
Baco, Sir Ranulph
Balfour, Arthur.

Balogh, Lord.
Bancroft, Baron Stormont.
Baring.
Barnato, B.
Barran, Sir John.
Baxendell, Sir Peter.
Beatrice of Savoy, Princess.
Beaverbrook, Lord.
Beck, Robert.
Beeley, Sir Harold.
Beit, Alfred.
Benn, Anthony Wedgewood.
Bennet, John W.
Benneton, Gilberto or alternate Carlo.
Bertie, Andrew.
Besant, Sir Walter.
Bethal, Lord Nicholas.
Bialkin, David.
Biao, Keng.
Bingham, William.
Binny, J. F.
Blunt, Wilfred.
Bonacassi, Franco Orsini.
Bottcher, Fritz.
Bradshaw, Thornton.
Brandt, Willy.
Brewster, Kingman.
Buchan, Alastair.
Buffet, Warren.
Bullitt, William C.
Bulwer-Lytton, Edward.
Bundy, McGeorge.
Bundy, William.
Bush, George.
Cabot, John. Family Designate.

Caccia, Baron Harold Anthony.
Cadman, Sir John.
Califano, Joseph.
Carrington, Lord.
Carter, Edward.
Catlin, Donat.
Catto, Lord.
Cavendish, Victor C. W. Duke of Devonshire.
Chamberlain, Houston Stewart.
Chang, V. F.
Chechirin, Georgi or Family Designate.
Churchill, Winston.
Cicireni, V. or Family Designate.
Cini, Count Vittorio.
Clark, Howard.
Cleveland, Amory.
Cleveland, Harland.
Clifford, Clark.
Cobold, Lord.
Coffin, the Rev William Sloane.
Constanti, House of Orange.
Cooper, John. Family Designate.
Coudenhove-Kalergi, Count.
Cowdray, Lord.
Cox, Sir Percy.
Cromer, Lord Evelyn Baring.
Crowther, Sir Eric.
Cumming, Sir Mansfield.
Curtis, Lionel.
d'Arcy, William K.
D'Avignon, Count Etienne.
Danner, Jean Duroc.
Davis, John W.
de Benneditti, Carlo.
De Bruyne, Dirk.

De Gunzberg, Baron Alain.
De Lamater, Major General Walter.
De Menil, Jean.
De Vries, Rimmer.
de Zulueta, Sir Philip.
de'Aremberg, Marquis Charles Louis.
Delano. Family Designate.
Dent, R.
Deterding, Sir Henri.
di Spadaforas, Count Guitierez, (House of Savoy).
Douglas-Home, Sir Alec.
Drake, Sir Eric.
Duchene, Francois.
DuPont.
Edward, Duke of Kent.
Eisenberg, Shaul.
Elliott, Nicholas.
Elliott, William Yandel.
Elsworthy, Lord.
Farmer, Victor.
Forbes, John M.
Foscaro, Pierre.
France, Sir Arnold.
Fraser, Sir Hugh.
Frederik IX, King of Denmark Family Designate.
Freres, Lazard.
Frescobaldi, Lamberto.
Fribourg, Michael.
Gabor, Dennis.
Gallatin, Albert. Family Designate.
Gardner, Richard.
Geddes, Sir Auckland.
Geddes, Sir Reay.
George, Lloyd.
Giffen, James.

Gilmer, John D.
Giustiniani, Justin.
Gladstone, Lord.
Gloucestor, The Duke of.
Gordon, Walter Lockhart.
Grace, Peter J.
Greenhill, Lord Dennis Arthur.
Greenhill, Sir Dennis.
Grey, Sir Edward.
Gyllenhammar, Pierres.
Haakon, King of Norway.
Haig, Sir Douglas.
Hailsham, Lord.
Haldane, Richard Burdone.
Halifax, Lord.
Hall, Sir Peter Vickers.
Hambro, Sir Jocelyn.
Hamilton, Cyril.
Harriman, Averill.
Hart, Sir Robert.
Hartman, Arthur H.
Healey, Dennis.
Helsby, Lord.
Her Majesty Queen Elizabeth II.
Her Majesty Queen Juliana.
Her Royal Highness Princess Beatrix.
Her Royal Highness Queen Margreta.
Heseltine, Sir William.
Hesse, Grand Duke descendants, Family Designate.
Hoffman, Paul G.
Holland, William.
House of Braganza.
House of Hohenzollern.
House, Colonel Mandel.
Howe, Sir Geoffrey.

Hughes, Thomas H.
Hugo, Thieman.
Hutchins, Robert M.
Huxley, Aldous.
Inchcape, Lord.
Jamieson, Ken.
Japhet, Ernst Israel.
Jay, John. Family Designate.
Keynes, John Maynard.
Jodry, J. J.
Joseph, Sir Keith.
Katz, Milton.
Kaufman, Asher.
Keith, Sir Kenneth.
Keswick, Sir William Johnston, or Keswick, H.N.L.
Keswick, William Johnston.
Kimberly, Lord.
King, Dr. Alexander.
Kirk, Grayson L.
Kissinger, Henry.
Kitchener, Lord Horatio.
Kohnstamm, Max.
Korsch, Karl.
Lambert, Baron Pierre.
Lawrence, G.
Lazar.
Lehrman, Lewis.
Lever, Sir Harold.
Lewin, Dr. Kurt.
Lippmann, Walter.
Livingstone, Robert R. Family Designate.
Lockhart, Bruce.
Lockhart, Gordon.
Linowitz, S.
Loudon, Sir John.

Luzzatto, Pierpaolo.
Mackay, Lord, of Clasfern.
Mackay-Tallack, Sir Hugh.
Mackinder, Halford.
MacMillan, Harold.
Matheson, Jardine.
Mazzini, Gueseppi.
McClaughlin, W. E.
McCloy, John J.
McFadyean, Sir Andrew.
McGhee, George.
McMillan, Harold.
Mellon, Andrew.
Mellon, William Larimer or Family Designate.
Meyer, Frank.
Michener, Roland.
Mikovan, Anastas.
Milner, Lord Alfred.
Mitterand, Francois.
Monett, Jean.
Montague, Samuel.
Montefiore, Lord Sebag or Bishop Hugh.
Morgan, John P.
Mott, Stewart.
Mountain, Sir Brian Edward.
Mountain, Sir Dennis.
Mountbatten, Lord Louis.
Munthe, A., or family designate.
Naisbitt, John.
Neeman, Yuval.
Newbigging, David.
Nicols, Lord Nicholas of Bethal.
Norman, Montague.
O'Brien of Lotherby, Lord.
Ogilvie, Angus.

Okita, Saburo.
Oldfield, Sir Morris.
Oppenheimer, Sir Earnest, and successor, Harry.
Ormsby Gore, David (Lord Harlech).
Orsini, Franco Bonacassi.
Ortolani. Umberto.
Ostiguy, J.P.W.
Paley, William S.
Pallavacini.
Palme, Olaf.
Palmerston.
Palmstierna, Jacob.
Pao, Y.K.
Pease, Richard T.
Peccei, Aurellio.
Peek, Sir Edmund.
Pellegreno, Michael, Cardinal.
Perkins, Nelson.
Pestel, Eduard.
Peterson, Rudolph.
Petterson, Peter G.
Petty, John R.
Philip, Prince, Duke of Edinburgh.
Piercy, George.
Pinchott, Gifford.
Pratt, Charles.
Price Waterhouse, Designate.
Radziwall.
Ranier, Prince.
Raskob, John Jacob.
Recanati.
Rees, John Rawlings.
Rees, John.
Rennie, Sir John.
Rettinger, Joseph.

Rhodes, Cecil John.
Rockefeller, David.
Role, Lord Eric of Ipsden.
Rosenthal, Morton.
Rostow, Eugene.
Rothmere, Lord.
Rothschild, Elie de or Edmon de and/or Baron Rothschild.
Runcie, Dr.Robert.
Russell, Lord John.
Russell, Sir Bertrand.
Saint Gouers, Jean.
Salisbury, Marquisse de Robert Gascoiugne Cecil. Shelburne,
    The Salisbury, Lord.
Samuel, Sir Marcus.
Sandberg, M. G.
Sarnoff, Robert.
Schmidheiny, Stephan or alternate brothers Thomas,
    Alexander.
Schoenberg, Andrew.
Schroeder.
Schultz, George.
Schwartzenburg, E.
Shawcross, Sir Hartley.
Sheridan, Walter.
Shiloach, Rubin.
Silitoe, Sir Percy.
Simon, William.
Sloan, Alfred P.
Smuts, Jan.
Spelman.
Sproull, Robert.
Stals, Dr. C.
Stamp, Lord Family designate.
Steel, David.
Stiger, George.

Strathmore, Lord.
Strong, Sir Kenneth.
Strong, Maurice.
Sutherland.
Swathling, Lord.
Swire, J. K.
Tasse, G. Or Family Designate.
Temple, Sir R.
Thompson, William Boyce.
Thompson, Lord.
Thyssen-Bornamisza, Baron Hans Henrich.
Trevelyn, Lord Humphrey.
Turner, Sir Mark.
Turner, Ted.
Tyron, Lord.
Urquidi, Victor.
Van Den Broek, H.
Vanderbilt.
Vance, Cyrus.
Verity, William C.
Vesty, Lord Amuel.
Vickers, Sir Geoffrey.
Villiers, Gerald Hyde family alternate.
Volpi, Count.
von Finck, Baron August.
von Hapsburg, Archduke Otto, House of Hapsburg-Lorraine.
Von Thurn and Taxis, Max.
Wallenberg, Peter or Family Designate.
Wang, Kwan Cheng, Dr.
Warburg, S. C.
Ward Jackson, Lady Barbara.
Warner, Rawleigh.
Warnke, Paul.
Warren, Earl.
Watson, Thomas.

Webb, Sydney.
Weill, David.
Weill, Dr. Andrew.
Weinberger, Sir Caspar.
Weizman, Chaim.
Wells, H. G.
Wheetman, Pearson (Lord Cowdray).
White, Sir Dick Goldsmith.
Whitney, Straight.
Wiseman, Sir William.
Wittelsbach.
Wolfson, Sir Isaac.
Wood, Charles.
Young, Owen.

CONSPIRATORS' HIERARCHY:
THE COMMITTEE OF 300
BIBLIOGRAPHY, SUMMARIES AND NOTES

1980'S PROJECT, Vance, Cyrus and Yankelovich, Daniel.

1984, Orwell, George.

AFTER TWENTY YEARS: THE DECLINE OF NATO AND THE SEARCH FOR A NEW POLICY IN EUROPE, Raskin, Marcus and Barnett, Richard.

AIR WAR AND STRESS, Janus, Irving.

AN AMERICAN COMPANY; THE TRAGEDY OF UNITED FRUIT, Scammel, Henry and McCann, Thomas.

AN INTRODUCTION TO THE PRINCIPLES AND MORALS OF LEGISLATION, Bentham, Jeremy. In this 1780 work Bentham claimed that "nature has placed mankind under the governance of two sovereign masters, pain and pleasure.... They govern us in all we do." Bentham went on to justify the horrors of the Jacobin terrorists in the French Revolution.

ANNUAL REPORT OF BANK LEUMI, 1977.

AT THAT POINT IN TIME: THE INSIDE STORY OF THE SENATE WATERGATE COMMITTEE, Thompson, Fred. I was told where to find Thompson, who was the Minority Counsel on the Ervin Committee, by Bernard Barker, one of the Watergate Burglars. My meeting with Barker took place outside an A&P Supermarket quite close to the Coral Gables Country Club in Coral Gables, Florida. Barker said Thompson was with his law partner who was on a short visit to his mother in Coral Gables, which was only about five minutes away from the A&P Supermarket. I went there and met Thompson who expressed his disappointment over the way Ervin had imposed such severe restrictions on evidence he, Thompson, could admit.

BAKU, AN EVENTFUL HISTORY, Henry, J. D.

BEASTS OF THE APOCALYPSE, O'Grady, Olivia Maria. This remarkable book gives details about a large number of historical figures, including William C. Bullitt, who conspired with Lloyd George to pull the rug out from under White Russian Generals Denekin and Rangle at a time when they had the Bolshevik Red Army on the very brink of defeat. It also gives a great deal of information about the utterly corrupt Petroleum Industry. Of particular interest is the information it provides on Sir Moses Montefiore, of the ancient Venetian Black Nobility Montefiores.

BRAVE NEW WORLD, Aldous Huxley.

BRITISH OPIUM POLICY IN CHINA, Owen, David Edward.

BRITISH OPIUM POLICY, F. S. Turner.

CECIL RHODES, Flint, John.

CECIL RHODES, THE ANATOMY OF AN EMPIRE, Marlowe, John.

CONFERENCE ON TRANSATLANTIC IMBALANCE AND COLLABORATION, Rappaport, Dr. Anatol.

CONVERSATIONS WITH DZERZHINSKY, Reilly, Sydney. In British Intelligence documents not published.

CREATING A PARTICULAR BEHAVIORAL STRUCTURE, Cartwright, Dorwin.

CRYSTALIZING PUBLIC OPINION, Bernays, Edward.

DEMOCRATIC IDEALS AND REALITY, Mackinder, Halford.

ERVIN, SENATOR SAM. Apart from obstructing the introduction of vital evidence in the Watergate hearings, Ervin, in my opinion, while holding himself out as a Constitutional authority, consistently betrayed this nation by opposing aid to church schools, citing the judicial opinions in the Everson case. Ervin, a Scottish Rite Freemason—which in my opinion is why he was given the Watergate Committee chair, was eventually honored, receiving the prestigious Scottish Rite "Individual Right's Support" award. In 1973, Ervin held a luncheon in the Senate Dining Room in honor of Sovereign Grand Commander Clausen.

EVERSON VS. BOARD OF EDUCATION, 330 U.S. I, 1947.

FRANKFURTER PAPERS, Box 99 and Box 125, "HUGO BLACK CORRESPONDENCE."

GNOSTICISM, MANICHEANISM, CATHARISM, The New Columbia Encyclopedia.

GOALS OF MANKIND, Lazlo, Ervin.

GOD'S BANKER, Cornwell, Rupert. This book gave some insight into P2 and the murder of Roberto Calvi—P2 Masonry.

HUMAN QUALITY, Peccei, A.

INTERNATIONAL JOURNAL OF ELECTRONICS.

INTRODUCTION TO THE SOCIOLOGY OF MUSIC, Adorno, Theo. Adorno was kicked out of Germany by Hitler because of his Cult of Dionysus music experiments. He was moved to England by the Oppenheimers where the British royal family gave him facilities at Gordonstoun School and their support. It was here that Adorno perfected "Beatlemusic Rock," "Punk Rock" "Heavy Metal Rock" and all of the decadent clamor that passes for music today. It is worthy of note that the name "The Beatles" was chosen to show a connection between modern rock, the Isis cult and the Scarab Beatle, a religious symbol of ancient Egypt.

INVASION FROM MARS, Cantril. In this work Cantril analyzes the behavior patterns of people who fled in panic following the Orson Wells experiment in mass hysteria, using H.G. Wells' "WAR OF THE WORLDS."

INVESTIGATION OF THE KENNEDY ASSASSINATION, THE UNCOMMISSIONED REPORT ON JIM GARRISON FINDINGS. Paris, Flammonde.

IPS REVISITED, Coleman, Dr. John.

ISIS UNVEILED, A MASTER KEY TO THE ANCIENT AND MODERN SCIENCE AND THEOLOGY, Blavatsky, Madame Helena.

JOHN JACOB ASTOR, BUSINESSMAN, Porter, Kenneth Wiggins.

JUSTICE BLACK'S PAPERS, Box 25, General Correspondence, Davies.

KING MAKERS, KING BREAKERS, THE STORY OF THE CECIL FAMILY, Coleman, Dr. John.

LIBERATION THEOLOGY. Information was drawn from work by Juan Luis Segundo, who in turn drew heavily upon the writings of Karl Marx. Segundo savagely attacked the Catholic Church instruction against Liberation Theology as found in "Instruction on Certain Aspects of the 'Theology of Liberation'" published August 6th, 1984.

LIES CLEARER THAN TRUTH, Barnett, Richard (Founder member of IPS).

McCalls Magazine, January 1983.

McGRAW HILL GROUP, ASSOCIATED PRESS. Portions of reports from 28 magazines owned by McGraw Hill, and AP stories.

MEMOIRS OF A BRITISH AGENT, Lockhart, Bruce. In this book we are told how the Bolshevik Revolution was controlled out of London. Lockhart was Lord Milner's representative who went to Russia to watch over Milner's investment in Lenin and Trotsky. Lockhart had access to Lenin and Trotsky at short notice even though Lenin frequently had a waiting room full of high-ranking officials and foreign delegates, some having been waiting to see him for as long as five days. Yet Lockhart never had to wait more than a few hours to see either man. Lockhart carried a letter signed by Trotsky informing all Bolshevik officials that Lockhart had special status and should be given the utmost cooperation at all times.

MIND GAMES, Murphy, Michael.

MISCELLANEOUS OLD RECORDS, India House Documents, London.

MK ULTRA LSD EXPERIMENT, CIA Files 1953-1957.

MR. WILLIAM CECIL AND QUEEN ELIZABETH, Read, Conyers.

MURDER, Anslinger, Henry. Anslinger was at one time the Number 1 agent in the Drug Enforcement Agency and his book is highly critical of the so-called war on drugs allegedly being waged by the U.S. Government.

MY FATHER, A REMEMBRANCE, Black, Hugo L., Jr.

NATIONAL COUNCIL OF CHURCHES, Josephson, Emmanuel in his book "ROCKEFELLER, INTERNATIONALIST."

OIL IMPERIALISM, THE INTERNATIONAL STRUGGLE FOR PETROLEUM, Fischer, Louis.

PAPERS OF SIR GEORGE BIRDWOOD, India House Documents, London.

PATTERNS IN EASDEA TITLE I READING ACHIEVEMENT TESTS, Stanford Research Institute.

POPULATION BOMB, Erlich, Paul.

PROFESSOR FREDERICK WELLS WILLIAMSON, India House Documents, London.

PUBLIC AGENDA FOUNDATION. Founded in 1975 by Cyrus Vance and Daniel Yankelovich.

PUBLIC OPINION, Lippmann, Walter.

REVOLUTION THROUGH TECHNOLOGY, Coudenhove Kalergi, Count.

ROCKEFELLER, INTERNATIONALIST. Josephson details how the Rockefellers used their wealth to penetrate the Christian Church in America and how they later used their Number 1 agent, John Foster Dulles—who was related to them—to maintain their grip on every aspect of church life in this country.

ROOM 3603, Hyde, Montgomery. The book gives some detail about MI6 British Intelligence operations run by Sir William Stephenson out of the RCA Building in New York; but, as is usual with "cover stories," the REAL events have been omitted.

SPECIAL RELATIONSHIPS: AMERICA IN PEACE AND WAR, Wheeler-Bennet, Sir John.

STEPS TO THE ECOLOGY OF THE MIND, Bateson, Gregory. Bateson was one of the Tavistock new-science scientists in the top five at Tavistock and later did much to formulate and manage the 46-year war on America conducted by Tavistock.

STERLING DRUG. William C. Bullitt was once on its board of directors and was also on the board of I.G. Farben.

TECHNOTRONIC ERA, Brzezinski, Z.

TERRORISM IN THE UNITED STATES INCLUDING ATTACKS ON U.S. INTELLIGENCE AGENCIES: FBI Files # 100-447935, #100-447735, and #100-446784.

THE CAIRO DOCUMENTS, Haikal, Mohammed. Haikal was the grand old man of Egyptian journalism, and he was present at the interview given to Chou En-lai by Nasser in which the Chinese leader vowed to "get even" with Britain and the U.S. over their opium trade in China.

THE CHASM AHEAD, Peccei, A.

THE DIARIES OF SIR BRUCE LOCKHART, Lockhart, Bruce.

THE ENGINEERING OF CONSENT, Bernays. In this 1955 book, Bernays lays out the modus operandi of how to persuade targeted groups to change their minds on important issues that can and do alter the national direction of a country. The book also deals with the unleashing of psychiatric shock troops such as we see in lesbian and homosexual organizations, environmental groups, abortion rights groups and the like. "Psychiatric shock troops" was a concept developed by John Rawlings Reese, the founder of the Tavistock Institute of Human Relations.

THE FEDERAL BUDGET AND SOCIAL RECONSTRUCTION, IPS Fellows Raskin and Barnett. A list of members of Congress who asked IPS to produce the alternative budget study and/or supported it is too long to include here but contained such prominent names as Tom Harkness, Henry Ruess, Patricia Schroeder, Les Aspin, Ted Weiss, Don Edwards, Barbara Mikulski, Mary Rose Oakar, Ronald Dellums and Peter Rodino.

THE HUXLEYS, Clark.

THE IMPERIAL DRUG TRADE, Rowntree.

THE JESUITS, Martin, Malachi.

THE LATER CECILS, Rose, Kenneth.

THE LEGACY OF MALTHUS, Chase, Allan.

THE MANAGEMENT OF SUSTAINABLE GROWTH, Cleveland, Harlan. Cleveland was commissioned by NATO to report on just how far the Club of Rome's Post Industrial

Society-Zero Growth blueprint to wreck the industrial base of the United States had succeeded. This shocking document should be read by every patriotic American who feels an urgent need for an explanation as to why the U.S. is in a deep economic depression at the end of 1991.

THE MEN WHO RULED INDIA, Woodruff, Philip.

THE OPEN CONSPIRACY, Wells, H. G. In this work, Wells describes how in the New World Order (which he calls the New Republic) "useless eaters," excess population, will be gotten rid of: "The men of the New Republic will not be squeamish either in facing or inflicting death.... They will have an ideal that will make killing worthwhile; like Abraham, they will have the faith to kill, and they will have no superstitions about death.... They will hold, I anticipate, that a certain portion of the population exists only on sufferance out of pity and patience, and, on the understanding that they do not propagate, and I do not foresee any reason to oppose that they will not hesitate to kill when that sufferance is abused.... All such killings will be done with an opiate.... If deterrent punishments are used at all in the code of the future, the deterrent shall be neither death, nor mutilation of the body...but good scientifically caused pain." The United States has a very large contingent of Wells converts who would not hesitate to follow the dictates of Wells, once the New World Order becomes a reality. Walter Lippmann was one of Wells' most ardent disciples.

THE POLITICS OF EXPERIENCE, Laing, R.D. Laing was the Staff Psychologist at Tavistock and, under Andrew Schofield, a member of the Governing Council.

THE POLITICS OF HEROIN IN SOUTH EAST ASIA, McCoy, Alfred W., Read, C.B and Adams, Leonard P.

THE PROBLEM OF CHINA, Russell, Bertrand.

THE PUGWASH CONFEREES, Bertrand Russell. In the early 1950's Russell led a movement urging a nuclear attack on Russia. When it was discovered, Stalin warned that he would not hesitate to retaliate in kind. This led to a quick "rethink" on the part of Russell, who almost overnight became a pacifist. Thus was born the "Ban the Bomb" Campaign for Nuclear Disarmament (CND) out of which arose the Pugwash anti-nuclear scientists. In 1957 the first group met at the home of Cyrus Eaton in Nova Scotia, a long-time American Communist. The Pugwash Conferees dedicated themselves to anti-nuclear and environmental issues and were a thorn in the side of U.S. efforts to develop nuclear weapons.

THE ROUND TABLE MOVEMENT AND IMPERIAL UNION, Kendle, John.

THE STRUCTURE OF THE POPULAR MUSIC INDUSTRY; THE FILTERING PROCESS WHEREBY RECORDS ARE SELECTED FOR PUBLIC CONSUMPTION, Institute for Social Research. This work explains how "Hit Parades," "The Top Ten"—now expanded to the "Top Forty"—and other charades are constructed to deceive listeners and convince them what they hear is what "THEY" like!

THE WORKS OF JEREMY BENTHAM, Bowering, John. Bentham was the liberal of his day and the agent for Lord Shelburne, British Prime Minister at the end of the American War of Independence. Bentham believed that man was no more than a common animal, and Bentham's theories were later written up by his protege, David Hume. Writing about instinct in animals Hume said, "...which we are so apt to admire as extraordinary and inexplicable. But our wonder will perhaps cease or diminish when we consider that the experimental reasoning itself which we possess in common with beasts, and upon which the whole conduct of life depends, is nothing but a species of instinct, or mechanical power that acts in us unknown to our-selves.... Though the instincts be different, yet still it is an instinct."

TIME PERSPECTIVE AND MORALE, Levin B.

TOWARD A HUMANISTIC PSYCHOLOGY, Cantril.

TREND REPORT, Naisbitt, John.

U.S. CONGRESS, HOUSE COMMITTEE ON INTERNAL SECURITY, REPORTING ON THE INSTITUTE FOR POLICY STUDIES (IPS) AND THE PENTAGON PAPERS. In the spring of 1970, FBI operative William McDermott went to see Richard Best, who at that time was Rand's top security officer, to warn him of the possibility that Ellsberg had removed Vietnam study papers done by Rand and had copied them outside of Rand premises. Best took McDermott to see Dr. Harry Rowan who headed Rand and who was also one of Ellsberg's closest friends. Rowan told the FBI that a Defense Department inquiry was going on and on his assurance, the FBI apparently dropped its investigation of Ellsberg. In fact, no inquiry was in progress, nor did the DoD ever conduct one. Ellsberg retained his security clearance at Rand and blatantly went on removing and copying Vietnam War documents right up to the time of his exposure during the Pentagon Papers affair which rocked the Nixon Administration to its foundations.

UNDERSTANDING MAN'S SOCIAL BEHAVIOR, Cantril. Cantril was primarily responsible for establishing the Association for Humanistic Psychology based in San Francisco that taught Tavistock methods. It is in institutions of this type that we find the lines between pure science and social engineering become totally obliterated. The term "social engineering" covers every aspect of methods used by Tavistock to bring about massive changes in group orientation toward social, economic, religious and political events and brainwashing of target groups who then believe that opinions expressed and viewpoints taken are their own. Selected individuals underwent the same Tavistockian treatment, resulting in major shifts in personality and behavior. The effect of this on the national scene was, and still is, devastating and is one of the principal factors in bringing the United States into the twilight, decline and fall state-of-being in which the country finds itself at the close of 1991. I did a report on this national condition under the title: "Twilight, Decline and Fall of the United States of America" which was published in 1987. The Association for Human Psychology was founded by Abraham Maselov in 1957 as a Club of Rome project. Another Tavistock-Club of Rome Commissioned opinion-making research center was established by Risis Likhert and Ronald Lippert who called it The Center for Research in the Utilization of Scientific Knowledge. The facility was under the directorship of Club of Rome's Donald Michael. The center drew heavily on the Office of Public Opinion Research established at Princeton University in 1940. It was from here that Cantril taught many of the techniques used by today's pollsters-opinion makers.

UNPUBLISHED LETTERS, Kipling, Rudyard. Kipling was a Wells disciple and, like Wells, believed in Fascism, as a means of world control. Kipling adopted the Running Cross as his personal emblem. The Running Cross was later adopted by Hitler and with slight modifications became known as the swastika.

UNPUBLISHED LETTERS, Wells, H. G. Gives interesting details of how Wells sold the rights to "WAR OF THE WORLDS" to RCA.

WHO OWNS MONTREAL, Aubin, Henry.

WHO'S WHO IN CANADA, several editions.

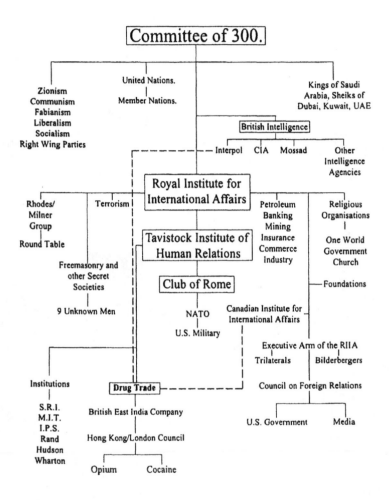

The Structure of Freemasonry

American Freemasonry resembles two sets of stairs that begin and end together, as this chart of Masonic structure shows. A Mason's first step is to become an Entered Apprentice. He climbs to the third step where most Masons stay. If he wants to go on in Masonic hierarchy, he enters either the Scottish or York rites. Many authorities say the Scottish Rite was begun by Scots émigrés in France; the York Rite is named after York, England where, by legend, the first Masonic body was organized.

In the Scottish Rite a Mason climbs 30 steps, or degrees. The name he takes on at each degree is written on each step in chart. Where there are two names the top is used by northern Masons, the italicized one by southern Masons. Some figures a Mason meets in Rite ceremonies stand on the steps (from bottom): King Solomon, King Cyrus, acolyte, George Washington, Sultan. Each degree teaches a moral. To earn degree candidate learns the moral and participates in ceremony dramatizing it. A 32° is the highest degree a Mason can earn. The 33° is awarded by the Supreme Council, ruling body of the Rite.

A Mason in York Rite advances 10 degrees, known by name and not by degree number. On chart are figures he meets at each degree or the degree symbol. Figures are temple workman, Past Master (Virtual), Israel tribesman, High Priest of Jews, King Hiram of Tyre, Knight of Malta, Knight Templar, equal in prestige to 33° in Scottish Rite. Under the arch are organizations allied to Freemasonry. Master Masons are eligible for Grotto and Tall Cedars of Lebanon. Girls with a Mason in the family can join Job's Daughters or Rainbow Girls; women, the Eastern Star; boys, DeMolay. Only 32° Masons or Knights Templar can join the Shrine. Shriner's wife can be a Daughter of the Nile. Most important of many Masonic symbols are the open Bible with square and compass on it (left); Solomon's temple (below Bible); and the G with the all-seeing eye inside (upper right). In the U.S. the G stands for God.

SCOTTISH RITE

33° Knight
32° Commander Knight Comr
26° Prince of Mercy
25° Knight of the Brazen Serpent
24° Prince of the Tabernacle
23° Chief of the Tabernacle
22° Prince of Libanus Knight of the Royal Axe
21° Patriarch Noachite Noachite or Prussian Knight
20° Master Ad Vitam *Master of the Symbolic Lodge*
19° Grand Pontiff *Pontiff*
18° Knight of the Rose Croix of H.R.D.M. *Knight Rose Croix*
17° Knight of the East and West
16° Prince of Jerusalem
15° Knight of the East or Sword *Knight of the East*
14° Grand Elect Mason *Perfect Elu*
13° Master of the Ninth Arch *Royal Arch of Solomon*
12° Grand Master Architect *Master Architect*
11° Sublime Master Elected *Elu of the Twelve*
10° Elect of Fifteen *Elu of the Fifteen*
9° Master Elect of Nine *Elu of the Nine*
8° Intendant of the Building
7° Provost and Judge
6° Intimate Secretary
5° Perfect Master
4° Secret Master

Tall Cedars of Lebanon   Order of the Eastern Star

AAONMS

ALLIED

INDEX

The Spiritual Laws and Lessons of the Universe

$19.95 + Shipping

382 pages   ISBN: 0-9640104-6-1

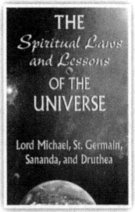

For eons of time in your human history, mankind has experienced and existed in blindness about his divine spiritual heritage, that is, his oneness with the Creation. Since the time of the "Fall" from "grace," many have continued to struggle with what is "their" purpose, and why it is so difficult to find and know THE TRUTH. Many, in their ignorance and confusion, have asked themselves why the Creator allows the seemingly unending ruthless and merciless inhumanity of man to continue; why HE allows suffering of children, wars, disease and pestilence and corruption. Often ones simply decide there is no Creator, which only keeps ones ever "separate" from KNOWING HIS PRESENCE WITHIN.

"The Spiritual Laws and Lessons" is deliverance of truth to YOU. The Creator is offering YOU the instructions for reaching the "lighted" path back home to HIM, AND THUS TO ONENESS. You will learn HOW to recognize the Anti-Spirit, (that which is AGAINST the Creator and therefore AGAINST LIFE) within YOU and why through your gift of free-will YOU allowed the Anti-Spirit within your temple. You will learn about what are the "Deadliest" Sins (errors) committed by you and also about the nature of YOUR personal responsibility for ALL consequences and experiences within this manifested physical "illusion."

NOW within these pages bringing forth the EIGHTEEN Logical Cosmic Laws of Balance of The Creation, written in explicit detail with MANY examples given for YOUR careful consideration and recognition of truth. Why? To let there be NO misunderstanding of HOW and WHY you, of humanity, have lost your inner as well as planetary BALANCE. You have broken EVERY law set forth herein and have, therefore, suffered the consequences of your errors against the Creator and against LIFE. You each now have before you YOUR "road map" back home to spiritual wisdom, knowledge and truth. Will YOU see? Will YOU hear? Each ONE of you, being fragments of THE CREATION must and will make this choice: To wisely learn your lessons in truth, abide by the laws and thus EARN your Spiritual UNITY and Freedom within the Kingdom OR continue in the darkness of deception, ignorance and spiritual poverty which will keep you bound in the Anti-Spirit's "illusion" of separation. THIS cycle is about to END. The new cycle will BEGIN anew in the GLORY and Celebration of cleansing within and without of ALL fragments of ANTI-LIFE. WILL YOU JOIN OUR FATHER/MOTHER CREATOR in the Divine Holy Kingdom of LIFE? The Creator awaits your decision. So be it.

Handbook for the New Paradigm
Volume I

$6.95 + Shipping
192 pages   ISBN: 1-893157-04-0

The messages contained in this handbook are
intended to lift mankind from the entrapment
of the victim consciousness that keeps the level
of experience ensnared in fear and frustration.
Humanity was intended to live, not in luxury,
but in abundance. The information found in
this book will lead all that read and reread with

an open mind to the discovery of the truth of who and what they truly are.
The end of the search for these answers is provided at last in clarity and
conciseness. There are no recriminations or feelings of guilt to be gleaned
from these pages. There is clarity and upliftment in each segment. It is the
intent and purpose of this small book to encourage every reader to live in
accordance with the plainly disclosed simple laws that underlay all that each
comprehends as life. Each segment leads to greater understanding and to a
simple application that encompasses them in entirety in a few words that
guarantee absolute change in your day to day experience.

Embracing the Rainbow
Volume II

$6.95 + Shipping
144 pages   ISBN: 1-893157-05-9

Volume II of the Handbook For The New
Paradigm contains the continuing series
of messages guiding its readers to accept
the concepts contained within them for the
purpose of creating a new life experience for
the "humans becoming" on planet Earth. Each
message broadens the conceptual understandings of the necessity to release
the limitations that have been thrust upon humanity preventing them from
understanding who and what they truly are. It contains surprising truths of
some of the shocking deceptions intentionally taught that limit and separate
mankind from their opportunities for spiritual evolvement. It defines how
it is possible to take back the heritage of self-determination, freely create
one's own destiny and heal the planet and humanity as a whole living entity
through the suggested dynamic process.

Becoming
Volume III

$6.95 + Shipping
180 pages   ISBN: 1-893157-07-5

The messages contained in this, the third book, are offered for the continued realization of who and what each human being truly is. The consciousness changing information each volume contains brings forth the understanding that humanity on this planet is, in reality, a whole and holy awareness. From the global myriad of belief systems arises a single picture that represents a composite awareness. This totality of thought creates the reality of the human experience, a great deal of effort is now focused with the intent of influencing how the individual and the total global awareness perceive the human experience. The mind discerns what it understands is its surrounding reality but the feelings determine its believability. Confusion masks the ability to choose between what appears to be true and what the feelings believe to be true. Beneath all the rhetoric that is focused on the conscious and subconscious levels within the current deluge of information in all its various forms is the human desire for the freedom to choose what is for the highest and best good of each individual and the planetary whole. Mankind stands at the threshold, the decision point of whether to accept what it is being told is for its highest and best good or to instead shrug off the programmed suggestions and choose for itself a future that is in total contrast. At the heart of the matter is the opportunity to choose cooperation rather than competition, brotherly love and assistance rather than hate and violence. It is time to observe the world situation that has resulted from competition and experiencing the premise of survival of the fittest. It is time to begin.

ORDER ENTIRE SET

(Vol. I, II, III)

for $19.95 + Shipping and receive

Messages for the Ground Crew FREE

Call 1-800-729-4131 or www.nohoax.com

More Suggested Reading:

One World Order
By Dr. John Coleman   ISBN: 0-9640104-9-6 $16.95
                            13 digit: 978-0-9640104-9-9

Diplomacy by Deception
By Dr. John Coleman   ISBN: 0-9640104-8-8 $19.95
                            13 digit: 978-0-9640104-8-2

What You Should Know About the United States Constitution and the Bill of Rights
By Dr. John Coleman   ISBN: 1-893157-03-2 $19.95
                            13 digit: 978-1-893157-03-3

PAN AM 103: The Lockerbie Cover-Up
By William C. Chasey   ISBN: 0-9640104-1-0 $21.95
                            13 digit: 978-0-9640104-1-3

Psychokinesiology: Doorway to the Unconscious Mind
Alexander S. Holub, Ph.D.   ISBN:1-893157-06-7 $19.95
                            13 digit: 978-1-893157-06-4

*plus shipping and handling

To order or for a FREE Catalog
Call 1-800-729-4131

Visit our website at www.nohoax.com